The Child Care Provider

Trusting that you'll
enjoy - learn from
[Arthur] & Janice's work
& thoughts about this
work

[signature]

The Child Care Provider
Promoting Young Children's Development

by

Carol S. Klass, Ph.D.

·PAUL·H·
BROOKES
PUBLISHING Co.

Baltimore • London • Toronto • Sydney

Paul H. Brookes Publishing Co.
Post Office Box 10624
Baltimore, Maryland 21285-0624

www.brookespublishing.com

Typeset by Eastern Composition, Binghamton, New York.
Manufactured in the United States of America by
Versa Press, East Peoria, Illinois.

The names of the children and adults described in the vignettes and interviews
recorded in this book have been changed to protect their identities.

The epigraph on page 1 is from "Us Two" by A.A. Milne, from *Now We Are Six*
by A.A. Milne, illustrations by E.H. Shepard. Copyright 1927 by E.P. Dutton, re-
newed © 1955 by A.A. Milne. Used by permission of Dutton Children's Books,
a division of Penguin Putnam, Inc.

Library of Congress Cataloging-in-Publication Data

Klass, Carol Speekman.
    The child care provider : promoting young children's development /
  by Carol S. Klass.
      p.   cm.
    Includes bibliographical references and index.
    ISBN 1-55766-396-3
    1. Child care—United States.   2. Child development.   I. Title.
  HQ778.63.K58   1999
  362.7—dc21   99-18542
                                                                    CIP

British Library Cataloguing in Publication data are available from the British
Library.

Contents

About the Author

In her long career, Carol S. Klass, Ph.D., has taught college, worked as an early intervention specialist and mental health consultant, and served as a field-based mentor of early educators. She has designed and directed two early intervention programs for high-needs young children, and three professional development programs for early childhood educators. Dr. Klass has used ethnographic action research to improve her own practice and the practice of the early educators with whom she works. Her prior books include *The Autonomous Child: Day Care and the Transmission of Values* (Falmer Press, 1986) and *Home Visiting: Promoting Healthy Parent and Child Development* (Paul H. Brookes Publishing Co., 1996). She is a sunrise walker, gardener, and mother of two grown sons, and she always knows the phase of the moon.

Foreword

Most books on child care for young children are jam-packed with activities, lessons, and plans for stimulating the development of children in groups. Thankfully, this book charts a different course. That children's emerging definitions of self and of self in relation to others are formed in and through significant relationships is the major message of this book. Rather than tell the reader specifically what to do to expand a child's intellectual capacity or how to handle biting, the book tells us something more useful. It tells us that the most truthful advice one can give on a myriad of child care topics is "it depends." It depends on the child's developmental stage. It depends on the child's temperament. It depends on the familial, cultural, and child care context. And, most of all, it depends on the relationship between the child and those who care for him or her. It is because this book doesn't give any pat answers that it is so important. This is a book about who infants and young children are, how they need close nurturing relationships with caregivers in order to prosper, and why certain types of care are better for the overall development of children in groups than in other types of care.

Much of group child care in the United States of America is low quality. One of the reasons for this is that the policies and training that influence the type of care that is provided are misguided. Many efforts are based on inaccurate visions of how children develop, of how to stimulate intelligence, of how to form groups, and of how caregivers should relate to children. Many child care programs are launched without a litmus test for the policies and training that drive them. This book provides the necessary information for that test and will be invaluable to policy makers, program managers, and trainers who work with child care providers because it gives them a solid foundation from which to make decisions about how to develop and operate programs.

In the introduction to the book and in the second chapter, for example, five propositions upon which good care should be based and five basic motives for infant behavior are put forward. These 10 statements give the reader a clear beginning, a grounding in how children best develop and learn, and an orientation toward defining a caregiver's role in care. More than two thirds of the child care programs I have observed do not operate in a way that reflects any understanding of these propositions and motives. The resultant care often ignores both the child's motivation toward mastery, self-revelation, and social commerce and his or her reliance on relationships with trusted caregivers for overall development. Just by using these 10 concepts, policy makers, program managers, and trainers will be able to improve care.

But the book has much more. As the book progresses we find other helpful conceptual aids for how to look at and evaluate care sprinkled throughout each chapter. There is, for example, a wonderful section on differentiating and explaining the various types of interactions that caregivers engage in with children as part of their daily modeling of language and social rules. This type of valuable information is almost never found in books on child care, yet it is essential for even a rudimentary understanding of the ongoing give-and-take between caregivers and children through which children learn. Research evidence supporting the positions taken by Klass is also quite plentiful. When, for example, Klass asks us to pay close attention to the caregiver–child interactions as we plan and train, we don't just have to take her word for it. Her recommendations are based on her review of research.

The frequent vignettes showing examples of points made in the text are also helpful aids to the reader. Program managers and trainers will see issues—similar to ones they have had to cope with themselves—presented, explored, explained, and dealt with in ways that reflect the philosophy of the book. These vignettes, I believe, will be ripe for use both for discussions during training and for planning when trying to solve similar problems.

A major strength of this book is that it gives complete and direct information about the early development of children as social and emotional beings and about the caregiver's essential role in that process. Klass' statement, *"Emotional development is a social achievement,"* concisely outlines the important role caregivers play in the development of a child's capacity to express and modulate emotions. So much of an infant's experience depends on the quality of his or her relationships with caregivers. Klass explains that children develop through the relationship and that a baby learns even something as individual as self-regulation through the caregiver and baby's working together. To Klass, how children come to express and regulate their social and emotional behavior through their attachment to and experiences with those caring for them is key. Her thoughts on this topic help planners and trainers understand why child care policies and practices must include attention to the dependence of children on caregivers.

In my work I have advocated that the care of infants and toddlers take place in intimate settings where special relationships with caregivers and other children are given time and opportunity to form. The policies that support this type of care are as follows: caring for very young children in small groups, having primary caregivers assigned to each child, and ensuring continuity of those assignments so that relationships not only are established but also have a chance to grow and deepen. What this book does that is different from most books about child care practice is get below the surface of those recommendations. The book explains why these conditions for care are so important to infants and why they should be a part of policy and practice. It shares information about why a child needs close, caring, and ongoing relationships with caregivers and how children build their early sense of self through these relationships. It also spells out in detail the critical nature of the child–caregiver interaction process in fostering child development.

To my great dismay much of the current advice about caring for young children in groups focuses on preparing caregivers to teach lessons and develop adult-directed experiences that will stimulate child learning. Many interpretations of how professionals should react to recent brain research findings are leading child care to ignore the child's motivation, curiosity, and interest and focus on adult-selected and driven activities. Klass resists this temptation. She does not give us specific ways to train young children. Instead, she tells us that the best way to help children develop is to respect their competencies and uniqueness, read their cues, and respond appropriately. She shows that responsiveness is not only the best way to support the development of a strong sense of self and healthy social exchanges but also the best way to support intellectual development. Unfortunately, many who advise us about how to stimulate brain growth have forgotten the work of years of solid cognitive and learning research that has proven that responsive care works best for both intellectual (including language) and social-emotional development. Klass has not. She shares that research with us and also shares how caregiver practice would look if based on that research.

One of the striking things about this book is the respect it shows young children. It points out their competencies and asks the reader to understand and work with their individuality. The chapter on play, learning, and development is a good example of this respectful stance. Klass walks us through the developmental stages, pointing out at the various stages what children enjoy doing and are curious about and how to best foster that enjoyment and curiosity.

In her last chapter Klass takes us in a different direction. She shares with us the personal lives of caregivers. We get a glimpse of the values and beliefs of people who provide care. This chapter dips us into a pond whose water has seldom been disturbed. Klass takes the first step in leading the field toward what I believe will be a major focus of child care training in the future, helping caregivers see that they bring to the care of young children ways of thinking, feeling, and acting that come from their own childhoods and life conditions and that these unexamined influences must be considered when hoping to move toward better practice.

If you are looking for a "cookbook"-type manual for child care, you have picked up the wrong book. If you are looking for something with depth and wisdom that will help you understand children and how they should be related to, you will not be disappointed. This is the book to read before you develop child care policies, before you engage in training, and before you put the finishing touches on your approach to caring for children in groups.

J. Ronald Lally, Ed.D.
Director
Center for Child & Family Studies
WestEd

Preface

I have included in this book the following: first, the experiences of family caregivers and center-based teachers; second, my understandings of how their work affects babies and young children; third, the scholarly literature on child development and early education; and, fourth, my own professional experience in helping teachers and caregivers.

Through writing this book, I have discovered that much of my work life prepared me for the task. In the spring of 1965, when Congress provided initial Head Start funding, I began studying child development at Tufts University. In 1974 I began working with out-of-home caregivers, first as part of the Child Development Associate (CDA) pilot training project and, 8 years later, as a CDA representative assessing teachers in child care, as well as Head Start and preschool teachers throughout the Midwest. In the 1980s and 1990s, as an early intervention specialist, I designed and directed an intervention/prevention program for babies and young children at risk of maltreatment. I also designed and directed a program focused on helping parents and child care teachers promote the healthy development of young children with substantive behavior problems. In addition to working on these programs, I designed and co-directed three professional development programs for teachers of babies and young children.

This work has helped me better understand the subtle, ever changing nature of early child development and the caregiving process. As I reflected on my everyday work, I gained insight into the meaning of adult–child interactions. In my work with adults caring for babies and young children in rural, urban, and suburban settings and in various Head Start, family caregiving, center-based caregiving, and preschool programs, I have observed not only differences in the caregiving contexts but also similarities in patterns of adult–child interactions.

Since the early 1980s, I have combined work with parents, teachers, and caregivers with *qualitative action research,* much of which has focused on adult–child interaction. Qualitative action research is a research process deriving from self- and collaborative reflection on everyday action, in which the researcher and participants gain new insights that lead to improved practice. As a doctoral student, I spent 6 months observing child care teachers who placed a great deal of emphasis on individual versus social learning, and, on a small scale, I noted how these teachers reproduced the valuing of individualism that is so much a part of American culture. While working for an early intervention program for a child protection agency, I hired and provided ongoing training in rural counties and factory towns to women who, in their own homes, cared for babies and young children at risk of maltreatment. I found that I could understand how the personal histories of talented family child care staff intersected with their caregiving skills.

In 1988, as research coordinator for the Missouri Parents as Teachers in Child Care Centers (PAT) program, I observed several PAT home visitors conducting visits so that I could write a case study on the home visitor's role. That work led to my writing a manual for home visitors entitled *Home Visiting: Promoting Healthy Parent and Child Development* (Paul H. Brookes Publishing Co., 1996). For 6 years, I assisted child care teachers and parents of young children having behavior difficulties at home and in the classroom. Through my work with the parents, home visitors, and other adult caregivers, we examined the taken-for-granted daily routines and adult–child interactions, and together we developed adaptations so that young children can succeed.

In all my work, I have moved back and forth between scholarly literature and my own clinical experience and qualitative research. Core themes have involved relationships as well as child, parent, and caregiver development and the complex interaction between relationships and development and the social environment. Over the years, as I read scholarly literature, I could see ideas being worked out in the day-to-day reality of caregiving. Often problems that perplex parents and caregivers are addressed in scholarly literature, but I saw that this scholarly information is not easily accessible to people in the field. In this book, I integrate my clinical and research work, developmental theory and research, and observations of the everyday encounters between out-of-home caregivers and babies and young children.

Throughout this book, I have been mindful of how very young children and their family caregivers and teachers both develop and can influence each other's development. I designed this book to assist those professionals engaged in improving the understanding and skills of out-of-home caregivers of young children. I hope this book can help in improving the quality of out-of-home child care for all our society's children.

Acknowledgments

I am very grateful for the emotional and cognitive support that my husband, my sons, and my close friends gave me throughout this book project. In extended conversations with them, I experienced both affirmation and challenge to delve into the task and make meaning from my years of lived experience with out-of-home caregivers.

As I wrote this book, I was very fortunate to have four skilled readers, each using a different lens to strengthen my work. My husband, Dennis, was my first reader, and he assisted me in speaking more directly and clearly. As with my home visiting manual, Marion Wilson helped me recognize when I either omitted or addressed a topic too briefly. Given her many years working with child care teachers, Eileen Borgia was quick to recognize when I needed to expand or address an issue more clearly. And my editor, Jennifer Kinard, gave comments that helped me tighten the final draft.

But my greatest appreciation goes to the family caregivers and center-based teachers and administrators who, over the years, have welcomed me into their workplace and have spoken with me openly about the meaning of their work with infants and young children. As I wrote this book, I felt the passion in these women's work, and I dedicate this book to them and all caregivers who work with our infants and young children.

Introduction

6:45 A.M.   As Sammy (age 2½ years) and his mother, Myrtrice, enter Sunshine Child Care Center, Sammy's teacher, Nina, greets them warmly. Half a dozen preschoolers are seated at the table eating their breakfast of milk, Cheerios, and bananas. Charisse sits next to her daughter, Brianna (age 3 years), and drinks a cup of coffee from the center's coffee urn. Charisse brings Brianna to the center 30 minutes before she goes to work so she and Brianna can have time together each morning. Myrtrice kneels next to Sammy and chats with him quietly, hugs him, and leaves the center. As she drives away, Myrtrice wishes she didn't have to be at work at 7 A.M.; then she, too, could linger with her child each morning. Myrtrice reminds herself, however, that she has a good relationship with Nina, who seems to truly care for Sammy. And, she is glad that at least she does not have to rush home in the afternoon when she picks up Sammy; she can relax with him at the center for a while. But it still doesn't make up for leaving her only child each morning, 1 hour after he has awakened. She knows the need to linger in the morning is her need, not Sammy's, because he loves the center and is eager to go each morning and see his teacher and friends, about whom he often talks at home.

In 1994, 69% of all mothers of preschool-age children were working; and, in 1995, 58.7% of mothers with children younger than 3 were in the workforce (Bureau of Labor Statistics, 1995). Our nation's children and their parents deserve the best child care out-of-home caregivers can provide. This book describes how to provide quality child care. The book begins with the overarching premise that the most salient feature of babies' experience is their relationship with their caregivers. Development occurs within this critical relationship. As D.W. Winnicott stated in 1965, "There is no such thing as a baby"; that is, babies only exist in interaction with their caregivers. In other words, babies do not develop alone; rather, their development occurs within the context of their everyday interactions with caregivers. Relationships and development are the two primary themes in this book. The book discusses some important points of development from birth through age 5 years and describes how the interactions within caregiving can promote children's optimal development.

The book begins by discussing the matrix of relationships within out-of-home child care: teacher–child, teacher–teacher, child–child, and parent–teacher. Using these relationships as the framework for discussion, the rest of the book examines the child's development, birth through 5 years, in four critical areas: social-emotional; language and communication; guidance and discipline; and play and learning. The book explores how caregivers' relationships with the babies and young children in their care promote the young children's development in each of these critical areas through their everyday child-rearing interactions. Next, the book discusses the social-environmental concerns that are affecting an ever increasing number of children and their relationship with their caregivers. The last chapter looks at how teachers' own personal histories are intertwined with their professional competence.

This book is primarily designed for teacher educators, administrators, and consultants engaged in preservice and in-service professional development of infant, toddler, and preschool teachers. Throughout the book, observations of and remarks by family caregivers and center-based teachers illustrate child development and effective practice. As readers come to understand how children develop and what effective practices nurture this development, they may gain new insights into their own work. Parents of young children who would like to learn what quality out-of-home child care looks like also may find this book helpful.

The observational vignettes and conversations of family caregivers and center-based teachers and administrators are a part of the qualitative action research that I have conducted over the past 15 years. These vignettes depict caregiving situations involving babies, toddlers, and preschoolers. After observing early educators in their work, I shared my written observations with them. Together we discussed my observations in the spirit of improving both our joint understanding and the educators' practice. For the last chapter, I interviewed family caregivers, center-based teachers, and directors to learn about how their life histories influenced their professional practice in early care and education.

GUIDING ASSUMPTIONS

Five propositions guide the discussion of child development and effective caregiving practice presented in this book.

1. *Development occurs within a relationship.*   Robert N. Emde stated that "the facilitation of infant development is virtually synonymous with the facilitation of the caregiving relationship" (as cited in Nelson, 1989, p. 34). From their first breath, babies have built-in abilities to initiate, maintain, and end social interactions with others. Babies and young children develop their sense of self, attitudes, values, and behavior within the taken-for-granted everyday child-rearing interactions of their parents and their out-of-home teachers, who are very significant others in their development. The child–caregiver interaction is like a dance in which each partner responds to and is synchronous with the other's movements.

2. *All relationships involve mutuality.*   Each person in a relationship influences the other at every moment and in important ways over time. Teachers of infants and young children influence the children, and, in turn, the children influence their teachers. When a teacher holds a 3-month-old on his first day at the center and sings softly to him, the baby smiles and coos. The baby experiences comfort and security and expresses these feelings by smiling and cooing in return. The baby's behavior helps the teacher know that she is being an effective teacher who is able to help a 3-month-old feel at ease in his first day of out-of-home child care.

3. *There is unity in development; young children develop as a whole.*   Babies and young children function as a totality. No developmental realm—cognitive, social-emotional, physical, or moral—can be understood apart from other realms. Development is an integrated process, so that each domain of development has significant implications for other domains. When a 4-year-old is on the climber with her friends and hangs from her knees successfully, she is experiencing a new gross motor skill. She also feels increased competence and is sharing her enjoyment on the climber with her friends (social-emotional and language/communication realms).

4. *Development is characterized by increasing complexity and qualitative change.*   As babies and young children develop, new and more complex behavior builds on previous behavior. Between 3 months and 18 months, a baby's cooing becomes babbling, which develops into single words, then two-word sentences, and so forth. Development is not linear. Rather, within this emerging complexity are qualitative

changes in development. For example, at 3 months the baby begins smiling and cooing, and cycles of wakefulness are extended; from 7 months to 9 months the baby experiences the onset of focused attachment, initiation, and response to social gestures along with the onset of motor exploration. These qualitative changes emerge as a result of new, more elaborated, and differentiated pathways in brain development.

5. *Development and the teaching/learning process are intertwined with the social environment.*   The literature describes ecology as a way of focusing on an individual's social environment. When out-of-home teachers take an ecological approach, they consider the young children within their total family environment and the interplay of the child's family with other social systems, such as the extended family, the neighborhood, and the parent's workplace. They understand that the quality of a family's life is interconnected with the quality of its members' social environment. This understanding helps teachers to be sensitive to parents' access or lack of access to resources, personal and social networks or the lack thereof, and potential restraints, all of which influence parents' relationships with their child as well as with their child's teacher. Similarly, when teachers try to understand the complex dynamics of their work experience, they should consider systemically the functioning of the center, relationships among teachers and the director, and teachers' relationships with parents and children.

OVERVIEW OF TOPICS

Relationships intertwining with development provide the structure of this book. This book is not a curriculum guide nor is it an activity book. Rather, the book examines the progression of development from birth through 5 years of age, and it explores how the teachers' and family caregivers' everyday interactions affect this development. Chapter 1 explains the wide array of relationships within out-of-home caregiving. Everyday interactions in out-of-home child care include teacher–child, teacher–teacher, child–child, and parent–teacher relationships. First, the chapter explains the levels of involvement and patterns of teacher–child interaction and how these interactions promote healthy development of babies and young children. Second, the chapter discusses how teachers interact with each other. Interaction between teachers can assist and enable co-teachers and can provide a climate in which babies and young children learn to act, to feel, and to understand. Third, the chapter describes babies' and young children's actions and interactions, the meaning of these interactions in terms of promoting development, and how teachers can promote these behaviors. Last, the chapter discusses how teacher and parent can develop an open, trusting relationship so that the young children can experience the parent–teacher relationship as a partnership.

Chapters 2 through 5 portray the progression of development from birth through 5 years. These chapters also discuss, within the descriptions of developmental progression, how out-of-home teachers' relationships with babies and young children promote their development. Chapter 2 describes the progression of social-emotional development and discusses how teachers' everyday child-rearing interactions with babies and young children can promote children's social-emotional development. The chapter explains how social-emotional development is integrated with development in other realms such as the cognitive and physical. The chapter also explores how, just as brain development influences social-emotional development, caregiving and the child's social-emotional behavior influence brain development.

Chapter 3 focuses on the progression of language and communication development and how out-of-home caregivers' everyday interactions with children can promote this important developmental area. This depiction clarifies how, beyond language learning, babies and young children are immersed in emotional communication, first with their caregivers and then with their peers in a process that is intrinsically social. The progression of language and communication also intertwines with cognitive development. The chapter closes with a discussion of emergent literacy.

Chapter 4 examines guidance and discipline, the topics about which both parents and out-of-home caregivers seem to be most concerned. As babies and young children develop, teachers can guide and discipline dimensions of their development, progressing from initial physiological and emotional regulation to responding to gestures of independence and autonomy and then guiding skills of social competence with peers and skill in attending to tasks.

Chapter 5 is about play and its important role in promoting children's learning and development. Babies and young children engage in playful activities as their primary way of acting, interacting, learning, and developing. Teachers' interactions with babies and young children influence the quality of children's play as well as the learning and development possible in this play.

Chapter 6 moves away from a discussion of babies' and young children's development and their relationships with teachers and focuses on the social environment problems that create maladaptive development as well as difficulties in the teacher–child relationship. The chapter describes babies and young children living in psychologically vulnerable families, such as families coping with marital discord and divorce, parental mental illness, parental substance abuse, domestic and community violence, and child maltreatment. The impact of these social environment problems on babies' and young children's development is discussed to assist out-of-home caregivers to recognize and better understand children who are living in these situations. The chapter closes with a discussion of the resilient child who manages to succeed despite many difficulties at home. Much of the discussion in Chapters 2 through 5 can assist teachers in working with such children. Teachers dealing with children with social environment concerns may also want to review the early intervention literature.

Chapter 7 returns to themes of relationship and development by examining the relationships and development of adults working in out-of-home caregiving. This chapter examines the personal and professional life histories of family caregivers, center-based teachers, and directors to explore how their histories intertwine with their professional competence. To learn how an early educator's personal and professional life is connected to her professional competence, I conducted interviews with family caregivers, center-based teachers, and center directors. These interviews form the basis for learning how early educators' personal histories and professional experience influence their work and how these individuals describe their understanding of themselves as early educators.

Working with family caregivers and center-based teachers and directors has helped me better understand the subtle, ever changing nature of early development and the caregiving process and how development occurs within caregiving situations. Throughout this book, I have been mindful of the lived experiences of babies, their parents, and their out-of-home caregivers and how each can influence the other's development. I wrote this book for academicians, child care administrators, and out-of-home caregivers. I hope this discussion is a useful step in the growth of a profession that is critical to the future of our nation's young children.

REFERENCES

Bureau of Labor Statistics. (1995). *Employment status of the civilian noninstitutional population by sex, age, presence and age of youngest child, marital status, race, and Hispanic origin.* Washington, DC: Author.

Nelson, K. (Ed.). (1989). *Narratives from the crib.* Cambridge: Harvard University Press.

Winnicott, D.W. (1965). *The maturational processes and the facilitating environment.* Madison, CT: International Universities Press.

To the silent heroes who care for our society's
infants, toddlers, and young children

The Child Care Provider

chapter 1

Relationships in Out-of-Home Child Care

There's always Pooh and Me.
"What would I do," said I to Pooh,
"If it wasn't for you?" and Pooh said, "True,
It isn't much fun for One, but Two
Can stick together," says he.
"That's How it is," says Pooh.

—*A.A. Milne (1927, p. 37)*

When we look closely at family- and center-based child care, we find an incredible variety of interactions and relationships, including teacher–child, teacher–teacher, child–child, and parent–teacher relationships. Caregiving relationships form the foundation of babies' and young children's developing social-emotional development. This chapter discusses the wide array of relationships within out-of-home caregiving and examines how the quality of these relationships influences the short- and long-term development of babies, toddlers, and young children.

TEACHER–CHILD INTERACTION

From the first moments after birth, babies are learning—about their bodies, about who they are, about those who care for them, and about their everyday environment. Many of the core human abilities such as the ability to trust oneself and others, to engage in intimacy, and to regulate one's emotions and behavior begin to develop in the first weeks and months of life. Critical to developing these abilities is *the quality of the love and authority patterns of everyday child-rearing interactions*. These interactions are taken for granted, subtle, and constantly changing and thus are hard to depict. Nevertheless, understanding the dynamics of concrete interactions allows us to grasp the meaning of out-of-home child care relationships.

The quality of the teacher–child relationship is influenced by individual attributes of both the child and the teacher. What the child brings to this relationship is central. Children have different temperaments that influence their activity level, their adaptability, and their responsiveness to people and their environment. During infancy, babies also have different states or levels of attentiveness that influence their interactions with others. Robert Emde provided a profile of basic motives of infancy that can be a helpful guide in understanding individual attributes of babies and young children:

> Activity is the first basic motive. Given a consistent care giving environment, the infant is active, exploratory, and motivated to master the world and realize developmental agendas.
>
> Self-regulation is a second basic motive, referring to the fact that there is an inborn propensity for regulation of behavior, as well as physiology.
>
> Social-fittedness, a third basic motive, summarizes research that indicates the extent to which infants are motivated and preadapted for initiating, maintaining, and terminating human interactions.
>
> Affective monitoring is a fourth basic motive referring to research that indicates that there is a propensity from early infancy to monitor experience according to what is pleasurable and what is unpleasurable.

From the mother's point of view, infant affective expressions guide care giving.

Cognitive assimilation, a fifth basic motive, is bolstered by research indicating that, from the beginning, the infant has a tendency to explore the environment, seeking what is new in order to make it familiar. The fifth motive overlaps with the first motive of activity, but it is added so that we can bring emphasis to a more directed tendency in the child to "get it right" about the environment. (1996, pp. 13–14)

Teachers, like young children, have different styles of interacting. Teachers also have different levels of sensitivity and different affective tones; for example, teachers differ in how much they enjoy caregiving and in their level of commitment and engagement. Some teachers are clearer and more direct in communication, for example, and speak in specific, concrete language ("Please speak quietly"); others use repetitive slogans ("Use inside voices"). Teachers also imitate the style of the significant interactions from their own early childhood histories, what Selma Fraiberg termed *ghosts in the nursery* (Fraiberg, 1980; Fraiberg, Adelson, & Shapiro, 1975). These representations often influence teachers' interactions with young children.

Early education research has consistently pointed to adult–child interactions as forming the basis for quality in early childhood programs (Kontos & Wilcox-Herzog, 1997). Research also has indicated a consistent link between increased professional development in early childhood education and quality of teacher–child interactions (Howes, Smith, & Galinsky, 1995). Furthermore, studies have indicated that when there are fewer children per adult, the teachers are more sensitive and responsive with the children. In processes that are primarily teacher-directed and didactic, research shows that teachers are less sensitive and engage in fewer verbal exchanges with their students (Kontos & Dunn, 1993).

Levels of Teacher–Child Interaction

Teachers vary in the amount of involvement and degree of interaction in which they engage with babies and young children. When out-of-home teachers are in close proximity to babies and young children, they can ensure children's safety and are available to the children emotionally. Teachers also can observe the children's behavior. When teachers are aware of children's behavior, they can consciously decide how to interact rather than let the flow of the day's activity schedule control their interactions.

Three different levels of involvement are possible in competent child care (Klass, 1986). First, the teacher can be near the children but not directly relating to them. For example, a family caregiver prepares lunch as toddlers are engaged in table activities such as drawing or playdough sculpting. At this level, the teacher is a *stabilizing presence*. At the second level, *facilitative intervention*, the teacher can enter the children's activity, interact with them, and then exit. At the third level, *shared participation*, the teacher can be a total participant in the children's activity, such as when playing "Ring Around the Rosie" with toddlers. The three levels of involvement are explained in more detail in the following sections.

Stabilizing Presence   When young children are involved in an activity, their teacher's presence has an affirming and stabilizing effect on the children's action. When their teacher is nearby, children know that the teacher is interested in their activity, is available to help if needed, can share in their delight, and can come to their aid. Pam's stabilizing presence is clear in the following example.

> Kumar and Eddie (both age 4 years) are building with large, colored rubber blocks. Eddie puts a toy figure inside a block as he says, "Here comes Dracula." Pam, their teacher, is seated nearby and is sorting paper for a group time activity. Another child, Hani (age 3 years), puts a figure inside a block as he says, "And the witch is flying." Hani and Eddie walk about the block area with their blocks in the air as though they were flying. Eddie tells Hani, "I turned him into a monster." Hani replies, "I turned her into a monster too." As Kumar watches his friends, he tells them, "And I am finishing the wolf house." Kumar moves the roof off of his "house," and Eddie places his "monster" inside, as does Hani. Kumar turns to Pam and says, "Pam, the wolf invited the monsters into his house because they are friends." Pam replies, "Just like you, Eddie, and Hani."

The children know that their teacher is nearby and can share in their play. Pam's presence stabilizes the children's play. Her reply to Kumar affirms their play together.

Facilitative Intervention   The next level of involvement goes beyond the teacher's being a presence. Teachers have many opportunities to enter into children's experiences, interact with them, and then withdraw from the activity. When they move in and out of children's experiences, teachers not only affirm the children's activity but also assist, clarify, or extend the children's play. In the next example, Jean, a family caregiver, demonstrates facilitative intervention as three toddlers play in her living room.

> Jean is sitting on the couch with Josh (age 20 months) and looking at a picture book with him. Ricky (age 21

months) brings a toy airplane to Jean, who asks, "Are there some people in it?" Ricky shakes his head no, and Jean suggests that he go find some people to put in the airplane. Ricky walks across the room and looks at the assorted toys. Jean suggests that he look in the bedroom, but he still does not find any toy people. Jean says to Josh, "Let me go find the people for Ricky, and I'll be right back." She then takes three play people out of the toy box as she tells Ricky, "I see one, two, and three here in the toy box." She gives Ricky two play people and then hands one to Nancy (age 23 months). Nancy then takes her play person across the room, sits down on the rug, and plays with the shape sorter as Ricky scoots the airplane about the room. Josh names the pictures in the book that Jean holds for him.

As Ricky puts the play people into his airplane, Jean asks, "Are the people going on a trip?" Ricky nods yes. After a few moments, Ricky brings another book to Jean, and she reads to Josh and Ricky.

Throughout the morning, Jean remains in the living room as the three toddlers engage in brief sequences of play. Jean's presence helps the children feel safe enough to initiate their own brief play sequences. Because she is able to observe the play, Jean is quick to assist Ricky find the play people. As Ricky begins to tease Nancy with a stuffed puppy, Jean's comments help make this playful interaction feel safe for Nancy.

Shared Participation   When teachers participate fully in activities with young children, the teachers can assist the children in completing a task, such as a puzzle, or lead an activity, such as story reading or dramatization, fingerplays and singing, eating together, cooking, games, or movement and music. Group activities may be spontaneous or structured by the teacher. Teacher–child shared participation offers young children social experiences of enjoyment and a sense of connectedness that enable the children to develop a sense of self in relation to others. In her shared participation, the teacher acts as a significant role model and facilitator of the children's learning. She affirms the young child's involvement, and she models language and turn taking.

Barb and Pam: Two Styles of Shared Participation

Preschool teachers Barb and Pam have different interaction styles and different understandings of children's play. During outdoor playtime, Barb often participates in spontaneous group activities with the children, for example, playing kick ball or games such as Duck, Duck, Goose. During daily small-group activities indoors, Barb reads or dramatizes a story, sings, and engages in fingerplay songs with the children. In contrast, during free play, when the children ask Barb to play with her, she chooses not to. Barb explained her position to me: "I hate when they ask me [to play with them during free play]. I usually reply, 'You get started, and I'll see what you can do.' Or, 'Why don't you find another child?' I feel like my attention needs to go to too many places. I hate to be seated, for when I do, I don't seem to get to places fast enough."

Barb was very nurturing and spontaneous with the children as she shared in their play outdoors and effectively led group activities indoors. At the same time, she did not see her teaching role as encompassing being a play partner with the children during free play; rather, she was there to observe, assist, and redirect when needed.

Pam also sang and engaged in fingerplay songs, read, and acted out stories with children during small-group time. Pam agreed to play with the children during free play, and she was an artist as she engaged in play with the children throughout the day.

> Callie (age 4 years) sits next to Pam and puts a coffee can full of colored, small plastic bears on the table. Callie makes a small circle of blue bears and surrounds them with a circle of red bears. Pam then makes a circle of green bears about 10 inches from Callie's circles. Pam says, "Let's see. One of these green bears is going to take a walk around the circle to pick up a friend." Pam "walks" one green bear around her circle, gets a yellow bear from the can, and puts it in back of the green bear in the circle. Then she says to Callie, "Now you do that." Callie puts a blue bear behind Pam's yellow one. Jim then comes to the table and asks Pam, "What are you doing?" Pam replies, "Taking our bears for a walk."
>
> Then Ned (age 3 years) comes to the table and sits on the other side of Pam. Ned places a tub of 6-inch wooden figures on the table. As he begins to stack the figures, making a sculpture, Pam assists him in balancing the structure. As soon as Callie sees Pam assist Ned, she says, "Pammy, will you play with me?" Pam replies, "What am I doing? Sitting here cutting my hair?" Callie then walks behind Pam

and pretends to cut her hair. Callie holds a bear in her hand as she says, "I'm giving you a bear cut." Pam laughs as she says, "You're giving me a bear cut." Ella (age 3 years) joins Callie in pretending to cut Pam's hair. Then the two girls continue role-playing with the bears as Pam assists Ned in making different structures with wooden figures. Ned, Pam, and the other children play at the table for about 20 minutes.

In this observed sequence, Pam added imaginative role play to Callie's play. Pam and Callie experienced shared enjoyment as they role-played with the small bears. As Pam began building with Ned, she provided a stabilizing presence for Callie, who was able to continue her role play with Ella. I asked Pam what she intends to happen when children ask her to play with them. Pam said, "I don't want always to just be sitting and observing. Yet I do some of that, too. When playing with the children, I see myself not directing them but helping them to maintain focus. And often they do remain at a task longer when I am playing with them. Besides, it's fun for me too!"

Pam had been teaching for 8 years. Like Barb, she was nurturing and spontaneous with the children. Unlike Barb, she was comfortable being a play partner with the children throughout the day.

Child development literature emphasizes the developmental value of adults being play partners with very young children (Greenspan, 1992; Greenspan & Greenspan, 1989). When parents and out-of-home teachers play with young children, the children feel a sense of connectedness and affirmation. It is the one time when the child can be the leader, and the adult can follow the child's emotional tone.

Eating periods offer opportunities for teachers to engage in daily shared participation with their children. As they eat with young children, teachers can promote the children's development in multiple ways. I observed Jean, a family caregiver, eating lunch with four toddlers. As they ate she promoted their language, cognitive, social, and physical development.

Ricky (age 17 months), Nancy (age 19 months), Trina (age 23 months), and Cindy (age 12 months) are seated at the kitchen table with Jean. Ricky, Nancy, and Trina feed themselves from a plastic bowl using a spoon. Jean is eating her lunch and feeding baby food to Cindy. In the center of the table is a pitcher of milk; three plastic bowls with tuna salad, Jell-O, and spaghetti noodles; and a plate with half-slices of toast.

Trina looks at me and points to Cindy as she says, "Sissy." Jean replies, "Sissy, yes, Cindy is your sister." Trina says, "Sissy…baby."

Jean says to Nancy, "You don't have a sister, do you?" Nancy replies, "No. Sister be here pretty soon." Ricky eats as the children and Jean are talking. Nancy continues, "Sleep at my home."

Jean asks Trina, "How is your spaghetti, Trina?" Trina replies, "Okay." Jean urges, "Then eat some." Trina takes a small bite of spaghetti as she points to Ricky. She then points to her sister as she looks at me and says, "Sissy," and Jean responds, "Yes, and Sissy is your sister."

A small piece of Jell-O falls on Nancy's chair, and she says to Jean, "I spilled." Jean hands Nancy a towel and says, "You can wipe it up." Nancy does.

As the children are eating, they hear the sound of a concrete mixer outside. Jean says to the children, "Oh, they are pouring concrete. I was hoping they would wait to do that until we are done eating so we can watch them."

Ricky responds, "We check out the truck when we're done eating." Jean nods yes.

As the children's lunch continues, they engage in conversation with Jean. When they want more food, Jean holds the bowl, and they serve themselves. Nancy then spontaneously begins giving Cindy a small amount of baby food. As she feeds Cindy, Cindy says, "Mmmm." Nancy replies, "Mmmm, good." Jean comments, "Yes, she does like it, Nancy." Nancy says, "Mmmm, she likes her food." Cindy reaches her arm toward her food, and Nancy says to her, "Want some more." Jean says, "She's reaching for it." Nancy puts some baby food onto the spoon, but it spills off. Jean suggests, "Try and scrape the spoon on the jar before you give some to Cindy." Nancy does as directed and Cindy eats as she says, "Mmmm." Nancy replies, "Mmmm, it's good."

Ricky asks Jean for a turn to feed Cindy, and Jean replies, "It's Nancy's turn today. Next time we eat you may have a turn feeding Cindy when you sit next to her."

As they ate lunch with Jean, the children feel connected to her and to each other. Jean facilitated their language development as she extended their speech, and the children took turns in conversations. As they fed themselves and cleaned up their own spills, they worked on self-help skills. Nancy showed a beginning sense of social responsibility as she assisted in feeding Cindy and cleaned up her own spill.

During infancy, especially early infancy, shared participation between baby and caregiver is a part of caregivers' biological and emotional regulation of the babies in their care. Split-second and several-second interactive sequences between baby and caregiver regulate the baby's affect, arousal, and attention. By age 3–4 months, as babies develop social smiling, social vocalizing, and laughter, babies and caregivers engage in repeated sequences of play exchange. By age 7 months, babies repeatedly initiate brief play interactions. They love turn-taking games such as Peek-a-boo. Raver noted that during play interactions, "coordination of joint interest in objects allows children to gain an appreciation that the other person is a subject" (1996, p. 851). By age 7 months, babies understand not only that their caregiver is an acting subject but also that the caregiver can understand what is going on in their mind. As they play with babies, caregivers regulate the amount of tension babies can tolerate. These experiences in emotional arousal and regulation are the building blocks of babies' developing self-regulation.

Teacher–Child Interaction Patterns

The three levels of adult involvement just discussed, that is, the stabilizing presence, facilitative intervention, and shared participation, encompass multiple teacher–child interaction patterns (Klass, 1986). I derived seven interaction patterns from my extended qualitative action research with early educators when I worked with children from birth through 6 years of age in a variety of program sites and program types. The patterns discussed are not meant to be exhaustive of all possible teacher–child interactions. Rather, they represent the patterns of interaction that I found to be most salient in my qualitative action research. The seven teacher–child interaction patterns include *physical intimacy, spontaneous communication and conversation, encouragement, assistance, turn taking, rule implementation,* and *conflict resolution*. When teachers are aware of and understand different interaction patterns, they can choose responsibly how they relate to a child. Conscious decision making makes effective teaching possible.

Physical Intimacy   Face-to-face interaction, holding, rocking, hugging, patting, and stroking are essential caregiving interactions that provide comfort and security to very young babies. Experiencing bodily contact with caring adults is essential to children's continued sense of belonging and security. These intimate contacts contribute to babies' and young children's sense of trust in others and in themselves.

Out-of-home teachers have daily opportunities to hold and rock babies as they give them their bottles, a task that is essential for fostering optimal development. Similarly, simple tickling or "I'll get you" games during diapering are a form of repeated intimate caregiving interaction. Story reading or singing are periods in which babies, toddlers, and preschoolers often enjoy sitting on their teacher's lap. In addition, teachers spontaneously can offer physical intimacy throughout the day, such as a light pat on the shoulder or a welcoming hug on a child's arrival.

Who a teacher is as a person is the primary tool she brings to her work, and teachers have different rhythms and manners of offering children physical intimacy. My 6-month case study of three child care teachers of 3- and 4-year-olds is illustrative (Klass, 1986).

Barb, Pam, and Anne: Three Patterns of Giving and Receiving Physical Intimacy

Barb, Pam, and Anne each provided the children in their care with affection, but each teacher did so in a different way, sometimes for different reasons. Pam expressed the most physical affection: a teasing tickle, a soothing arm, or an enthusiastic enveloping hug. She was exceptionally affectionate with needy children, such as Joey, who typically was sad during his first ½ hour at the center; Ronnie, who lacked self-control; or Jimmy, who resisted adult directions. On first seeing Joey each day, Pam hugged him or gave him a quick, tickling greeting. She allowed Ronnie to "shadow" her most of each day, which assisted him in gaining increased self-control and the ability to focus in play. It was not uncommon to see Pam with her arm around Ronnie when speaking to him as Ronnie leaned against her. Pam knew that Jimmy loved music, so she often sat next to him, joined his table activity, and sang with him. I asked Pam if she sees her role in the center as one of mothering.

Pam: Well, I now share a house with a friend who has a 5-year-old. I'm very aware that my "teaching behavior" is very different from mothering. And yet if by mothering you mean nurturing, I think that is the most important thing that I do at the center with the children—nurturing.

Barb was intimate physically with the children; however, her spontaneous actions most often involved the children in her small group. As each of these children arrived, Barb gave them a warm welcoming hug. Two periods in which she was affectionate to all of the children were during story and singing time for all children and during the nap period when she would rub their backs. I also asked Barb if she thought one of her teaching roles is mothering.

Barb: Sometimes I think that mothering is as important as anything else. I do a lot of hugging, a lot of contact, and I think that is part of our job. [She chuckles lightly.] And I think I sometimes need it too. When I taught half days, there was none of that; but those kids were with us 3½ hours, whereas our kids are with us 9–10 hours each day. I think kids in my group feel close to me. And when I arrive, I go to each of them and say hello and try to make them feel special, that they are in my group. And they seem to love this little extra.

Anne agreed with Barb and Pam as to the importance of providing physical affection. Anne also used intimacy, however, as a form of control. She told me, "The children know that if they follow the rules they get a hug." Often Anne would tell the children, especially those in her small group, "I love you," as she observed them act appropriately.

Barb, Pam, and Anne each have different personal histories, education, and prior work experience. Also each woman has her own unique personality and temperament and current personal life, separate from her work at Rosehill Day Care Center. It is not surprising that we see significantly different ways these three women provide affection to the children for whom they care.

   Spontaneous Communication and Conversation   Babies are prewired for social interaction. From birth babies interact with their parent and/or caregiver in daily, repetitive nonverbal interaction sequences, what Daniel Stern (1995) termed *microevents*. Stern spoke of split-second microevents as "mutual microregulations of affect and activation" (p. 63). As family and child care center teachers feed, diaper, and hold these very young babies, what the teachers do with their eyes and faces and what they say when the babies look or smile at them make up the repetitive interaction sequences that allow babies to feel secure and develop a sense of who they are.

   When very young babies are awake and alert, teachers can talk to these babies; and through this talking babies feel comforted and experience a sense of belonging and connectedness. Emma entered her child care center at 8 weeks of age; Joy is her primary teacher. In her second week at this center, Emma did not seem attached to her teachers. She did, however, maintain a sense of calm when alert because her teachers provide repetitive, nurturant interactions not dissimilar from those of her parents.

> *Joy sits on the rug area and holds Emma (age 9 weeks) as she interacts with several other babies and toddlers playing near her. Joy has just finished giving Emma a bottle of milk. She says, "We need to get out a burp. I'll help you. And we'll help you take more than 1 ounce of formula." As Joy speaks, Emma looks at her and smiles. For about 10 minutes Joy holds Emma and alternates speaking with the nearby babies and toddlers and Emma. Then she places Emma in the infant swing.*

Teachers often talk to the babies in their care about what they themselves are doing or what they see the babies doing, as do Joy and her co-teacher, Alicia, in the following vignette.

> *Three toddlers push plastic vacuum cleaners in the gross motor room. Alicia comments, "You are vacuuming our rug." Mia (age 20 months) replies, "Vacooming."*
>
> *Joy changes Mimi's (age 18 months) diapers as she talks to her. "I'm changing your diapers, and then you'll feel better. Then you can play with the other kids at the sensory table."*
>
> *Sunita (age 12 months) stands at the sensory table and picks up one noodle at a time and puts them into a plastic bottle. Alicia comments, "You're putting noodles into a bottle." Sunita smiles.*
>
> *Emma (age 10 weeks) sits in the infant seat, which has a small infant "gym" attached to the front. Mark (age 12 months) sits next to Emma and twirls the rattles on the gym. Joy comments, "Mark, you're keeping Emma happy when you twirl her toys." Mark smiles.*

As Joy and Alicia talk with these toddlers and describe their actions, the children feel affirmation and a sense of belonging, and they are stimulated to respond, as did Mia when she repeated, "Vacooming."

When toddlers do begin speaking, teachers have innumerable opportunities to repeat the toddlers' speech and expand on it.

> *Alicia has just arrived, and Rezi (age 17 months) runs to her and gives her a hug as he says, "Brella." Alicia replies, "You brought an umbrella today so you wouldn't get wet in the rain." Rezi smiles as he nods yes.*
>
> *Mia (22 months) plays at the sensory table, which is covered with oatmeal, small plastic cups, and plastic spiders. Mia picks up a spider as she says, "There." Joy replies, "There you have a spider, don't you?" Mia nods yes and begins filling a cup with oatmeal.*
>
> *Alicia and five toddlers are playing "Ring Around the Rosie." Each time they finish the game, Carrie (18 months) says, "gain," and Alicia replies, "You want to play again, Carrie." It is as if Carrie's comment and Alicia's reply become part of the children's game.*

As the children play, their teachers' extensions of their one-word sentences let them know that their teachers have entered into their experiences and are affirming their actions. At the beginning of each day, young children and their teachers can talk about happenings at the children's homes. Conversations about the children's home lives help the children feel a sense of connection between home and child care.

> *Carrie says to Alicia, "Swing." Alicia replies, "You got a new swing, didn't you?" Carrie nods yes. Alicia says, "And daddy pushed you." Carrie nods and says, "Daddy work." Alicia replies, "Yes, your daddy is at work now."*

Because Alicia and her co-workers talk to each parent on the child's arrival, Alicia knew that Carrie's dad had put up a new swing set over the weekend. Carrie no doubt feels secure as she watches Alicia and her parents engaging in pleasant conversation at the start and end of each day. Alicia's extension of Carrie's one-word sentence invited Carrie to continue thinking and talking about her daddy whom Alicia had mentioned. As young children speak, they are more involved in thinking about themselves and the world. Toddlers' brief conversations foster the toddlers' cognitive development.

Out-of-home teachers have unlimited opportunities to talk spontaneously with the children in their care, both when they are engaged in routine activities and when the children are playing.

> *Jean sorts laundry on her living room couch as Ricky (age 21 months) and Nancy (age 23 months) play on the rug in front of her. Both toddlers have their shoes off.*

> *Ricky says, "Wear Nancy's shoes." Jean replies, "Ask*
> *Nancy if it's okay."*
> *"Okay, Nancy?" asks Ricky.*
> *Nancy says, "Okay."*
> *Ricky goes to the table and gets Nancy's shoes, saying,*
> *"Here are them."*
> *Jean says, "Here they are. Have a seat."*
> *Ricky sits down in front of Jean and says, "Have a seat."*
> *As she assists Ricky with Nancy's shoes, Jean asks*
> *Nancy, "Do you want to wear Ricky's shoes?" Nancy nods*
> *yes and gets Ricky's shoes and brings them to Jean. Ricky*
> *says, "Wear Nancy's shoes. Okay, Nancy?" Nancy nods yes,*
> *and both toddlers smile. Ricky then looks at his shoes on*
> *Nancy's feet and asks Jean, "Nancy tie?" Jean says, "Tying is*
> *pretty hard for little kids. I think I'll do it," and ties both tod-*
> *dlers' shoes. The two children then stand up, and Ricky ini-*
> *tiates playing "Ring Around the Rosie." Both toddlers twirl*
> *around and around until each falls down as they say, "Fall*
> *down," and giggle.*

In child care settings, teachers can limit their conversations with children to the tasks at hand and thereby maintain focus on children's learning of task mastery. In addition, they can engage in many spontaneous conversations that are not goal directed but are instead more like friendly small talk in which teacher and child share personal experiences, thoughts, and feelings. As children and teacher engage in informal conversation throughout each day, a relaxed informal ambience is created in the caregiving environment. Furthermore, as the young children engage in conversation with one another and their teachers, the children develop a sense of companionship and belonging.

Encouragement   Teachers affirm children's actions when they describe what the children are doing in positive terms and thereby influence the children's self-understanding, as illustrated in the following vignette.

> *Alicia sits next to the large plastic-covered foam shapes*
> *in the gross motor room as toddlers climb up the foam blocks*
> *and jump onto a foam mat. As the toddlers climb, Alicia says*
> *softly, "You're climbing higher and higher." Mia (age 16*
> *months) hesitates before she jumps. Alicia says to her, "It*
> *looks really high, but I saw you jump yesterday. Remember?"*
> *Mia nods yes and jumps. Alicia claps as she says, "You did*
> *it!" Mia chuckles gleefully.*

By describing the toddlers' actions, Alicia is encouraging them. As she encourages Mia and then responds enthusiastically, Mia feels proud of herself as she chuckles.

When teachers repeatedly describe children's actions and accomplishments aloud, children feel competent enough to explore actively and to attempt new tasks. This form of encouragement differs from the global repetitive praise that some adults give young children, praise using terms such as "good," "nice," or "good job." Young children quickly learn that these global evaluative comments mean that they are pleasing their teachers. The children understand that the value of their actions is tied to pleasing an adult. Rather than encourage curiosity and exploration, repetitive, nonspecific praise fosters young children's dependence on adult approval.

Assistance   A significant proportion of child rearing involves assistance. Emotional and physiological regulation are the first forms of assistance teachers provide. Between ages 7 and 9 months, babies begin pointing, raising their arms, and vocalizing to gain their teacher's assistance, for example, to give them food or to lift them up. Throughout early childhood, teachers assist children in routine tasks such as diapering, toileting, and feeding; in task initiation or completion; in learning self-help skills; and in learning rules and routines. Adult availability and responsiveness allow young children to feel secure enough to explore, attempt new tasks, and relate positively to their peers.

Once a baby becomes mobile, teachers make decisions as to whether the child needs assistance or whether the child's development would be better fostered by the child's experiencing a little frustration, learning through trial and error, or problem solving in response to a given need. Once children are walking, teachers make choices about assisting a child themselves or encouraging another child to provide the assistance. Carmeletta often encourages children to help each other.

> *Emma (age 30 weeks) lies in an infant seat and begins to fuss. Carmeletta suggests that Mia (age 22 months) rock Emma's infant seat and talk to her. Mia does so, and Emma stops fussing.*

When the toddlers in her care eat meals together, Carmeletta usually asks a toddler to pass the plastic bowls of food to another child rather than do it herself. Similarly, she encourages the toddlers to learn to serve their own second helpings. As Carmeletta encourages these young toddlers to assist each other, she fosters their sense of self in relation to others and thus a beginning sense of social responsibility.

Turn Taking   Mutuality is a core feature of teacher–baby interaction. Young babies' vocalizations, smiles, or gestures encourage their
teacher to respond; often this teacher response triggers the babies' continued interaction. Teachers' sensitive timing and behavioral responses
facilitate give-and-take communication. Brazelton and Cramer explained
adult–baby communication as follows:

> While each separate gesture or expression is a communication, the tim-
> ing and sensitive clustering of behaviors communicates more than the
> behaviors themselves. For example, a mother will lean over her baby,
> reach for a flailing extremity, hold the baby by the buttocks, enclose
> him or her in an envelope made up of her intense gaze and her soft vo-
> calizations. Out of this cluster of five behaviors, she will heighten one
> of them, her voice, to elicit a response. As her voice increases gently,
> the baby responds with a cluster of behaviors—relaxation of the whole
> body, softening of facial features, intense looking at her, then a soft
> "coo." The mother's clustering of behaviors around each vocalization
> is as important in producing the response as her voice alone. A baby
> needs to be "contained" in order to attend to her. The mother also needs
> to learn her baby's system of clusters. The capacity of a mother to form
> a behavioral envelope to contain the baby, to maintain the baby's alert
> state, and to allow the necessary rhythms of attention-withdrawal be-
> comes critical to her ability to communicate. (1990, p. 98)

Repeated sequences of this type of interaction provide young babies with the tools for learning to communicate. To engage in this communication, babies need to be alert and attentive for a prolonged period.
In turn, the teacher learns how to read the baby's emotional state, thereby
anticipating when the baby needs to withdraw and when to develop a
tempo that extends the baby's attention span.

By 3–4 months of age, babies can engage in repetitive give-and-take
games with their teachers, in which baby and teacher exchange vocalizations, smiles, and gestures. By 7 months of age, babies enjoy repetitive games such as Peek-a-boo. Once babies develop an understanding
of object permanence, somewhere between 9 and 12 months of age, they
delight in Hide-and-Seek or "what's hidden" games (e.g., looking for a
toy that the teacher has covered with a cloth). These simple games provide babies with turn-taking experiences that allow them to develop expectations and to test themselves as well as their teachers.

Out-of-home teachers often have opportunities to structure simple
activities that provide toddlers with turn-taking experiences.

In the gross motor room of her child care center, Alicia
structures turn taking for five toddlers who delight in climb-

ing up foam shapes and then jumping from the large square shape to the tumbling mat.

Another caregiver provides repeated turn-taking experiences as she cooks at least twice a week with the toddlers for whom she cares.

> *Jean and four toddlers, Ricky (age 19 months), Nancy (age 21 months), Mark (age 30 months), and Tracy (age 38 months), are making biscuits for lunch. Jean sets a mixing bowl on the table and pours some flour into a measuring cup as she says to the children, "Okay, it is Nancy's turn to put some flour into the bowl." Jean scoots the bowl in front of Nancy, who dumps the flour into it.*
>
> *Then Jean says, "Now it's Ricky's turn." Jean repeats the process for each of the children. Jean then brings some baking powder to the table and says, "Now it's Nancy's turn again." Jean helps each child put some baking powder into the bowl. As they wait for their turns, the toddlers enjoy making circular motions with their hands in the flour on the table.*
>
> *Then Jean gives each child some salt to put into the mixing bowl. Ricky and Nancy begin pounding the table with their fists. Each child has a turn pouring the milk into the bowl. Jean asks Mark, "Can you stir this while I put the milk away?" Mark nods yes and begins to stir. Jean places the dough on the table and then gives each child a round cookie cutter. They each help cut out the biscuits.*

These children may seem exceptionally young to be able to engage in a project involving so many turn-taking sequences. But because Jean organizes these cooking experiences every week, the young children have learned to expect that they will have a turn preparing the food and thus can enjoy the process.

The nature of turn taking is an individual act within a social context. By the time they are 3 years old, young children can engage in many forms of turn taking, especially when it is structured by their teachers. Turn taking can have an individual or a social emphasis. When individual children have to wait for their turn to practice reciting their address and telephone number, the activity has a distinctly individual tilt. When young children and their teacher engage in a small-group movement activity, in which children and teacher rhythmically chant each child's name and move their hands and arms in the manner initiated by the named child, the activity has a social tilt. Here the individual act transforms the group process into a new social experience.

A potential problem can emerge when teachers zealously emphasize individual turn taking in group activities because the waiting children typically become restless. Then teachers often have difficulty maintaining effective group management. If a teacher chooses to repeatedly call on the restless children, their own redirection can rupture the flow of the other children's attention. This fragmentation of the group process illustrates the dynamic that Kounin (1970) termed the *ripple effect*, when a teacher's handling of one child's misbehavior distracts the attention of the other children.

Developmental Anomalies: Child Behavior Representing the Spectrum of Autism

Over the years, teachers may have a child in their class who rarely, if ever, seems connected or able to engage in turn taking, either in conversation or in simple games. Babies who are unable to engage in turn taking, either in communication or through games, may be indicating the first signs of an autistic disorder.[1] Out-of-home teachers can be keen observers of the children in their care and may be the first to identify this type of disorder.

Erin's child care teachers asked me to observe Erin and consult with them when she was 16 months old. Erin had entered the center at 8 weeks of age and throughout her first year seemed to be developing normally. By age 12 months, Erin spoke approximately three intelligible words and delighted in play with the other children and adults.

When she was about 14 months old, however, Erin's daily behavior changed significantly. She no longer made eye contact with children or adults, had no spontaneous speech, did not engage in any give-and-take exchange, and did not follow adult directions or redirection. Rather, she seemed to play in her "own little world" alone, and she would spend long periods of time lining up her toys.

Although Erin did have speech, her speech consisted only of repetition of numerals and letters, over and over. Her vocalization also changed and seemed to come from her throat, not from her palate.

Once Erin's parents initiated a full evaluation of Erin, they discovered that she had Asperger syndrome, a pervasive de-

velopmental disorder with the social and behavioral features
of autism but no significant language or cognitive delays. With
rigorous occupational, speech-language, and play therapy, Erin
is slowly developing skill in communication and the ability to
play with her peers.

Rule Implementation   Rules are guidelines that contribute to
young children's ability to be together for extended periods of time and
are the scaffolding of teachers' group management. Group management
is an essential skill of family- and center-based teachers for without it,
disorder and confusion would emerge. Understanding and following
rules are essential for young children to develop self-control, a primary
task of the early years.

Teachers will need rules as soon as babies become mobile because
then the babies' actions might be dangerous or might bother other young
children. With very young children, teachers often can anticipate potential hazards and redirect the children safely. When teachers observe
the children in their care closely, they are able to implement rules within
the context of the children's activity. Rule implementation thus becomes
a learning experience for the children.

> *Jean is seated on the living room couch while four tod-*
> *dlers play near her. Ricky (age 21 months) picks up a small,*
> *wooden toy person; opens the back door of a large toy*
> *school bus; and says to Jean, "There's one people."*
>
> *Jean responds, "Okay, let's take him up the steps." Ricky*
> *pretends that three play people are climbing up the back*
> *steps of the school bus.*
>
> *Ricky then comes to Jean with two play people and says,*
> *"Pocket." Jean answers, "Well, let's check and see if you*
> *have any pockets."*
>
> *During this time, Nancy (age 23 months) gets on the*
> *school bus and begins to ride it about the living room. Ricky*
> *goes to Nancy and begins to push her off the bus.*
>
> *Jean redirects by saying, "Nancy is going to take her*
> *people on a ride, Ricky. Let's wait until her people get back.*
> *Then you can take your people up the steps." Ricky then*
> *leaves Nancy and gets a car out of the toy box. He lies on*
> *his stomach as he makes motor sounds and moves the car*
> *back and forth.*

As Ricky and Nancy played, Jean was available to assist, extend, or
redirect the toddlers' play. Jean understood the project on which Ricky
was working with his play people and the school bus. When Ricky at-

tempted to push Nancy off the school bus, Jean could redirect Ricky's action within the context of his play. By explaining Nancy's intentions to Ricky—"Nancy is going to take her people on a ride"—Jean helped him understand another child's perspective. Often young children act impulsively with little or no awareness of their own intentions or feelings. When Ricky heard his own intentions expressed—"Then you can take your people up the steps"—he was more willing to hear Jean's report of Nancy's intentions and was thus more willing to wait his turn or become distracted by a different activity.

If Jean had not been near the playing children, Ricky probably would have pushed Nancy off the bus, and there would have been an emotional outburst. Jean would then have responded to the emotional outburst and implemented her rule that forbids pushing other children. Jean's response would have ended the children's dispute. If Jean were only aware of the emotional outburst resulting from the conflict, her strategy to resolve the situation would have been external to the children's ongoing project that led to the conflict. Jean would have reinforced the rule about no pushing; however, the children would not have been able to recognize their own and the other child's intentions involved in their play, an important outcome of Jean's intervention.

When teachers are not observing the children keenly, their interventions often end the misbehavior successfully; however, the children's only learning involves the rule being reinforced. Anne, a teacher of 3-year-olds, illustrates this form of rule implementation.[2]

> Darnell, DeVonne, Jessica, and Ria are crawling about the housekeeping floor as they pretend to be lions. Ria swings a necktie as though it were a training whip as Darnell and DeVonne jump up and down. Ria then leads Darnell and DeVonne to the dress-up cupboard, which she opens as she says, "Now get into your cage." Darnell and DeVonne climb into the cupboard, and Ria closes the door.
> Anne is seated with children at a nearby table. She calls to the boys and says, "Darnell and DeVonne, the clothes closet isn't a good place to climb in." The boys then climb out of the cupboard.

Young children often are quite malleable and quick to learn rules, especially if their teachers are consistent in implementing those rules. Redirection experiences, however, can be opportunities not only for learning rules but also for learning about oneself and other children. In the previous story, Anne "catches" the children's rule violation and is not punitive in her redirection. But she neither enters into the children's experience to understand the project they are working on, nor does she give the children an explanation of the need for rule adherence. Alternatively, Anne could have explained to the boys that the cupboard was for dress-up clothes and might break if they climb in and out of it.

Conflict Resolution When young children bother one another, it is not uncommon for the conflict to escalate into a fight, either verbally or physically. Teachers not only can redirect young children but also can teach them strategies to respond to their peers when a conflict arises. In the following example, Joy helps Carrie learn how to respond to peer interference.

> *Mia (age 22 months) and Carrie (age 18 months) play at the sensory table with oatmeal and assorted cups. Mia grabs Carrie's cup, and Carrie screams, "Mine!"*
>
> *Joy says, "Mia, I hear Carrie's words. You need to give it back to her." Joy walks over to the children to ensure that Mia follows through with her directive, and Mia responds by giving the cup back to Carrie.*

Joy and her co-teachers have many opportunities to help toddlers learn simple ways to defend themselves or to redirect toddlers who are not quite old enough to remember the rules.

> *Cory (age 12 months) and Mia (age 22 months) play in the gross motor room with five other toddlers and two teachers. Cory grabs Mia's plastic lawn mower. Alicia says to Mia, "Tell Cory it's your turn to play with the mower."*
>
> *Mia shouts, "Mine!"*
>
> *Alicia explains, "Cory, now it is Mia's turn. I'll make sure you can have a turn in a couple of minutes."*
>
> *Cory then goes to two toddlers seated on a foam square and tries to push them off the square. Alicia takes Cory's hands and walks him to the ball tub as she tells him, "You play in the ball pit now." Cory delights in lying in the ball tub and tossing the balls.*

Alicia and her co-workers have cared for Cory since he was 8 weeks old. Alicia knows that Cory often interferes with the other children's play. At age 12 months, Cory sometimes needs specific rule implementation; other times he merely needs quick redirection.

Often young children are not able to figure out how their actions affect others. They especially don't think about the consequences of their actions in advance. When young children hear that their teacher recognizes and cares about their own feelings and intentions, they are more apt to hear when the teacher explains the feelings and intentions of the other child in the dispute. With the teacher's assistance, children in a dispute can reach a joint solution to the conflict; and conflict can become a social learning context for perspective taking and joint problem solving.

Cultural Diversity within Out-of-Home Caregiving

Teachers' ethnicity and culture are intertwined with the manner in which they interact with babies and young children. It is not uncommon, especially in urban communities in the United States, for child care teachers to work with young children of varying ethnicities and cultures, such as Asian American, Hispanic, Native American, African American, and Caucasian. Effective caregiving of children across diverse cultures is possible when teachers are eager to learn about cultures different from their own and can accept and respect others' differences. An extended discussion about caregiving across cultures and ethnicities is outside of the scope of this book (see Lynch & Hanson, 1998, for more information). A brief discussion, however, can point to areas needing consideration.

Effective teachers understand that emotions and patterns of relating are learned within the everyday child-rearing interactions of parents and their young children. A wide variation has been found in patterns of relating and valuing across cultures (Bateson, 1994; Heath, 1983; Klein, 1996a). Some parents may promote their babies' and young children's exploration, creativity, and independence, whereas other parents may promote cooperation, sensitivity to others, and sociability. Parents from different cultural backgrounds may vary significantly in their use of disciplinary practices. Some children in a caregiving program may come from extended families with multiple strong emotional attachments; others may come from single-parent families with minimal informal or formal support.

What is a teacher to do when confronted with significant cultural differences among the children for whom she cares? First, it is important to understand that what people see, value, and understand is filtered through their own cultural background. Teachers' sensitivity to how their own behavior and values reflect their age, gender, ethnicity, and income level can be the first step in relating to children and parents of a different culture. Second, teachers can strive to be open and flexible and sensitive about any stereotypical assumptions about children or their families whose cultural backgrounds may be different from their own. Third, they can engage respectfully in dialogue with parents and express eagerness to know what parents expect of their young children and of out-of-home teachers. When differences emerge, such as differences in discipline strategies, teachers can explain their own disciplinary practices and choices. Teachers can observe each child carefully and be open to varying behaviors and expressions. Furthermore, teachers can be sensitive about when they need to vary their own approach to better match the parental approach with which the young child is most familiar.

Multiple Teachers within the Course of a Day

Some babies and toddlers are cared for by several different teachers and caregivers, sometimes by four or five within 1 day. Working parents sometimes rely on caregivers other than those in the child care setting, such as before or after the program. Sometimes these caregivers are different on different days of the week. In addition, because of the minimal financial resources that out-of-home child care programs typically have, some programs have teachers who work for a few hours at the beginning or end of a day.

For babies and toddlers to feel secure, they need to have the *same teachers* who provide *consistent schedules and expectations.* Having too many teachers and caregivers creates a serious dilemma in the lives of many babies and toddlers. Daily changes in teachers can confuse babies and toddlers and lead to feelings of insecurity, which they are not old enough to communicate. In reality, *every moment of a baby or toddler's day has an impact on his or her care, development, and education.* There is no "down time" in young children's development. When they have multiple teachers and caregivers, young children may not feel secure enough to experience these times as contexts for promoting development.

The dilemma of multiple teachers is difficult for both parents and caregiving programs to address. Some programs manage this issue by staggering the teachers' daily hours so that they can make certain that at least one primary teacher is present during the entire day. Finding solutions to this dilemma for families, however, may be more difficult. Parents can become aware of the risks associated with multiple caregiving and committed to reducing the number of people caring for their child. Often child care programs can assist parents merely by informing them that having different, multiple teachers inhibits their young child's development, a fact that many parents may not know.

Concluding Comments on Teacher–Child Interaction

The teacher–child interaction patterns just discussed may be conscious or unconscious, intentional or unwitting. Regardless, each interaction is significant in terms of the development of the babies, toddlers, and young children with whom the teacher interacts. Now that babies' and young children's social-emotional context of child rearing has expanded to include out-of-home caregivers as well as parents, these children are forming very significant secondary attachments, which affect their development of self and internalization of attitudes, values, and behavior patterns. Just as these teacher–child interaction patterns are pivotal to the young children's development, so too are the other recurring interaction patterns within the out-of-home caregiving setting. The next section examines teacher–teacher interaction patterns.

TEACHER–TEACHER INTERACTION

Babies and young children thrive in environments that are calm and even-tempoed. The quality of teacher–child and teacher–teacher relations is the key dynamic to creating the climate in which babies and young children act, feel, and understand. Most caregiving environments involve a minimum of two adults working together. Beyond affecting the climate or ambience of a caregiving environment, the manner in which teachers interact with each other affirms or ignores, assists or inhibits, and enables or threatens the teachers' actions, feelings, and abilities to interact with the young children for whom they care. The following sections discuss the possibilities of teacher–teacher interaction and how this interaction promotes young children's development.

Interaction as Professionals

Many, if not most, out-of-home caregivers work in a team-teaching environment. Each teacher in a team brings his or her own personal history, personality, teaching style, education, and expertise to the team relationship.

Not surprisingly, teachers express individual differences in their actions, interactions, and understandings. Jill, Ellen, and Coreen, for example, are co-teachers of a classroom of 3-year-olds. Each teacher brings different strengths and weaknesses to the co-teaching situation. Jill is a very skilled play partner with the children; however, when she plays, she tends to lose her ability to supervise all of the children. Jill also creatively improvises in total-group movement activities. Her co-teacher,

Ellen, closely supervises the children, loves music, and has wonderful extended singing sessions with the children each day. Ellen likes structure; thus, her small-group activities tend to be very teacher directed and structured. In contrast, the third co-teacher, Coreen, improvises small-group activities in which the children are active participants. Coreen is exceptionally skilled in observing and interpreting the behavior of the children that she, Jill, and Ellen teach.

Given the inevitability of individual differences as well as the complexity of providing care for a group of babies and young children, clarification of roles and expectations can facilitate open, respectful relations among co-workers. For example, Jill and Ellen, knowing that each have different strengths and weaknesses, explicitly agreed on taking more responsibility for different aspects of the day. Ellen, 20 years older than Jill and skilled in relating to parents, took responsibility for having brief exchanges with parents on children's arrival. Given her aptitude for playing with the children, Jill usually was responsible for the housekeeping and block area during free play. Jill and Ellen knew what to expect of each other during the course of the day, and this clarity allowed them to play off each other in an easy manner.

At the same time, however, Ellen sometimes unwittingly ordered Jill about, especially with regard to maintaining order in the classroom. Ellen was not always aware of how she was coming across to Jill, nor was she aware of how her behavior humiliated Jill. Given the length of a child care day and the multiplicities of both attention and interaction in which each teacher engages, it is difficult always both to be aware of one's own feelings and actions and to be sensitive to those of others, especially one's co-workers.

For teachers to work smoothly together as a team, *daily or regularly scheduled planning and evaluation* is essential. Often teachers use the initial part of the children's afternoon nap for these meetings. Some programs provide a weekly planning and evaluation time for teachers. Collaboration skills are not easily learned or promoted in the American society. Most teachers have grown up with individualistic, competitive patterns of schooling. Developing collaborative work can be a new and challenging experience that takes time, self-reflection, and open discussion among co-workers. Teachers can use team meetings to share observations and reflections of ongoing caregiving activities and to discuss the young children's and the teachers' behavior. Teachers can evaluate what activities and actions are working and what needs to be changed. On the basis of these reflections, teachers can collaboratively plan their work together. Productive team meetings involve open sharing of each person's thoughts and feelings as well as questioning of one's assumptions. When teachers collaboratively plan and evaluate their work together, they are more likely to have open reciprocal classroom interactions that model healthy relationships for the very young children in their care.

A relationship based on trust, respect, and open communication is critical to successful team teaching. It takes time, however, for this relationship to develop. Spending time together organizing and cleaning the classroom and planning the curriculum can promote a healthy relationship. Inevitably differences arise, and feelings get hurt; therefore, an openness to confront feelings and differences by honestly discussing them is essential to the growth of the teacher–teacher relationship. Developing a framework around which tasks to share can be helpful; for example, it is productive to explicitly decide who will greet the children or lead total-group activities for 1 week. Once teachers know each other as individuals by working closely together over time, their professional relationship often develops into a personal one as well.

Structures of Team Teaching: Lead Teachers or Co-teachers

Team teaching can involve either a situation of lead and assistant teachers or a structure of co-teachers working as equals. Professionals often debate the pros and cons of either structure, but, regardless of the structure, it is essential that each teacher assume responsibility. Pam is assistant director of a child care center with 160 children, ages 6 weeks to 6 years old. Pam first worked in this center as a co-teacher for 10 years prior to assuming her position as assistant director. Pam discussed with me her experience in team teaching.

Pam: When I was teaching, all teachers were co-teachers; and I just did it all. And I always was frustrated because other teachers didn't do things that I thought were important. But at that time, I didn't have team skills.

Ten years ago, when I became assistant director, we continued to have co-teaching. But we began to see that no one was taking responsibility, and things were not happening on a timely basis. So we changed to the structure of Lead Teacher, Cooperating Teacher, and Aide. But a couple of teachers with years of experience were horrified that they didn't get the lead position. And many Cooperating Teachers expressed dissatisfaction. If they took initiative they didn't feel recognized; rather, the Lead Teacher got the credit.

Over time, we realized that everyone has to do the same work. It is the same quality care that is essential to the children every moment of the day. So if the responsibility is the same for everyone, then everyone should be co-teachers. We abolished the differentiation and everyone became co-teachers.

We realized that even though responsibilities are the same, everyone brings different strengths. We wanted our goal to be to help each teacher reach her optimal level. At the same time, we have some teachers who intuitively are master teachers. Realistically, we don't have that many.

Once we decided to change the structure to co-teaching we met with the entire staff, and they helped to develop a new job description. Interestingly, the first three items were communication/relationships—with children, with teachers, and with parents. I continue to find the hardest part of my work the adult-to-adult relationship. For the most part, teachers do a wonderful job with the kids, but they may not be able to relate successfully to other adults.

Carol: What do you think the primary problem is in terms of relating to other teachers?

Pam: It's a different skill and not why they chose the field. They chose the field because of their love of being with kids; and they may have had skill with kids but no clue in terms of communicating with adults.

Carol: How do you know when it is not working?

Pam: Interestingly, the kids are a barometer; that is, when there are fewer difficulties with the children, I have a sense that the team is working together. And individual teachers can be a barometer in terms of their willingness to engage in conversation with me. Some teachers are so even keeled, I know they'll do their job regardless. Others have their hearts on their sleeves, and I always know if something is going on with them.

When interacting with co-workers, it is important that teachers are able to ask themselves the following: "How am I coming across? When a young teacher asks for my opinion, do I reply as an authority or as a co-inquirer?" Similarly, it is important for teachers to be aware of how they are feeling and how they are expressing those feelings, for example, "When my co-worker consistently does not clean up her area, I know that I feel anger and resentment. How am I going to respectfully approach this co-worker about the conflict?"

Teachers always need to strive to be aware of their own and other's feelings—for example, when a teacher is "battling it out" with a non-compliant child, when a co-teacher snaps at another teacher, or when a co-teacher chooses *not* to respond to a child-to-child conflict. When teachers pause to reflect and to ask themselves what their co-worker is experiencing and feeling in a particular situation, they can interact in a thoughtful, caring, and supportive manner. Rather than intervene to approach the noncompliant child, for example, the teacher observing the situation might discuss it empathetically with the acting teacher at a later time. Together the two adults can brainstorm both about the child's behavior and intent and about possible adult interventions. Effective teachers are quick to help very young children understand another child's feelings, saying, for example, "That really hurt Leroy when you hit him." In the same way, effective teachers internally strive to be aware of their co-teachers' feelings, especially when the co-teacher is immersed in a difficult situation. When co-teachers do *not* develop this reciprocity in relating to each other openly, a climate of tension that is destructive to the babies and young children prevails.

Interaction as Peers

When teachers can relate together informally as peers as well as professionals, these interactions can provide release and relaxation. Throughout the day at Rosehill Day Care Center, teachers engage in a great deal of informal conversation. The adults seem to enjoy being with one another and relating socially, primarily as peers. Because they frequently share the same space during outdoor play, early and late care, and lunch and nap periods, they have many opportunities to share personal anecdotes.

As teachers are talking with each other, their dialogue often involves telling each other stories, perhaps personal stories about themselves or their families or stories about their work with the children. In myriad ways, these stories enrich both the teachers who are speaking and their partners in the dialogue. As teachers talk with each other, they are reflecting on their experiences and weaving their experiences into the meaning they make of their lives. In other words, telling stories is one way that teachers give meaning to their personal and professional lives.[3] In these dialogues each teacher shares her own stream of thoughts; and by sharing their thoughts with one another, teachers often develop a new stream of understanding. As they tell each other stories, each person's experiences are being heard and validated. The dialogue process enhances the collegial partnership of teachers. Often storytelling can be the first step in reflection for teachers to begin planning new action.

When teachers such as those at Rosehill enjoy each other's companionship, they are providing an informal, calming ambience for the young children in their care. Furthermore, they are modeling mutual respect and companionship. In turn, the children feel comfortable and secure enough to initiate their own activities and enjoy the companionship of both their peers and their teachers. Unfortunately, in my observations of teachers at Rosehill, the teachers' enjoyment of peer conversation sometimes superseded their close supervision of the children and their focus on interacting with them.

Integration of the Professional and the Personal

How teachers get along personally influences their ability to work together professionally. Alicia has been teaching babies and toddlers for 4 years. She spoke about her work with Joy and Carmeletta, her co-teachers:

Alicia: We are a lucky team. We seem to be able to read each other's minds. Of the four infant-toddler teams, we're the only ones with no turnover. Four years ago, when I first began teaching in this room, I didn't get along with the other teacher. We'd go through the day and only talk about the children. In fact, I'd get an update at 9:30 A.M. when I arrived, and that's where the talking stopped. You feel like you're alone with the kids, and there is no one to talk with.

        Then for 6 months, Joy and I were alone. We had long hours to cover the 11½-hour day, so it was hard. But we had fun getting closer. We thought there was no room for a third person. But we knew Carmeletta because she was a floating teacher. We asked her to be the third teacher; and we all get along wonderfully. When I am in the room, I can turn my back and know that Joy or Carmeletta is taking care of the kids. When I'm off there is a new person here, but I don't worry because Joy and Carmeletta are here. And I know that when we get along, it is better for the kids.

        We are team teachers, and decision making is easy. One does something and asks if it's okay, and we usually say okay. We each have our duties. The first person arriving does morning diapers, the second person does midday diapers, and the third does afternoon diapers. Whoever gets a child up from a nap changes the diaper.

        In every infant-toddler room, there is a primary teacher for each child. But for us, primaries don't matter, except for parent conferences and handling medicine. Whoever has a free hand relates to the child.

Alicia is a soft-spoken, nurturant teacher. She not only loves working with the babies and toddlers, but she also enjoys the companionship she has with Joy and Carmeletta. She explains that because she and her co-teachers care for and respect each others' competence, they engage professionally in an easy give-and-take sharing of responsibilities. It is as though their personal and professional interactions blend. As she spoke, Alicia shifted from describing her current classroom to discussing her prior work environment:

Alicia: You know, child care is usually a working environment for women, and environments can be very different. In my first job, there was a lot of gossip and cliques—sort of like high school. Here we have a relaxed environment, almost like a family. The teachers tend to share with each other like in a family.

   My brother is a vice president at Miller Bank, and he keeps urging me to work at the bank and make more money. But I'd never be happy there. We're so spoiled by the closeness we have with each other. Each day, like at naptime, we can chat together in a relaxed environment.

Alicia experiences a sense of belonging to a community of early education teachers. Not all teachers have as close and as trusting a relationship as do Joy, Carmeletta, and Alicia, nor do they feel a part of a close community. At the same time, teaching teams in which the teachers do not share a close personal relationship can still be effective, as long as each person respects the others, expectations and roles are openly discussed, and everyone regularly plans and evaluates together.

Rebecca is the infant-toddler coordinator in the center where Alicia, Carmeletta, and Joy teach. This center has five infant-toddler rooms and two 2-year-old rooms. Rebecca's discussion of team teaching involved themes similar to those expressed by Alicia:

Rebecca: Teacher–teacher interaction is a great model for the kids to see. The problem is, if it doesn't click, it doesn't work. When I hire infant-toddler teachers, I hire "from the gut." It's something inside that cannot be taught—working with infants and toddlers and team teaching. . . .

   It takes time for a relationship to develop [among teachers]. I think they have to develop an intimate relationship with each other. . . . They need to trust, respect, and understand each other. I cannot teach team building; it either happens or it doesn't happen. An infant-toddler teacher must be intuitive with adults as well as the kids. Trust is essential—knowing that if I'm not available, someone will be there for the kids.

Rebecca understands that it takes time for individuals to develop personal relationships, which she sees as a key ingredient to successful team teaching of babies and toddlers. She believes that every teacher and teaching team can learn from workshops on team building.

Rebecca also addressed the issue of high staff turnover when it comes to infant-toddler teachers and explained how working with babies and toddlers demands skills different from those required of preschool teachers:

Rebecca: Our highest turnover is with the infant-toddler teachers. But why should we be surprised, given their low salaries and early education training? They have minimal or no infant-toddler education and are *clueless* as to knowing what to do. Sometimes all they seem to experience is a lot of diaper changing and feeding of messy babies. They don't understand the meaning and purpose of their work or what they could be doing to promote their kids' development. And you know, I'm not sure every early educator understands that infant-toddler care is so different from teaching preschool.

Concluding Comments on Teacher–Teacher Interaction

Individual differences in teachers' values, attitudes, understanding, and behavior have an impact on how teachers relate to their co-teachers. Various factors contribute to a teacher's ability to work with other adults. Though these factors are discussed separately here, more than one of these dynamics may occur at the same time, and often they are reflexively intertwined. For example, the given environment of a center may be parallel to the personal style of a teacher.

A teacher's personal needs and personal history influence his or her interactions with co-teachers. Every out-of-home caregiver brings different pedagogical skills and knowledge. Many caregivers have minimal or no professional education, and many preservice education programs give only minimal attention to team teaching. Thus, it is not surprising to learn that how a teacher relates to other teachers has more to do with personal style than with educational knowledge or skill. Finally, the caregiving environment as well as the program characteristics can influence teacher–teacher interaction. Given this complexity, how teachers interact with each other creates a climate that influences how babies and young children act and interact within out-of-home caregiving.

CHILD–CHILD INTERACTION

Teacher–child interactions provide the framework in which young children interact with each other. Teachers' arrangement of the environment and the way in which they interact with each other and with the children enable reciprocal and mutually beneficial, unilateral, or aggressive relations among the children. A democratic society nourishes mutuality and reciprocity in relations with all people.

In the large meeting room at Rosehill Day Care Center, during early care (6:30 A.M. to 9:00 A.M.), the art table and about eight tables for table toy play were open for use by the 3- and 4-year-old children. The block and housekeeping areas, which invite spontaneous groupings of children and children's prosocial interaction, were closed. As a result, Rosehill children engaged primarily in individually focused play: drawing; puzzle completion; and building with Legos, Unifix cubes, and so forth. Given the nature of these children's quiet, low-activity play, their teachers often were able to gather together and chat informally. In contrast, in other centers some teachers open the block area, housekeeping area, and/or sensory tables—areas that invite spontaneous groups of children in play. In these two contexts, teachers are dispersed into different areas to care for the children effectively. These two different environmental arrangements invite two different patterns of teacher–child, teacher–teacher, and child–child interaction.

I derived children's action and interaction patterns from extended qualitative action research. Over extended periods of time, I observed teachers and young children and shared my observations with these teachers. The purpose of this action research process was to improve the understanding and implementation of practice. *Individually focused activity with teacher distance* refers to children's activity that involves minimal or no social exchange. Prosocial patterns typify child–child interactions, interactions that involve positive, mutual give-and-take exchange. Seven prosocial patterns include *spontaneous conversation, structured mutuality, joint projects, assistance, social role play,* and *association as friends.* As with teacher–child interaction patterns discussed previously, these child–child interaction patterns are not meant to portray all possible child–child interaction but instead to portray those patterns that I found to be salient across caregiving sites, teachers, and young children.

Individually Focused Activity with Teacher Distance

In many child care environments, during much of each day, young children control the choice and duration of their involvement in activities. During my 6 months of observation at Rosehill Day Care Center, the 3- and 4-year-olds were quite skilled at initiating their own activities. During 3 hours of early care and 3 hours of late care, materials invited primarily individual focus. Children were allowed to work with art materials, puzzles, and a wide assortment of manipulative toys at several small tables. Interestingly, although almost all of the children could initiate their own activities, only a few were able to maintain sustained focus. The most typical pattern I observed was frequent changing of materials and engaging in surface play; that is, children remained at a play task for very brief periods, and their play did not involve much creativity or complexity. Teachers often were in the adjoining kitchen preparing breakfast and chatting during these play periods. It seemed to me that it was possible that the teachers' maintaining distance from these individual activities led to the surface quality of much of the children's play. It seemed apparent that the young children had internalized their teachers' rules (e.g., the child who chose first did not have to share a toy); so the children required minimal adult intervention, thus allowing the teachers to maintain their distance. Given the surface quality of the play, not much was happening in terms of play promoting the children's development. At the same time, some teachers might see this experience as promoting independence.

Spontaneous Conversation

Teachers frequently talk about either what they are doing or what they see babies and toddlers doing, or they spontaneously talk with older children. This type of conversation promotes children's language development and encourages a sense of belonging.

> *Five toddlers play in water with baby dolls and wash small plastic dishes and clothes. Darnell (age 16 months) picks up his doll as he says, "baby." His teacher, Carmeletta, replies, "Yes, you're going to give your baby a bath." Mia (age 21 months) responds, "Wash baby."*

Darnell and Carmeletta's comments sparked Mia to join in the game. Toddlers often do not take the perspective of the other child or adult. Thus, sometimes a toddler's comment will spark another toddler's comment, but often the second comment may be unrelated to the first. For example, Mia may have said, "Alicia," as she was watching Carmeletta's co-teacher on the other side of the room.

Preschool children not only engage in informal chatting together but also often talk together as they construct something or engage in social role play. These conversations often involve joint planning and decision making. As Chunsey and Shalona, both 3 years old, play together with farm animals and a small plastic fence, they illustrate this pattern.

> *Chunsey and Shalona set up farm animals inside a small plastic snap-together fence. Chunsey suggests, "Let's lay them down." The children lay the animals down; as they do so, some of the fence tumbles down. Shalona says, "They are taking a nap," and Chunsey responds, "Our farm is breaking."*
>
> *The children stand the animals up as Shalona says, "Now their nap is over." Chunsey takes a duck and puts it on the rug, saying, "Now he is swimming." Shalona gets a cow and puts it on the rug as she says, "And it's so hot he needs a drink."*

Chunsey and Shalona are creating a world together. In their play, they use language to substitute for actions, and they are able to play off each other verbally.

Structured Mutuality

When two or more children play together, the structure of the materials or rules of the game can define the parameters of the play. Structured mutuality involves prosocial interaction because the children share materials and engage in cooperative interaction. When these play sequences are extended, the children experience shared enjoyment. The following are examples of children playing together:

- *Suzie and Rachel put together wooden train tracks and trains on the rug area.*
- *Mimi and Keisha shake film cans to match similar sounds.*
- *Emmet and Jimmy flip small plastic discs as if they are Tiddly Winks.*

Throughout my 6-month observational study at Rosehill Day Care Center, the four teachers I observed consistently emphasized individual rather than social learning. Thus, the observed structured mutuality of the children was predominantly child initiated; rarely did the teachers initiate this type of play. Similarly, the teachers rarely chose to focus on or interact with the children during this play. Yet the children's shared enjoyment led to their extended focus in these types of activities, even without adult participation or reinforcement.

Joint Projects

Joint projects refer to play in which children implement a plan together to create something new, such as when children build together with blocks, Tinker Toys, plastic snap-together toys, or engage in creative movement. Kumar and five other 3- and 4-year-olds illustrate this form of imaginative play.

> *During free play, Kumar takes an empty coffee can from the art area and begins tapping it as he chants rhythmically. Eddie, Rachel, Jennie, Mark, and DeVonne begin chanting with Kumar, who begins marching in a circle and chanting. Kumar changes his rhythm and step, and the other children follow him. Then Eddie and Rachel take the lead.*

In this spontaneously formed group, Kumar, Eddie, and Rachel took a leadership role as the children engaged in rhythmic chanting and movement. For approximately 10 minutes, these children experienced shared enjoyment and creative self-expression. In other sequences of joint projects, children also experience give-and-take cooperation, planning, and decision making as illustrated in the following vignette.

> *DeVonne (age 4 years), Derrick (age 4 years), and Jimmy (age 3 years) build with unit blocks. As they begin making a rectangular structure, DeVonne says, "Let's make a big fire-house." No one replies, but everyone adds to the building. Derrick then brings over a tub of zoo animals and suggests, "Let's make a zoo. This is the big cage for the lions."*
>
> *DeVonne says, "Okay, but we'll need lots more cages." The children together make several other "cages" out of simple squares and rectangles. With the completion of each cage, they discuss what animal will live in the cage. After they have made six cages for six animals, DeVonne announces that he will be the zookeeper. Derrick and Jimmy say that they will be the animal feeders. Derrick takes the empty zoo animal tub and pretends to be throwing food on the bottom of the cages for the animals.*

DeVonne and Derrick are friends and often play cooperatively during activity period. This was Jimmy's first time playing with DeVonne and Derrick, but he was quick to follow along with the older children.

Social Role Play   During their second year, toddlers engage in simple pretend play in which they act out everyday experiences, such as brushing their hair, pouring milk, and cooking eggs. With increasing age, young children engage in pretend play together, and this play is termed *sociodramatic* or *social role play*. In social role play, children take on roles and use imitation and their imagination to create sequences of action and conversation. Children incorporate real or imagined props, and they use words to describe imaginary objects, actions, or situations. The following vignette illustrates how two young children engage in social role play.

> *Bria (age 4 years) and Latoya (age 3 years) are sitting outside in the old wooden boat. Bria says, "This is our ice cream store. What kind of ice cream cone do you want?" Latoya replies, "Strawberry," and Bria pretends to hand Latoya a cone. Bria then leaves the boat and walks about the playground chanting, "Ice cream cones, 25 cents for ice cream cones." Several children place an order, and Bria returns to the boat to get their cones.*

Initially, young children act out their present and past experiences. Bria and her parents have gone to ice cream stores together; and, in play, Bria can reenact these experiences in her own way, as leader. As other children play along with her, she gains a sense of competence and self-worth, knowing that her actions can influence her peers.

Assistance

Young children are providing assistance when they help another child complete a self-help or play activity, such as tying shoes or completing a puzzle. Before their second birthday, toddlers feel uncomfortable when they see that another person is unhappy, and they tend to try to comfort that person. Mia illustrates this pattern.

> *In the gross motor room, Kurt (age 13 months) walks briskly about the room with a plastic lawn mower. He stumbles accidentally, falls on his face, and begins to cry. Mia (age 21 months) is playing nearby and walks over to Kurt. She pats his head repeatedly as she says, "Okay, Kurt. Okay, Kurt."*

Mia is quick to comfort Kurt when she sees him fall down and begin to cry. She is most likely imitating the comforting responses of her parents and teachers to her own crying.

During my 6-month observation at Rosehill Day Care Center, I saw one child assist another child only two times. Given the Rosehill teachers' emphasis on individual learning, this lack of child-to-child assistance was not surprising. In contrast, when I was working with approximately 20 Head Start teachers, in four urban areas, I observed a great deal of child-to-child assistance, where children helped each other in tying shoes, completing puzzles, zipping coats, and pushing each other on the swing. Clearly, teachers have significant influence on developing young children's natural tendency toward assisting their peers.

Association as Friends

Young children, 3 years old and older, often develop special friendships in their out-of-home caregiving setting. This companionship develops spontaneously without teacher facilitation. Young children have a simple understanding of the meaning of these friendships. Children younger than 6 years of age understand friends as "associates with whom one plays or comes into frequent contact. . . . There is no sense of liking or disliking the stable traits of another" (Damon, 1977, p. 153). A child calls another child his or her friend simply "because I play with him." Young children's play with friends involves a lot of give-and-take mutuality, but children have neither an awareness nor an understanding of this mutuality.

Interestingly, much of friendship play with preschool-age children involves prosocial behavior, such as sharing toys, helping, cooperation, and joint decision making and planning. Friendship play often is quite complex and of long duration. Friendships thus seem to promote both prosocial development and task focus. The children who have special friends often are the children who have developed more mature social skills.

Teachers of young children can choose to promote, ignore, or inhibit children's friendships. Most early educators speak very positively about the value of friendships; however, they sometimes find friendships to be disruptive to the flow of group activities. Furthermore, some children's play with a special friend can quickly escalate into loud, high-activity play. Anne, a teacher at Rosehill Day Care Center, spoke positively about friendships. But given her focus on control issues, Anne separates friends before she begins group activities. And she explained that she sometimes breaks up a friendship by promoting a child to the next, older class to simplify her management.

In caregiving environments that are well managed, and when teachers understand the role of social interaction, antisocial behavior such as children's being overly aggressive, tattling, or fighting occurs only infrequently. Very young children do not seem by nature to be competitive; rather, *competition* seems to emerge with certain environmental arrangements, adult expectations, and structuring of activities. When a very high adult–child ratio exists, young children feel competitive in their need to gain adult attention, approval, and affirmation. Competition also arises when teachers structure group activities with extended turn taking, thus causing young children to wait for long periods for their turn. A pattern of adult management that is fueled by a philosophy of behavior management or assertive discipline can also spark competition. Singling one child out for praise (e.g., "I like the way Joey is seated quietly") can breed competitive feelings among the children who are being left out.

Young children tattle not only to tell the adult about another child's misbehavior but also to gain that adult's attention. Usually only one or two children in a group spontaneously tattle on their peers. And most often, the young children who develop patterns of tattling are the most needy of adult attention. Effective teachers strive to break patterns of tattling; they usually can quickly end the pattern by letting the tattlers know that they need to take care of themselves and the adult will take care of the other children. Once teachers recognize this pattern in a child, they can strive to make the tattling child feel more secure and decrease this tattling need.

Child-to-child conflicts are inevitable; it is natural for very young children to grab toys from their peers or hit another child who has frustrated them. One of a teacher's primary tasks is to help young children learn simple rules for getting along with others. The majority of young children become aggressive when they are feeling frustrated. At the same time, however, very anxious children are often aggressive, and this aggression can be unprovoked. Chapter 4, Guidance and Discipline, discusses children's conflicts and offers effective strategies that teachers can utilize to intervene in such situations.

The Isolated Child

Friendships do not come easily to all children, and out-of-home teachers may find that one of the children in their care is isolated. Often children who are social isolates demonstrate behavior patterns that indicate that they may be depressed. The following vignette illustrates these patterns.

> Katie (age 4 years) did not choose an activity during free play; instead she sat or stood alone, rocking back and forth. Occasionally she would follow her favorite teacher, Anita; but she did not initiate conversation with Anita or the other children and adults. When teachers tried to interest her in an activity, she most often would shake her head no unless the activity was story reading or playing on the computer.

Katie often licked her face above and below her lips. When a teacher would read Katie a story, she often would seem to relax suddenly and enjoy talking about the story with the other teachers. In this context, she was very verbal and seemed quite intelligent. Katie would become quiet again, however, when another child began to talk about the story.

I was called on to consult with Katie's parents, who are both successful professionals, an attorney and an accountant. Katie has been in child care since she was 8 weeks old. She had been in her current child care for 5 months prior to the author's consultation. Katie's parents seemed surprised to hear that her teachers had serious concerns about her. They stated that her prior child care had not given them this type of report. The parents expressed concern and interest in working with the center to improve Katie's sense of comfort and ability to actively engage in center activities. Katie's father disclosed that he was seeing a psychiatrist who had prescribed an antidepressant and that both his father and his grandfather had histories of depression. After this consultation visit, Katie's parents arranged for her to see a psychotherapist weekly. Six months later her teachers reported that she continues to see the psychotherapist and that she is not quite as withdrawn or depressed.

Katie's behavior seems to have a genetic basis. Other young children who are social isolates may also demonstrate characteristics of depression; however, the basis of their behavior may be environmental. Two Head Start children, Bonnie and Tracy, are an example of children whose depression may be environmental in nature.

During free play Bonnie (age 4 years) plays alone each day in the same area of the classroom. In housekeeping she repeatedly strokes the hair of the same doll. She does not seem able to enter into give-and-take conversation with adults, nor does she play with the other children. During group activities and free play, she most often is staring off into space. When she does talk her speech is very immature.

I observed Bonnie in the classroom, met with her teachers, and then met with her mother and teacher. Bonnie's mother, Laconda is a very quiet 19-year-old single parent who also has a 12-month-old son. She and her children live in a four-room apartment in a small community's housing project. As a child, Laconda attended classes for children with mental retardation. Laconda left school at age 15, 4 months before Bonnie was born. Both of Laconda's parents are deceased, one brother is in jail, and her sister lives about 50 miles away. Laconda appears to have no informal or formal social support, and she spends a great deal of time watching television. Laconda has agreed to assist in the classroom once a week; her infant son will be cared for by the Head Start social worker during that time. Head Start has arranged for Bonnie to have a receptive language evaluation and begin language and communication therapy.

Tracy (age 5 years) also spends most of her day in the classroom staring off into space. She often has a finger in her mouth and hums to herself. Tracy's teachers report that she always plays alone and, in fact, seems oblivious to the other children. When riding a tricycle, Tracy will enter other children's space, and a teacher has to redirect her before she crashes into them. Tracy does not participate in singing, fingerplay, or music activities. Tracy is the oldest of four children. When she was 3 years old, she was with her father when he was killed in a drive-by shooting. The Head Start social worker has made several appointments with Tracy's mother; however, the mother does not come to the center, nor is she ever present when the social worker goes to her home.

Both Bonnie and Tracy demonstrate features of depression, stemming from different causes. Bonnie lives in severe deprivation; her family is isolated, and she appears to receive minimal stimulation from her mother. Tracy may be experiencing posttraumatic stress and has not received any professional intervention. Paley (1990) depicted a child similar to Tracy and offered strategies for teachers to help this type of child.

Concluding Comments on Child–Child Interaction

In any caregiving environment, different children have different styles and abilities in relating to their peers. Young children who are emotionally secure can be comfortable playing with other children and often enjoy their companionship. Many factors influence young children's emotional security. The child's immediate environment is one factor. A neatly arranged caregiving environment with materials that are accessible to children, an even tempo of activity, and a reasonable number of adults per children are factors that influence a child's sense of security. Sometimes, however, children have different temperamental dispositions, resulting from genetics or environmental causes alone or in combination, that influence their sense of ease with peers.

PARENT–TEACHER INTERACTION

Very young children feel secure when they know that their parents and teachers are partners working together. Both parents and teachers learn from each other when they speak openly and respectfully in their everyday conversations and in their formal meetings. Parent–teacher relationships do not form instantly; they take time to develop. Opportunities to develop this kind of relationship occur in many ways throughout the year, for example, during informal encounters on arrival and dismissal, social events at the school, parent conferences, and telephone chats. Usually parents have difficulty leaving their baby or young child for 8–10 hours per day. They want to know what happens during the course of their child's day and how their child is relating to the adults, the children, and the activities within the caregiving program. It is important for teachers to understand that parents want information. They want information about the school's philosophy, forthcoming events, and classroom activities, and they especially want information about their own child.

Teachers have myriad ways in which they can relate to parents and be supportive of them. Methods vary according to the community being served and the age of the children enrolled. Workman and Gage identified three conditions that make partnerships between child care programs and families possible:

> First, that we truly believe each of us brings something meaningful and valued to the relationship; second, that we have something in common—the welfare of the child; and, third, that we feel a sense of shared responsibility around our common goals. (1997, p. 11)

Some child care programs have an ecological view of family participation, and they expand their focus beyond just the child to embrace the whole family. An ecological approach recognizes the mutually supportive roles that child care programs and parents play in young children's development; thus, this type of program strives to have parents and teachers work as partners. The developers of such programs understand, however, that no one strategy works for all families. Programs with an ecological approach provide activities for the entire family, such as family socials, or family and child care staff weekend camp-outs. Parents are involved in the program, for example, joining a field trip, sharing family customs and traditions in their child's classroom, or being on the child care program's board of trustees. Parents may use their child's program as the site for single-parent or other support group meetings. Sometimes parents use the center one weekend night to alternately care for each other's children so that the other parents can use the night for recreation or to run important errands.

Some programs reach out by setting up an initial home visit prior to a child's entry into the caregiving setting. Home visits can be a time for parents to share their expectations of their child's out-of-home caregiving experience. Teachers can share explicitly their goals, objectives, and expectations of the young children for whom they care. Home visits also can be an opportunity for teachers to gain a small perspective into the child's everyday home life.

Teachers and parents often have different styles, expectations, and manners of interacting with young children. It can be helpful for teachers to explain to parents how they guide and discipline children because discipline practices can vary among individual families and across different ethnic and cultural backgrounds (Garcia, 1994). Young children can be secure with different discipline strategies as long as teacher and parent are each consistent and each respects the other's method. Difficulties may arise when children hear a parent or a teacher critique each other for their disciplinary choices.

Parents' Feelings About Out-of-Home Child Care

Regardless of the large number of employed mothers whose babies, toddlers, and young children are in family and center-based child care, the ideology of women being full-time mothers of very young children still dominates Americans' beliefs and value systems. As a result, America is the only Western nation whose government does not fully subsidize child care for young families. Given this disparity between ideology and reality, many parents feel ambivalent and guilty when placing their children in out-of-home child care. Each parent makes peace with his or her decision to use child care in his or her own manner.

In the following vignette, Kerry, an administrative social worker, discusses her feelings about placing her daughter, Patricia (age 38 months), in out-of-home child care. Kerry's husband, Dennis, is a special education teacher. Next month Kerry will give birth to their second child.

Kerry: Dennis and I were very lucky that when I returned to work full time when Patricia was 8 weeks old, a neighbor whom we knew well was able to provide child care for Patricia during her first year. Since then Patricia has been attending Mrs. Stevens's family child care full time during the school year and part time during the summer.

Mrs. Stevens is a mother and grandmother who cares for approximately four babies and young children in her home. All the children except for Patricia have their care paid for by the state.

I trust Mrs. Stevens. She is very organized, predictable, and warm with the children. For me it's always important to feel that I spend enough time in the morning to talk with Mrs. Stevens and to help Patricia feel comfortable but mostly to reassure myself that Patricia is settled and okay. Usually I can gauge how Patricia is doing within about 10 minutes; then I know she's comfortable with me leaving. Actually, Patricia has developed a routine for when she arrives. She sits in the high chair with a snack. That's how she decided she wanted to begin her day.

Mrs. Stevens always has charged $80 per week, but we pay her $90. We can afford to give her $10 more; and, you know, it's our way of prompting her to be more positive with Patricia. Dennis picks her up around 3:30, so her day is shorter than many of the children.

I know there is a down side to this arrangement. The children rarely play outdoors, and the TV is on quite a bit. Sometimes I hear Mrs. Stevens speak louder or sharper to some of the other children. But I don't think she speaks that way with Patricia. Often Mrs. Stevens and I have talked about her, and I have stressed how sensitive Patricia is. We live in a quiet home, and both Dennis and I are quite quiet. Mrs. Stevens understands that. In the fall, Patricia begins Delmar School, a private school for children 3 years through 12 years. Dennis will be able to pick her up at 3:30 so she won't need after-school care.

At the same time, I'm not real comfortable knowing the baby, at 8 weeks, will be cared for by Mrs. Stevens. A new baby—it's not ideal. She's not me.

In the next vignette, Phoebe, the Director of Human Services for a small social services agency, discusses her conflicting feelings about placing her daughter, Lela, in child care. Phoebe's husband, John, is a social worker. Lela was born in Russia, and she lived in an orphanage for the first 10 months of her life before Phoebe and John adopted her. A week after Phoebe, John, and Lela returned to America, Phoebe called a nearby child care center. Rebecca, the infant-toddler coordinator, told Phoebe that a baby had withdrawn that very morning and that in 2 weeks they would have an opening for Lela. Thus Lela began child care less than 1 month after coming to America.

Phoebe: When Lela was in the orphanage she was well cared for physically. But at 10 months she was not able to sit up, and she expressed herself very little emotionally. In the orphanage she was with many children all the time, with no personal space and minimal one-to-one attention from adults. Within 3 weeks of living with Phoebe and John, she had figured out how to sit up and began cruising around. And within 6 months she was quite emotionally expressive.

The transition to child care seemed easy for Lela probably because she had been living with so many babies her age. I had a more difficult time because I felt guilty. I should be at home with her. I kept asking myself, "Why am I not with my baby?" But I knew we basically live on my salary, so working was a given. During the first few weeks, I often returned midday, just to look through the window and know Lela was doing well. And she was!

I appreciated Carmeletta [Lela's teacher]. I think Lela felt familiarity with Carmeletta. They are very close. And even though Lela is now 29 months old and in the 2-year-old room, Carmeletta continues to babysit for us.

Lela had 2 weeks to make the transition to the 2-year-old room, and the teachers said she was doing fine. Well, at first she probably was overwhelmed because there was more space, more kids, and more activities; and she was the smallest. For me, it was very hard to say good-bye to the infant-toddler teachers, because each day we chatted together at the beginning and end of the day. And I knew those teachers better than I'll ever know Lela's current teachers.

The biggest down side to this child care is when I pick up Lela I know she often has learned something new, and I wasn't there to see it. She talks about the kids at the center all the time. And some days she isn't ready to go home. She tells me she wants to play outdoors. I'm pleased I have the flexibility that I can stay with her a little while so she can play outdoors.

Phoebe knows her daughter is in a high-quality child care center, and Lela is very happy there. Because Phoebe knows she has to work, she has made peace with her child being in out-of-home child care. At the same time, she knows she is missing out on the joy of sharing some of Lela's advancing development.

Working with Parents of Babies and Toddlers

Parents and teachers need to synchronize their caregiving by communicating with one another regularly. They need to discuss aspects of the child's life, such as his or her routine, eating and sleeping schedule, and any situations that could be affecting the child (e.g., the child's grandparents have just arrived so the daily schedule at home has been different). As the baby enters and leaves the caregiving setting each day, parents and teachers might choose to write such information on a form or in a notebook provided for each child. In addition, the babies' arrival and departure can be a time for parents and teachers to chat with each other. In these brief encounters, parents can feel affirmed and supported. As illustrated in the previous section, it can be very difficult for many parents to leave their young babies, and many feel guilt and remorse; thus, teacher support can be very helpful. When teachers are not available during arrival and departure times, parents may feel a lack of respect. Two caregivers, Joy and Alicia, spoke about how individual parents related initially to placing their child in out-of-home care.

> **Alicia:** Cynthia entered at 8 weeks, and for 3 weeks her mom hung around to get to know Cynthia's teachers. Her mom was very respectful of our process, so her presence didn't bother us.
>
> **Joy:** Before Mia [began child care], her mom spent about 5 hours watching our classroom process. Once Mia entered our classroom, her mom spent about 3 hours with us for a couple days. It seemed as if she wanted to see how we would relate to Mia, who was a colicky, fussy baby. Actually, it seems as if parents who have [fussier] babies hang around a little longer than the others.
>
> **Alicia:** None of the parents want to leave if our room seems a bit chaotic to them, and that's okay for us because they can often be helpful. If a parent's baby is sad, they will ask, "Shall I stay?" We usually reply, "No, but you can watch from the window." Usually we can distract and comfort the baby very quickly, and it is reassuring for the parents to see that.

Both Joy and Alicia understand that some parents need to linger and make sure that their babies are receiving quality care while they are at work. These teachers make it clear that they are available to parents if a parent needs to chat with them. In another example of healthy parent–teacher communication, a mother entered Joy and Alicia's classroom and described how her baby's sleep schedule was off over the weekend. Joy responded by assuring the mother that she and Alicia would watch to see if the baby was unusually fussy, and if so, they would put her to bed early. Joy actively listened to this mother and reassured her that she would make any accommodations necessary to ensure that the baby had an easy day at the center. The mother left knowing that her caregiver would watch over her daughter.

Rebecca, the center's infant-toddler coordinator, discussed dimensions of infant-toddler teachers' relationship with parents:

Rebecca: We value home visiting because we find that parents usually feel most comfortable on their own "turf," so in their home they seem more free to share. And teachers appreciate getting a perspective of families that is different than meeting parents within the center.

Each infant-toddler and 2-year-old classroom has at least one teacher who is involved in [the center's] Parents as Teachers in Child Care Centers [PAT] program. Each of these classrooms has four parent meetings a year, and about 80%–100% of the parents attend these meetings. Most often the meetings are topical—what the parents want to discuss in the moment.

Most frequently issues of sickness trigger problems between teachers and the parents. Our staff is so involved with their babies. They truly love them. They often take it personally when they think a parent does not want to pick up their sick baby quickly.

And it's not a given that parents are respectful to teachers. They are often so busy they just forget. For example, they may have had several conversations with the physician regarding their child's illness but never think to share this information with their child's teacher.

A final dilemma that does not occur really often but is the toughest to address is the difficulties when we need to tell a parent that there is a potential that their child has a developmental delay. First of all, parents don't automatically respect the judgment of our teachers. Second, they feel threatened, as though if [the] delay is true, they are failures as parents. And often, if their child is very young and they approach their pediatrician, the pediatrician will say, "Give it time," or "Boys will be boys." We stress to parents that they are the decision makers. Often it has been helpful if we specifically describe what we are doing to help their child, and we make suggestions as to what they can do. When they follow these suggestions, they often return to us and say, "Yes, we are seeing [the child's delay] at home!"

Working with Parents When Their Child Is Having Difficulties

It is not uncommon for child care teachers to have at some point a child in their class who has behavior difficulties. Most common behavior difficulties among young children involve hyperactivity, impulsivity, and aggression; however, other children may have problems such as being depressed, withdrawn, or electively mute.

Although a child care teacher may be very skilled in working with young children, he or she may find it difficult to approach the parents of a child with behavior problems. Some child care teachers have neither the experience nor the professional education that would enable them to feel comfortable sharing their concerns with parents. Several guidelines can assist child care teachers in this task:

1. Teachers can strive to develop an open and trusting relationship with each parent.

2. Prior to meeting with parents, the teacher and director can plan together the parent–teacher conference. As the teacher shares her concerns with the director, the director can ask questions to help the teacher clarify and be more precise in her statements. The teacher will feel more comfortable if she knows that the director supports this often difficult task.

3. When meeting with parents, teachers can list specific classroom behaviors that are a concern and the specific steps the teacher has taken that have not worked. Teachers also can invite parents to share their experience with this difficult behavior and how they have dealt with it.

4. Teachers can share alternative strategies to address the concern, for example, strategies for parents to use at home, such as bedtime rituals to calm the child, or can offer referrals to other sources, such as a child psychologist or an occupational therapist, so that parents can gain additional assistance.

5. Teachers always need to be aware that the responsibility to address the child's difficulties is the parents' choice. It is natural for parents initially to resist and deny, but usually they already see the problem at home.

6. After the initial conference, parents, teachers, and the children involved can benefit from continued dialogue regarding the child's progress at home and at school.

7. Teachers can be aware of early childhood special education resources in the community so that these resources can be called on when necessary.

When a child is having difficulty, teachers usually try to address the problem on their own prior to approaching the child's parents. Parents probably are not the only ones who feel guilty. Most child care teachers accept responsibility for helping a child through a behavior difficulty, and they immediately try to solve the problem within the classroom prior to calling the parent.

Facilitating the Transition from Infant-Toddler to Preschool Care

Parents and teachers of babies and toddlers often spend quite a bit of time together and develop close relationships. Suzanne and Pam are Director and Assistant Director of a child care center for approximately 260 children ages 6 weeks to 6 years. In their center, most children enter at age 2–4 months, and they remain in the same classroom until they are 2 years old. The children then spend 1 year in a 2-year-old classroom before they enter a mixed-age preschool classroom at age 36 months. Suzanne and Pam discussed how the transition first from infant-toddler to 2-year-old classes and then to the preschool affects both parents and children.

Pam: We give the toddlers 2 weeks to visit the 2-year-old classroom that they will enter, and we give the 2-year-olds 2 weeks to visit the preschool classroom that they will enter. This transition is smooth for most children. It is their parents who seem to have quite a bit of difficulty with this transition.

Suzanne: Both parents and teachers of children 6 weeks to 24 months complete a daily form and discuss happenings during each day. The infant-toddler teachers are close to the parents. Lots of the infant-toddler teachers are young and single; babysit for parents; and, thus, have extended time in the families' homes. They seem to be bonded much closer than our 2-year-old and preschool teachers and parents.

Pam: For years, we have had difficulties in the transition from 2-year-old to preschool, and parents have more difficulty than do their children. Constantly we try to make improvements; yet one or more parents feels disappointed and shares their concerns. [Parents are concerned that] their kids are no longer getting the same amount and quality of attention. The preschool classes are bigger groups, with mixed age, and that can be very frightening to parents. And the rooms are bigger and louder. And the routines are different.

We've learned that these parents do not have enough information regarding preschool expectations. And now I'm trying some new changes. Just as the kids have a 2-week transition period to visit their new classroom, I am encouraging parents to visit the preschool classroom. I'm increasingly understanding that this is a significant transition for parents. Interestingly, when new parents enroll their child of the same age, 36 months, [for the first time] they do not seem to have this problem.

Suzanne: All infant-toddler and 2-year-old classrooms are in the same wing, separate from the preschool wing. The parents of infant-toddlers and 2-year-olds felt close to the teachers, not only their child's teachers; but, over 3 years, they would get to know other teachers in this wing. Now all preschool teachers are strangers, not friends, in a different wing of the school—the preschool section.

Pam: It's not just a new classroom but a new culture. And in fact, preschool teachers are not as available when parents bring their child to the center. Now the older kids are more demanding. All the children are old enough to talk and demand a teacher's attention, and some teachers feel obligated to make certain each child immediately becomes involved in an activity. In other words, there aren't as many opportunities to build parent–teacher relationships.

Suzanne: And [the same is true] for the parents. They now are more comfortable in their parenting and their needs are not as great, so they don't initiate as many informal conversations on arrival as they did with infant-toddler teachers.

Over the years, Suzanne and Pam have learned that the structure they have established allows toddlers to make a smooth transition into their new classrooms. They did not initially understand, however, that this transition was difficult for many of the toddlers' parents. They realized that they needed to develop transition activities for the parents to help them feel as comfortable with the transition as were the parents' children.

Structured Meetings Between Parents and Teachers

Many caregiving programs have structured periods for parent conferences or group meetings. In one-to-one parent–teacher conferences, teachers can inform parents about their child's progress; how the child is relating to adults, children, and the daily activities; areas needing further improvement; and any concerns the teachers may have. When parents and teachers have developed an open and trusting relationship, the parents can use this time to share family happenings or concerns that they think may help the teacher understand their child. Or, the parent may have questions or concerns about the teacher's caregiving. Conferences thus serve both teachers and parents as they help each to learn from the other for the benefit of the child.

When parents and teachers develop a healthy, open relationship during the parents' everyday delivery and pick-up of their child, parent conferences can offer a relaxed, extended time for parents and teachers to engage in dialogue. Just as teachers can gain new meaning and closer relationships via their storytelling and conversing with each other, storytelling among parents and teachers can provide new meaning for each person as well as strengthen the parent–teacher relationship. Bruner (1986) explained that a person's story not only involves the individual's memory but also his or her interpretation of the story's meaning. Dialogue about a story and its meaning provides new insights both for the storyteller and the listener. As a teacher listens to parents tell a story about their child, both teacher and parent gain a deeper understanding about the child. And often this dialogue leads to planning how to specifically move forward together to support the child.

Parent group meetings offer an opportunity for presentations and discussions about child development, caregiving, or other topics parents might find helpful, such as the issue of television violence. Attending meetings after a long day of working can be very difficult for young parents. Child care programs often accommodate parents at these meetings by providing dinner and child care for parent meetings and scheduling meetings immediately at the close of the caregiving day. Some meetings can provide a time for parent and child to play together. When parents and teachers develop open and trusting relationships, they often enjoy sharing time together. In these settings, a spring or fall joint weekend camp-out or a holiday feast can be enjoyable for everyone. These events also help the children know that parents and teachers are united in caring for them.

Suzanne and Pam work in a child care program that serves predominantly middle-income families. When a caregiving program serves a majority of families with low incomes, the center can become the environment in which children and sometimes family members can receive services from other community agencies. For example, administrators can arrange for professionals from different disciplines, such as psychologists, speech-language pathologists, and physical and occupational therapists, to gain Medicaid certification so that they can treat young children at the center. Sometimes early educators can be ombudsmen with community agencies and their families. In one metropolitan area an early educator arranged for a large counseling organization to offer up to 12 free psychotherapy sessions for children, parents, and teachers at the United Way Child Care Centers.

Openness of the Caregiving Setting

Each caregiving program has guidelines regarding parents' coming and going during the day. Often it helps to have an area with comfortable chairs and coffee or tea where parents can feel at ease to chat with other parents or a staff member. Mothers who work nearby often are able to continue nursing their babies during the working day, and establishing a nursing area in the caregiving setting will help mothers feel comfortable. Parents who work nearby also can join their young children during mealtimes.

Current Family Issues

In 1994, 69% of all mothers of preschool-age children worked, and 56% of married women with children age 1 year or younger were working (Bureau of Labor Statistics, 1995). Mothers of very young children experience multiple pressures as they not only work full time but also are homemakers and mothers. Fathers often strive to assume some formerly "traditional" homemaking tasks, yet they too have long work days and minimal time at home. In turn, the very young children often experience little spontaneous, extended shared time with their parents.

It may be that work is an easier environment for some parents of young children than is the home. Some working parents find orderliness, harmony, and camaraderie at work, whereas family time is minimal, uncertainties are rampant, and laundry and housecleaning never seem to get done. For many families with young children, relaxed, spontaneous shared time with family members is in short supply. Homemaking tasks and family time often are subverted by a "cult of efficiency" that used to be reserved only for the workplace (Hochschild, 1997). Many parents speak of "quality time": time that they reserve for relationships that is separate from everything else, such as homemaking chores. Quality time with young children on the weekends, between errands and chores, becomes like a scheduled appointment. Some children are rewarded with "time credit," time to be spent with parents during the weekend. Arlie Hochschild poignantly described this reversal of work and home life:

> Paradoxically, what may seem to harried working parents like a solution to their time bind—efficiency and time segmentation—can later feel like a problem in itself. To be efficient with whatever time they do have at home, many working parents try to go faster if for no other reason than to clear off some space in which to go slowly. They do two or three things at once. They plan ahead. They delegate. They separate

home events into categories and try to outsource some of them. In their efficiency, they may inadvertently trample on the emotion-laden symbols associated with particular times of day or particular days of the week. They pack one activity closer to the next and disregard the "framing" around each of them, those moments of looking forward to or looking back on an experience, which heighten its emotional impact. They ignore the contribution that a leisurely pace can make to fulfillment, so that a rapid dinner, followed by a speedy bath and bedtime story for a child—if part of "quality time"—is counted as "working the same" as a slower version of the same events. As time becomes something to "save" at home as much as or even more than at work, domestic life becomes quite literally a second shift; a cult of efficiency, once centered in the workplace, is allowed to set up shop and make itself comfortable at home. (1997, p. 212)

Parents whose very young children spend 40–60 hours per week in child care have to cope with multiple complexities; caregivers who understand parents' issues can be more supportive, respectful, and empathic with parents. When a toddler is exceptionally fussy on the Monday after his mom has just returned from a 4-day business trip, the teacher can perhaps be a little more patient with the child.

Because many working parents have very little free time, teachers can be exceptionally supportive by speaking with parents in an unhurried manner. Understanding the stressful lives of working parents with very young children, teachers need to strive to ensure their availability at arrival and dismissal time and structure relaxed conference times with each parent. Sometimes it can be very difficult for teachers of young children to be accepting of all parents; often working parents can be so harried that the last person they think to relate to openly and respectfully is their baby's teacher. Yet the most disrespectful and brusque parent is often the one who is most in need of support. Teachers need to trust that it takes time to develop a personal relationship; and their availability will prevail, even if it takes weeks or months for a parent to relax and openly, respectfully relate to his or her child's teacher. Understanding the stress and dilemmas of being a working parent can help a teacher avoid taking a parent's harsh comments personally. Likewise, having close relationships with one's co-teachers can help a teacher "bounce back" when a parent has been disrespectful and abrupt.

Concluding Comments on Teacher–Parent Interaction

Like all relationships, it takes time for teachers and parents to develop a trusting, open relationship. When this relationship is successful, both parent and teacher know that each is important to the child's development and share common values regarding the child's welfare. The goal and the process of teacher–parent interaction involve a partnership.

Teachers understand that they will have different relationships with different parents; so, too, parents learn that each teacher has a different personal style.

When teacher–parent relationships are successful, parents will feel that their child's teacher is accessible and can give them the time they need. Optimally, parents know that they can relate to their child's teachers in many ways: spontaneous, informal exchanges at delivery and pickup, structured conferences and parent meetings, and informal family socials. Different parents will feel comfortable relating openly in different situations. Similarly, different teachers will bring different skills in relating to parents. It is not uncommon for most early educators to love working with very young children; however, often they did not consider establishing a good relationship with parents as part of their chosen field. In fact, some teachers may not be comfortable or skilled in working with parents. In these situations, administrators can offer teachers support and guidance for developing these skills.

CONCLUSION

The way teachers of babies and young children interact with the children in their care, with each other, and with the children's parents makes a difference in how the children develop. The love and authority patterns of teachers' everyday child-rearing interactions are the framework in which the babies and young children develop an ability to trust themselves and others, to express themselves emotionally and socially, and to learn to regulate their emotions and behavior.

Different levels and patterns of teacher–child interaction make a difference in how children act, interact, and develop. In addition, the way teachers relate to adults, both co-teachers and parents, influences the children's experience in child care. Teacher–child interaction does not occur in a vacuum; rather, it occurs within a specific child-rearing environment. A key factor in creating the climate of this environment is how teachers interact with each other, as both professionals and peers. Other significant adults with whom teachers interact daily are the children's parents. For children to feel secure, they need to feel that both parent and teacher are working together in a partnership. Children in out-of-home child care who see their parents and teachers getting along are being given the optimal opportunities to develop social skills and emotional strengths as a foundation for subsequent growth and development.

chapter 2

Social-Emotional Development

The self is something which has a development; it is not initially there, at birth, but arises in the process of social experience and activity, that is, develops in the given individual as a result of his relations to that process as a whole and to other individuals within that process.

—*George Herbert Mead (1934, p. 135)*

When an adult cares for an even-tempered baby, the caregiver and baby have many positive interactions. These positive interactions help the caregiver feel competent; and in turn, the caregiver's competent feelings promote relaxed and calm interactions between the baby and the caregiver. The caregiver's calm behavior helps maintain the baby's even temper. In contrast, an irritable baby can spark a caregiver's sense of incompetence, which may lead the caregiver to feel anxious. In turn, the baby experiences the caregiver's tension and the baby's irritability increases. Caregivers shape babies' actions at the same time that babies shape their caregivers' actions. This mutuality of child-rearing interactions is a key developmental principle guiding this book.

SOCIAL-EMOTIONAL DEVELOPMENT AND THE CHILD–CAREGIVER RELATIONSHIP

Social-emotional development from birth through 5 years is a social achievement; that is, babies and young children develop through living with others. Social-emotional development unfolds within the everyday, taken-for-granted interactions of baby and caregiver. Social-emotional development is an inclusive concept that comprises sense of self and is intertwined with all other developmental areas, such as physical and sensorimotor, language, communication, and cognition. Development is a unified, integrated process in which development in one domain has an impact on the development of other domains. The unfolding of emotion is coordinated with the physiological, social, and cognitive aspects of development (Sroufe, 1996). Whether a 10-month-old feels pleasure or wariness in the grocery store depends on the baby's cognitive understanding of the meaning of going to the grocery store. This understanding depends on the baby's memories of prior experiences at the store, which are stored on the cognitive map that the baby has about being in grocery stores.

In addition, social-emotional development and emotional regulation are part of the same whole. Emotional regulation is the baby or young child's ability to respond spontaneously to the ongoing demands of his or her experience in a manner that is socially appropriate. Emotional regulation is initially a dyadic process that babies and caregivers accomplish together—that is, emotional regulation is first a social event. Babies cry, and caregivers soothe them; babies coo, and caregivers respond with a warm smile and a softly spoken comment. The baby's signals influence what caregivers attend to, as illustrated in the following vignette:

> *Timmy (age 10 months) plays with the xylophone that his teacher, Julie, has given him. He then lies down and be-*

gins fussing. Julie sits him up and plays the xylophone as she talks to him softly. Timmy stops fussing and plays with the xylophone again as Julie strokes his hair and says, "Timmy is making a beautiful sound."

Julie is quick to respond to Timmy's signal of unhappiness as she helps him regulate his feelings. Once he is calm and begins playing with the xylophone again, Julie reassures him further by talking to him softly as she strokes his hair. In her daily interactions, Julie often "contains" a baby; that is, she helps the baby remain involved in an activity.

Both babies and caregivers sometimes engage in mismatched interactions—in which signals are unclear, are misread, or are unsynchronized or in which stimulation is overloaded. Caregiver and baby cannot maintain mutual regulation at all times, but they can accommodate or repair such mismatches in interaction. Babies develop behaviors, which stabilize around 6 months of age, for repairing interactive mismatches (Tronick & Gianino, 1986). To let their caregiver know that they are unhappy, for example, babies will frown or will switch their focus from the caregiver to objects in the room. As babies gain more experience with their caregivers' soothing responses to their signals of unhappiness, babies begin to develop their own pattern of soothing self-regulation, for example, by babbling to themselves before going to sleep or on awakening. A key component of self-regulation is the baby's emotional security. Emotional security emerges from multiple factors and is strongly influenced by family functioning, especially the quality of the parent–child attachment (Cummings & Davies, 1996). Just as the baby–caregiver relationship is critical to emotional development, the parent–child relationship likewise becomes the scaffolding for babies' developing ability to regulate tension and establish expectations.

By the end of the first year, babies experience and express emotions such as joy, anger, and fear. Babies develop the capacity to experience different emotions in a parallel fashion; for example, the same processes and developmental principles underlie the development of fear as underlie joy.

Emotions are a part of every experience. When parents bring their baby to out-of-home child care, the baby and his or her child care teacher respond to each other emotionally. Similarly, parents respond emotionally to leaving their baby to go to work. Emotions can involve multiple aspects of behavior and can be complex in expression. Many factors influence a baby's emotional security, including the baby's past interactions with his or her parents, the presence (or absence) of the parents, and the baby's immediate context, such as a regular versus an ever-changing schedule of daily events. Similarly, very different outcomes, whether adaptive or maladaptive, can result from the same caregiving activity, given the different histories of each baby. A nurse can bathe babies in the same way, and yet each baby may experience his or her bath very differently.[1]

Emotions involve physiological arousal, cognitive appraisal, and behavioral expression, and they are central to personal relationships (Cummings & Davies, 1996). Sroufe identified three functions of emotions: "1) to communicate inner states to important others, 2) to promote exploratory competence in the environment, and 3) to promote adequate responses to emergency situations" (1996, p. 16). At about age 10 months, babies develop memory, and the emotional meaning of an event is affected not only by the baby's present experience but also by the baby's experiential history. When a young child experiences an event that evokes an emotional response, the response often guides the child's interactions (Thompson, Flood, & Lundquist, 1995). For example, fear can trigger the communication of a need, such as the need to be comforted; a self-defensive act, such as hiding; or a positive social signal, such as climbing on the caregiver's lap. In infancy and early childhood, emotions occur within everyday caregiving interactions, that is, within a social context; thus, this area of development is referred to as social-emotional development (Sroufe, 1996). The sections that follow discuss emotional self-regulation, the neurophysiology of emotion, and the parallel development of emotion and cognition within the context of the baby–caregiver relationship.

Emotional Self-Regulation

Initially, a caregiver's nurturing interaction with babies, such as cuddling or rocking babies, regulates young babies' emotions. Over time, however, babies develop an increasing internal ability to regulate their emotions by themselves. Emotional self-regulation consists of processes in monitoring and modifying emotional reactions to accomplish one's goals and adapt to environmental demands. By age 9 or 10 months, brain development allows the baby to inhibit responses and to cope with emotionally arousing events (Chugani, 1998). The face-to-face caregiver–baby interaction makes possible the neurological changes that allow babies to develop self-regulation skills. Vision is the primary mode of connection with the caregiver for most babies.

Different emotional regulation strategies may be used in different situations and for different goals (Thompson & Calkins, 1996). Thompson et al. (1995) identified three qualities of effective emotional regulation: 1) ability to express a full range of emotions appropriate to the situation, 2) ability to function competently and accomplish one's goals with emotions that have sufficient intensity and duration, and 3) ability to smoothly shift from one emotion to another.

Emotional regulation strategies can alter emotional experience in different ways. For maltreated babies, emotional regulation becomes not only a strategy for them to elicit nurturance but also a means for them to avoid harm. For example, a baby may learn that his or her crying triggers a parent's rage, resulting in physical harm to the baby. Babies who have been abused physically may learn to stifle their crying and express minimal affect. Babies at risk of being abused may learn to become astonishingly adept at self-monitoring to protect their well-being. Neglected babies who are unsuccessful in gaining their caregiver's attention often develop behavior to compensate for the lack of caregiver attention, such as switching their focus to objects to control the negative emotion generated by their caregiver's rejection (Tronick & Gianino, 1986). In other at-risk environments, babies may learn to heighten their arousal rather than inhibit it. Babies who witness a lot of domestic violence become hypersensitive and often have persistent feelings of sadness or anxiety. These strategies may enhance resiliency in some contexts, especially in interactions with a maltreating parent, but they can also lead to increased vulnerability, such as being excessively fearful in the child care environment where the baby is receiving nurturant care. Babies and toddlers who are emotionally abandoned or neglected or who have disorganized attachment with their caregivers are deprived of the warm, nurturant everyday child-rearing interactions that promote the formation of neural pathways. This deprivation undermines neurological development, which can lead to difficulties in brain-mediated functions such as empathy, attachment, emotional regulation, and emotional expression (Karr-Morse & Wiley, 1997). The lack of emotional regulation also can lead to a lack of motivation (Schore, 1998).

Neurophysiology of Emotion

It has long been held that the central nervous system controls the complex processes of regulating signals from the environment as well as from within our bodies. Neurobiological research has explained a great deal about the connection between the biological and psychosocial aspects of development.[2] Neuroimaging allows researchers to measure chemical functions within the brain, such as glucose utilization, cerebral blood flow, oxygen utilization, and protein synthesis (Chugani, 1997). This research indicates that emotional development and emotional regulation parallel brain development. Changes in brain development trigger qualitative changes in babies' behavior and social-emotional life. The babies' experiences, especially their everyday caregiving interactions, influence their brain structure and chemistry, especially in the first months of life.

Brain development refers to structural and neurochemical changes in the brain. We might think of the brain's complex structure as a "wiring system." This network is not really made up of wires but is made up of brain cells (*neurons*) that communicate to each other like circuits in a computer. Neurons connect with each other to form networks, termed *synapses*, which link up to form neural pathways. These neural pathways make up the "wiring" of the brain and allow for different brain areas to communicate and function together. Every neuron waits for stimulation to call it into action. The vast majority of synapses develop in the first 24 months of life, and experience determines which neurons will be activated. Infancy and toddlerhood is a critical time of accelerated and continuing brain growth that is dependent upon environmental influences, especially child-rearing interactions. Between ages 10 and 12 months, the baby's prefrontal cortex, which is uniquely involved in social-emotional development and makes focused attention possible, is growing (Schore, 1998). By the time a child is 3 years old, his or her brain activity is double that of adults (Chugani, 1998). In the early 1980s, scientists assumed that the baby's brain structure was genetically determined. Research now indicates, however, that *babies' and toddlers' everyday experiences, especially their interactions with their caregivers, have a decisive influence on the development of synapses in the brain and on how children learn.* Brain research demonstrates that not only does brain development have an impact on the emotions but also that experience within the caregiving relationship reciprocally influences the development of the brain (Schore, 1994). Repeated positive caregiving experiences make a decisive impact on the architecture of the brain, which is unique to each individual. Once we understand this dynamic, we understand that neurological development is like muscular development; that is, you use it or lose it! As this chapter tracks young children's social-emotional development from birth through 5 years, it becomes apparent that qualitative advances in social-emotional development are intertwined with qualitative changes in the brain, which are made possible by nurturant, responsive caregiving.

Parallel Development of Emotion and Cognition

The antecedent of any mature emotion is based on the baby's developing understanding of the meaning of events. By age 10 months, a baby's emotional reaction to an event is related to the baby's memory of prior related events, that is, to the baby's cognitive understanding of the event. Emotion and cognition mutually influence each other; the baby's emotions influence the significance of an event, and the baby's cognitive appraisal of an event influences the emotion tied to that event. When a young puppy jumps up onto the chest of a standing 15-month-old, for example, the puppy may frighten the toddler who then cries. Given the memory of this unsettling experience, the toddler may have a fear response every time he sees a furry four-legged animal, dog or cat. Baby–caregiver interactions are critical components of the memory of events and contexts. In any experience, a baby's feeling will depend not only on the current situation but also on the baby's experiential history with this or similar situations. Familiarity of setting and the presence of the caregiver are critical indicators of the baby's sense of well-being. Developmentalists historically have elevated the importance of cognition over emotion; however, it is now well known that the two realms are parallel and influence each other. Noted infant psychiatrist Stanley I. Greenspan stated, "Emotions, not cognitive stimulation, serve as the mind's primary architect" (1997, p. 1).

Summary

Emotional development is a social achievement; thus, this chapter uses the term *social-emotional development*. A central principle of this development is *mutuality*. Caregiver–child interactions are created mutually, and these interactions mutually influence brain development in the same way that cognitive and social-emotional development influence each other reciprocally. This mutuality points to the *unity of development*; that is, each experience and each area of development influences all areas of development. The remainder of the chapter illustrates the principles discussed thus far as it traces social-emotional development from birth through 5 years of age.

SOCIAL-EMOTIONAL DEVELOPMENT: BIRTH TO 7 MONTHS

From birth, babies are developing a sense of competence as they learn from experiences. When babies' environments are nurturant, each caregiver interaction fuels babies' development. During the first 6 months, development proceeds at astonishing speed. Emotions are the scaffolding of development across each developmental realm (Greenspan, 1997).

Physiological and Emotional Regulation

From birth, babies respond to and interact with their caregivers. A mother speaks softly as she comes toward her newborn, and he or she turns toward the mother in response. When the mother sneezes loudly, the newborn turns away his or her head. The baby cries, and the father comforts him or her. Initially, caregiving interactions primarily involve physiological regulation, such as regulating the baby's sleeping and eating. Child care providers also regulate the baby's emotional state. In the following observation, Joy, an infant-toddler teacher, illustrates how she helps regulate a young baby both physiologically and emotionally on the baby's first morning in child care.

> *Emma (age 8 weeks) has just awakened from a 5-minute nap in her crib. Joy picks up Emma and returns to sitting on the rug next to Jake (age 7 months). Joy rocks Emma and talks to her soothingly: "Are you in a new place today? Hello, Miss Emma, are you going back to sleep? Am I that boring?" In fact, Emma has gone back to sleep, and she remains in Joy's lap for the next 30 minutes as Joy talks to Jake and the toddlers that are moving about nearby.*

Although Emma is only 8 weeks old, she clearly recognizes that all the voices in her child care center are different from those of her parents. Joy not only helps Emma's physiological regulation by helping her to sleep, but she also holds her and talks to Emma quietly so that Emma begins to feel safe. Over time, Emma will associate a sense of emotional security with the sound of Joy's voice, the child care environment, and the nurturing interactions with the care providers, as long as Joy and her co-teachers can respond empathically to Emma's signals.

Research indicates that during the newborn period, babies have six states or cycles of consciousness that allow for their physiological and emotional regulation (Brazelton, 1992; Brazelton & Cramer, 1990). Knowing these six states of consciousness helps caregivers to understand when it is appropriate or inappropriate to interact with a baby. This infant cycle of states of consciousness is listed next:

1. Deep sleep
2. Light sleep (REM, or rapid eye movement, sleep)
3. Drowsy, in-between state
4. Awake, alert state
5. Alert but fussy state
6. Crying

During the awake, alert state, for example, 3-week-old babies' eyes are quick to follow objects; during the drowsy, in-between state, their eyes may open and close and they may whimper softly. Newborns' state influences whether and how they can take in information, and it also influences the kind of response they make (Brazelton & Cramer, 1990).

From birth, babies can give different signals with different kinds of crying. Sensitive caregivers learn not only to recognize the baby's state but also to recognize and differentiate among different kinds of crying—for example, among cries of pain, of hunger, and of discomfort. Brazelton and Cramer clarified the purpose of fussing for the very young baby as follows:

> By the second or third week, a kind of fussy crying occurs periodically throughout the day—usually in a cycle pattern—which seems to discharge and help to regulate the states that ensue. After a period of such crying, the newborn may be more organized for a while and may sleep more deeply. (1990, p. 66)

Tracking Development

Changes in the development of the brain bring changes in the baby's emotional life. Around age 3 months, a significant change in the baby's neurophysiological makeup occurs, which is marked by the disappearance of some reflexes, such as sucking, rooting, the Babinski sign, and the Moro reflex; a decrease in fussiness; and the beginning of babies' social smiling and vocalizing.[3] Now the babies' movements are primarily voluntary. Smiling and vocalizing affirm the caregiver's actions, and such signals encourage the caregiver to continue the interactions. Babies react pleasurably in their interactions with caregivers and in response to a positive novel experience such as watching a moving mobile. These behaviors point to babies' cognitive engagement (Sroufe, 1996). Now baby and caregiver enjoy extended periods of spontaneous socializing. Often caregivers' behavior is exaggerated, such as when they engage in "baby talk," in which the speaker's pitch is raised and the rate of speaking is slowed. Babies have their own optimal range of positive excitation, and caregivers learn to read this optimal range and adapt their behavior accordingly. Max's teacher, Alicia, for example, has learned that Max (age 15 months) can get overstimulated easily in the gross motor room when six other toddlers are roaming about and some are using noisy push-pull toys. Thus, Alicia often initiates involving Max in an activity that has clear boundaries, such as playing in the ball tub or in the 4-foot square playhouse. Regulation is a dyadic process; the child also regulates his or her levels of excitation, for example, by turning away from stimulation—a reaction that can be read by a sensitive caregiver. In out-of-home caregiving this adaptability can be challenging because a child care teacher may be interacting with several babies who have their own comfortable levels of excitation.

By 3 months of age, babies' responses change from global and diffuse total body reactions to more specific coordinated actions. For example, a 2-week-old baby's outstretched arms and legs could be her star-tle response to a sudden loud noise; whereas, the same noise would pro-duce a facial grimace in a 3-month-old. As cognitive development pro-gresses, babies begin to recognize specific objects and people. By age 3 months, babies favor those who care for them regularly. Now babies en-joy watching their hands; and, as they learn to turn their hands around, their eye–hand coordination develops. Simple objects such as mobiles over the crib become fascinating. At this age, babies have excellent mo-tor memories, which help promote a sense of continuity with their pre-vious motor experiences.

By 5 months of age, babies can both initiate interaction and turn away from it. These new interactions with caregivers point to babies' growing independence. Interestingly, this independence is grounded in babies' certainty of the predictability of their caregiver's responsiveness. By 6 months of age, babies can laugh, especially in response to vigorous visual, tactile, and auditory stimulation. As babies are increasingly awake and alert, they actively participate with the people and objects within their environment. As they engage in novel situations, these novel situ-ations produce tension. Sroufe (1996) described how a baby's engage-ment in novel situations advances the baby's cognitive development. From a Piagetian perspective, as babies experience novel situations, they cannot assimilate or incorporate these new situations without develop-ing their mental capacities. Through these experiences the baby's men-tal organizations, termed *schemes*, accommodate, or become reorganized, to adapt to the situation and the baby's cognitive advances. Child care teachers and parents play a critical role in helping babies and toddlers remain organized mentally and emotionally when they experience novel or unfamiliar situations. With the support of teachers, young children can master new situations, and through this mastery their cognitive de-velopment advances, as in the following observation:

> Ricky (age 19 months) and Nancy (age 21 months) sit in the sandbox, which is full of assorted plastic containers, spoons, and strainers. This is the second day the children have used the new sandbox; and because of rain the previ-ous night, the sand is slightly damp. Nancy uses her hands to put sand in the strainer. When she sees that the sand sticks to her hands she begins fussing as she holds up her hands to show Jean, her family child care provider. Jean says, "Rub your hands together, Nancy, and it will go away." Nancy looks at Jean as she rubs her hands together. Jean says, "That's it! It's kind of like Patty Cake." Nancy smiles as she looks at her clean hands.

Jean was available to Nancy when Nancy experienced the feeling of sticky wet sand for the first time. With a simple suggestion from Jean, Nancy was able to learn a new strategy for cleaning her hands; when frustrated, Nancy was able to resolve her frustration and gain mastery with Jean's support.

As their motor development and eye–hand coordination increases, babies love to play with their hands and feet as well as reach for and hold objects. All experiences are opportunities for exploration and learning. Babies consistently explore small objects by putting them into their mouths. They creep about the floor on their stomachs. Babies experience pleasure in these movements, but they also become frustrated when attempting something that developmentally is a little difficult. This frustration, however, often pushes the baby forward to achieve success. Teachers learn to be available to their babies as they try new skills and patiently allow for some frustration to spark babies' striving toward success. Alicia and Joy, two infant teachers, discussed some of the frustrations the babies in their care experience and how they deal with frustrated children to facilitate their striving for success:

Joy: Josh easily gets frustrated when I am holding another child. For example, yesterday I was holding Bria as I gave her a bottle, and Josh, on the other side of the rug, began whining for me. I talked him through it. That is, I encouraged him to crawl to me so that I could rub his back and comfort him as I fed Bria. Then he could wait.

Alicia: Sometimes it's easy for the kids to feel frustrated because we don't always have the hands [available to get to them]. We think it's important for the infants who just learned to crawl or walk to crawl or walk down the hall to the gross motor room. You know our room is so small the babies don't get a lot of practice crawling or walking. We encourage the new crawlers and walkers to crawl or walk on their own. Some don't mind crawling, but others want to be carried and need our encouragement.

Joy: And we sometimes get a lot of jealousy, especially if we are caring for a baby from another room. It's as if the kids are telling us, "That's not one of us!"

Self-Calming

By around 8–10 weeks of age, babies usually learn to calm themselves (Sammons, 1989). As babies go from one state to another, they learn ways to comfort themselves, such as sucking on their fingers or moving to the corner of their crib. Self-calming is the first form of independence a baby learns. This independence is achieved by baby and teacher working together. For example, the teacher can distinguish the baby's different cries and know when the softly crying baby can put herself back to sleep, one of the first self-calming behaviors babies learn. It is critical that teachers understand that all babies need to learn to put themselves to sleep. Sometimes teachers can speak to babies quietly or give them a soothing massage to reassure babies and assist them to calm themselves. If teachers always rock babies to sleep, the babies in those teachers' care will come to expect rocking anytime they awaken, including the middle of the night.

Teachers will need to adapt their guidelines for interacting with babies when they are caring for children with severe difficulties. For example, babies with prenatal substance exposure have greater difficulty going to sleep and probably will awaken more often. Teacher–baby rituals can assist in calming these babies prior to getting them to sleep. Babies sometimes can be calmed by being wrapped tightly in a soft, snug blanket, which gives the babies a sense of security. Some babies are sensitive to stimulation; caregivers of sensitive babies can avoid bright lights or sudden loud noises. Gentle massages can also help babies relax (Villarreal, McKinney, & Quackenbush, 1992).

Temperament

Beginning at birth, babies are different in activity level, in their responsiveness to people and their environment, and in how adaptable they are. These inborn patterns are termed *temperament* and shape how individual babies respond to experiences. For example, some babies are primarily cheerful; others are primarily fussy. Some babies have prolonged attention in activities; others are easily distractible. Some babies move very actively; others move more slowly. Chess and Thomas (1987) studied 133 people from infancy to early adulthood. A primary focus of this study was the identification and categorization of temperamental characteristics. At the beginning of their longitudinal study, Thomas and Chess classified temperament using a threefold scheme: first, regularity and adaptability to change; second, irregularity in biological functions and nonadaptability; and third, slow adaptability and regularity of biological functions (Thomas & Chess, 1977). Babies are born with different temperaments; however, as the baby develops, the expression of temperament is dependent upon the quality of caregiving and other everyday environmental factors. In other words, temperament is not "what is"; instead, temperament and environment interact to form patterns of behavior.

Alicia described some of the different temperaments of the children in her care and how she accommodates them as follows:

I never cease to be amazed at the differences in these children. Jake is calm and even-tempered, even though his 3-year-old sister, when in our room, always was fussing. Mimi (age 19 months) and Carrie (age 21 months) are out-going and cheerful almost everyday. Emily (age 11 weeks) seems very even-tempered. As young as she is, she seems content to alternatively be held in the infant swing or infant seat. Meanwhile, Mark (age 17 months) is just fussy, espe-cially during transitions. In fact, since Mark started moving about at 9 months, he cannot tolerate transitions from one activity to another.[4] We always warn Mark before changing an activity and have taught him to say "bye-bye" to the ac-tivity. These strategies have helped somewhat, but it never is easy.

To nurture babies' emotional growth, caregivers can adjust their re-sponses to fit individual children's temperaments. Alicia and her co-teachers have learned that they need to interact differently with differ-ent babies and toddlers. Because Mark is a sensitive child, his teachers have adapted their behavior (e.g., providing warnings when changing activities), and they have helped Mark develop some skill in regulating his own behavior (e.g., saying "bye-bye" to an activity).

Affect Regulation

Affect and emotion often are discussed interchangeably in the early child development literature. *Affect regulation* is a term designating a teacher's empathic response to a baby's signal. For example, the baby fusses and the teacher picks him up and rocks him as she talks to him softly. The teacher's response contains the baby, that is, allows the baby to main-tain a calm, alert state. Everyday child-rearing interactions, such as hold-ing, touching, caressing, rocking, and softly talking or singing, are ways that caregivers provide babies with loving responses and comfort. Joy, an infant child care teacher, illustrates this responsiveness in her in-teractions with Antoine (age 10 weeks) during his second day at the center.

Antoine sits in an infant seat and begins fussing. Joy picks him up and takes him to the rocking chair where she holds and rocks him. As she rocks Antoine, Joy talks to him softly: "See Susie and Demetrius playing. You don't know them yet, but soon they'll be your friends." As Joy speaks, Antoine calms down and begins reaching toward her face. When Joy returns Antoine to his infant seat, he remains calm.

By the time Antoine is 3 months old, he enjoys sitting in the infant seat close to where two or three older babies are playing with toys and interacting with a teacher. He seems at ease in this daily setting, and he engages with teachers socially through smiling and simple cooing. He is developing increased regularity in his physiological cycles of sleeping and eating.

Infant massage can be a powerful way to soothe babies who tend to be irritable or who have difficulty eating or sleeping. Infant massage can trigger the release of nerve signals that promote a baby's sense of well-being. Bernal (1997) conducted a case study on the use of massage to calm babies and toddlers in a child care center. Her research showed that after about 1 month of massages three times a week, infant behavior changed in the following ways:

- Less repetitive crying
- More tranquil sleep
- Muscular relaxation
- Better adaptation to the group
- Improved feeding habits

In some countries, especially parts of Africa, Asia, and India, infant massage is a common caregiving practice. In the 1990s, American researchers have found that massage helps to lessen babies' anxiety, both with typically developing and at-risk babies (Field, 1993).

Often teachers respond empathically to a baby's emotion with a behavior that matches the emotional tone of the baby's behavior. The teacher may move her or his body in a way that matches the baby's vocal sounds, or the teacher may make a sound that matches the way that the baby is moving. Stern termed these interactions *affect attunement*, and he provided a poignant example:

> An eight-and-one-half-month-old boy reaches for a toy just beyond reach. Silently he stretches toward it, leaning and extending arms and fingers fully out. Still short of the toy, he tenses his body to squeeze out the needed extra inch of reach. At that moment, his mother says, "uu-uuuh . . .uuuuh" with a crescendo of vocal effort, the expiration of air pushing against her tensed vocal chords. The mother's accelerating vocal-respiratory effort matched the infant's accelerating physical effort. (1985, p. 4)

The mother responded empathically to the baby's internal state. Although the mother's behavior was different from the baby's, Stern noted that caregivers match their babies' intensity (e.g., rapid acceleration, deceleration), timing (e.g., beat, rhythm, duration), and shape (e.g., up, down).

Bonding and Attachment

The parent's initial attachment to a baby is termed *bonding*. Parents seem to engage in an automatic array of bonding behaviors, such as exaggerated greeting responses and imitation of the baby's facial and vocal expressions. Babies' ties to their caregivers, which generally begin to form around 5–6 months of age, are termed *attachment*. Babies may show strong attachments to both their parents and to their out-of-home teacher. Babies' and teachers' strong positive bonds and attachments serve as a buffer during stressful experiences. Brain research suggests that *familiarity* may be a key protective dynamic for babies' inner states (Schore, 1998).

With repeated everyday child-rearing interaction, babies develop an attachment and an *internal working model* of their relationships with their teachers. Babies' internal working models are a representation, a memory of their interactions with teachers. An internal working model includes such information as whether the teacher usually responds when the baby cries for help and whether affection and responsiveness are reliably available. Internal working models permit babies to form expectations. For example, when caregivers put 12-month-old babies on the diaper-changing counter, babies will expect their caregivers to sing, talk softly, or engage in tickling or Peek-a-boo games.

Mutuality is central to the attachment behavior of babies and their caregivers. Babies smile and coo, and teachers return the smile as they talk to babies softly. Teachers lightly bounce babies who laugh in delight, and this laugh motivates the teachers to continue the bouncing.

> *Jake (age 6 months) has been seated on the rug with an array of infant toys for about 20 minutes. Nearby, five toddlers are playing at the sensory table and "talking" to their teacher, Alicia. Her co-teacher, Carmeletta, arrives and sits next to Jake. Carmeletta picks up Jake; puts him on her lap as she tickles his tummy; and says, "So how are you doing Jake?" Jake chuckles and begins babbling to Carmeletta, who repeats some of his babbling sounds. Carmeletta then stands Jake on her lap and continues to talk to him softly.*

Carmeletta's warm greeting to Jake is an affectionate way for her to let him know he is special and connected to his teachers. In turn, Jake responds with a chuckle and babbling. A two-person infant–teacher dance like this one is the dominant mode of effective everyday child-rearing interactions.

SOCIAL-EMOTIONAL DEVELOPMENT: 7–19 MONTHS

At about 7–9 months of age, a maturation takes place in babies' front cortical regions, which coincides with the appearance of new cognitive and behavioral abilities (Chugani, 1997). Now babies can sit up and begin to crawl. By sitting and moving about, babies see and understand their everyday world in new and exciting ways. Increased motor development coincides with cognitive advancement. Now out of sight is no longer out of mind; this concept is termed *object permanence.* A 10-month-old will lift up the blanket to find the ball underneath. The baby's experience becomes more organized. With recall memory and recognition, present and past experiences can be related, and often expectation is part of the baby's experience. Teachers now can talk to babies about prior experiences, and together they can tell stories of these experiences. Babies can begin to understand the connections of means to ends—*if I run away from my teacher when we're on a walk, she'll chase after me; when daddy comes to pick me up, we'll go home for supper.*

At 7–8 months of age, babies have advanced from merely being aware of others to initiating mutual interactions with others. For all of these changes to occur, babies must have both *memory* and *means of communication.* With memory, expectations become an important part of babies' experiences. During the second half of babies' first year, anticipation and intention are part of babies' emotional reactions. Stern (1985) termed this capacity *intersubjective relatedness,* and he identified three shared mental states: *shared joint attention, shared intention,* and *shared affective states.* Babies who are 7–12 months old can communicate their feelings through eye contact and vocalizations, and they can obtain information about how others feel. Babies' gestures of pointing and following their caregiver's line of vision are the first behaviors that permit inferences about establishment of joint attention. When the mother points to the kitchen to indicate that her child should go there for lunch, for this pointing to work, her baby must know to stop looking at the pointing hand and look in the direction the hand indicates. Intentions also become shared experiences. When a caregiver holds a cookie and the baby reaches out a hand as he or she says, "Eh! Eh!" these behaviors imply that the baby understands not only his or her intention to have the cookie but the caregiver's intention to satisfy him or her. Around age 7–8 months, babies smile not merely in response to stimulation, but with a social intention to communicate well-being, and to encourage teachers to repeat interactions. Around 10 months, when babies are in situations in which they feel uncertain and become ambivalent about approach or withdrawal, they look toward their caregivers to read their face to see if the situation is safe—a process termed *social referencing.* These three examples indicate that babies have the capacity for sharing affective states.

Sroufe summarized these changes in babies' behavior, which he described as being "increasingly under the control of psychological (anticipation, memory, intentionality) as opposed to physiological processes" (1996, p. 41).

Brain and Cognitive Development

Neuropsychological research shows that by about age 9 or 10 months, maturation of the frontal lobe of the cerebral cortex fosters the baby's ability to sustain attention, to inhibit a response or a negative emotion, and to manage emotionally arousing events (Thompson et al., 1995). Just as brain development underlies new abilities; so, too, experiences, especially caregiving interactions, continue to influence the brain.[5] In fact, the experiences that babies and young children have affect brain structure and function so profoundly that *absence of quality experiences may profoundly affect the development of the brain* (Gunnar, 1996a). With their new skills in self-regulation, babies have new capacities to respond to a negative situation. If an activity is too emotionally arousing, such as the robust singing of teacher and toddlers, babies can shift their attention to another activity or environmental space. Often babies reach out to their teacher for assistance. Some babies turn to a favorite toy, blanket, or other security object to comfort themselves. These objects, sometimes called *loveys* (Brazelton, 1992), are often most helpful during transition times such as between waking and sleeping. For this reason, child care teachers often allow babies to take a lovey from home with them to bed.

By the end of the first year, with advancing cognition, babies' memories of past experiences influence *how* they experience new events. Memory includes not only rationale and verbal recall but also nonverbal, essentially emotional, memory, especially memory of strong emotional experiences. With memory babies can anticipate events, and their actions can be specific and intended, for example, hiding their faces to play Peek-a-boo. Now that memory and anticipation of experiences play a part in present experiences, the *meaning* of an event will determine whether babies react emotionally and how they will react. The nature of the situation and whether the teacher is present become important in determining babies' emotional reactions.

Novel or incongruous experiences continue to promote cognitive development because such experiences make possible the development of new mental representations or schema, as in the following example:

> Charmaine (age 17 months) is out for a walk with her teacher. She says, "Bird," as she points to a butterfly. Her teacher replies, "It looks like a bird, but we call it a butterfly. Butterflies are lots smaller than birds."

Charmaine already knows the mental representation *bird,* which she expresses in this exchange with her child care teacher. Her teacher's response allows Charmaine to develop a new schema, *butterfly.* Whether babies can use novel or incongruous experiences to trigger cognitive growth often depends on their sense of security and their ability to regulate tension.

By age 9 months, the baby understands that experiences are sharable. By 9 months, babies point and can follow their teachers' pointing. They seem to know that "if I put my hands up, my child care teacher knows I want her to pick me up, or if I point to a bottle, she'll know I want one." This social signaling points to increased self-regulation, one way in which the baby is learning to be adaptive.

By age 10–12 months, babies can deal with feelings of uncertainty by pausing, turning away from the desired goal, and looking to their teacher to make certain it is okay to move forward. Thus, emotion also influences how babies assimilate new experiences. Developmentalists term this behavior *social referencing*—behavior that indicates cognitive advancement and secure attachment. Sroufe discussed the intertwining of emotions with cognitive development:

> Certain emotions require some capacity for the representation of relationships with others (e.g., grief, affection). Some require an evolving sense of self (e.g., shame). Other emotions require a comparison of behavior with an internalized standard (e.g., pride, guilt). Each of these makes demands on cognition (though again they reciprocally influence cognitive development). (1996, p. 126)

Schore (1994) also described the enormous change from the first to the second year in the caregiver's role as socialization agent. During the first year, babies experience primarily positive exchanges with their caregiver. Then, in the second year, they gain the motor skills to begin exploration, and suddenly they confront restrictions. They act, and the caregiver restricts—this is for them a new experience! Schore (1998) explained that the emotion of shame is involved in these restrictions. The baby acts and is restricted, and this restriction leads to feelings of shame, of being exposed. Baby and caregiver no longer are sharing the positive state of attachment. Unexpectedly, the baby sees his caregiver make negative facial expressions, and the baby responds with feelings of shame. Synchrony is replaced with dissynchrony. The baby then tries to avoid the caregiver's negative response by turning away, as though to escape being seen.

Schore (1998) emphasized that caregivers are not conscious of these half-second processes. The caregiver's skill in alleviating the baby's feelings of shame is critical. Can the caregivers reinitiate eye contact and reconnect with the baby? A caregiver's capacity to contain the baby's negative affect is critical. When the process of dissynchrony and reparation is successful, babies learn that negative experiences can be endured and conquered. In turn, the baby feels a sense of efficacy, similar to the efficacy the baby felt once trust was established. Schore noted that this process of restriction-shame-reparation involves the operation of two systems: self-regulation and interactive regulation. These interactive sequences lead to developmental advances of the prefrontal cortex, which enhances the baby's cognitive capacity to mentally represent these caregiver–baby transactions and the toddler's ability to learn self-control (Schore, 1994).

As babies mature, parents and teachers develop new strategies to foster babies' emotional regulation. Pipp-Siegel and Pressman identified three principal techniques that parents and teachers of 9- to 16-month-old babies can use to enhance the babies' self-regulation:

1) Ignoring behavior the mother [or caregiver] does not like
2) Diverting baby through rhythm, fun, and interest
3) Addressing prohibition situations by removing the baby or removing the forbidden object rather than by scolding (1996, p. 20)

As babies develop new strategies of emotional regulation, their teachers likewise do the same. Baby and teacher learn to read each other's signals, and the process is mutual.

Teacher Availability

As mentioned previously, emotions are essentially social, and the baby–caregiver interaction is the social scaffolding of development. The teacher's availability—both physical *and* psychological—is critical to the baby's social-emotional and cognitive development. Whether the teacher is available influences how much emotional tension 7- to 18-month-old babies can tolerate, how they respond to strangers, and how they respond to novel events. Teachers can be physically present but not psychologically available; for example, they may ignore or not respond empathically to a baby's initiative.

At age 9 months, as discussed previously, babies begin to resolve uncertainty in new situations by looking to their teacher. As babies mature and develop memory, it is very important that their teacher is present and attentive; babies' expectations arise from the full course of their history of interaction with the teacher (Sroufe, 1996). Over time, as teachers playfully interact with babies, for example, swinging the babies or hiding from them, babies learn to tolerate increased levels of tension integral to this play. At about 1 year of age, the range of emotional exchanges between babies and teachers is the basis of not only babies' sense of security (e.g., the baby feels secure even if the teacher is not present) but also of their ability to regulate arousal (e.g., the baby moves to a different activity if the current experience is too threatening).

Trust

Once babies become mobile, active exploration of their everyday environment becomes a primary preoccupation. When they feel secure, they will be more explorative because they know that their teacher is nearby if they get into trouble. Erikson (1950) noted that babies' first psychosocial developmental task is feeling trust as opposed to mistrust. When teachers are available and respond empathically, positively, and consistently to babies' signals, babies learn not only to trust their teacher but also to feel that they are of value and can influence their social environment. Trust fosters the baby's feelings of self-worth and competence— the baby's self-concept. When teachers encourage babies to explore, make choices, and take initiative, they are encouraging the babies' sense of competence, as in the following observation:

> Alicia is sitting on the floor with four babies and toddlers. The children are trying to snap together plastic ladders. Brad (age 17 months) snaps two pieces together successfully. Alicia hugs Brad as she says to him, "You did it! Yes!" Brad smiles as he repeats with glee, "Yes!"

Brad gains a sense of well-being in this affectionate interaction with his caregiver. In simple, brief interactions such as this, Alicia encourages Brad and his friends to attempt new tasks; and she is sure to encourage their efforts along the way. Her involvement also lets the children feel connected and helps them to maintain focus on a task.

Stranger Anxiety

At around 8–10 months of age, during a strong period of attachment with primary teachers, many babies often begin expressing fear with strangers. This fear response to strangers indicates that babies can distinguish their teacher as the person with whom they feel satisfied and protected. Usually when teachers comfort a baby who is dealing with an unfamiliar person, the anxiety disappears. Context is important in determining whether a baby responds to a stranger fearfully. If the teacher allows the baby to become familiar with the setting first and then introduces the stranger gradually, maybe even encouraging the stranger to play a familiar game such as Pat-a-cake, the baby will be less likely to feel afraid. In contrast, in a novel setting when a stranger approaches a baby without hesitation, most 10-month-olds will respond fearfully. Babies in out-of-home child care may have already learned to handle strange situations and strangers, but they still may undergo a period of adjustment during which they become upset when their parent leaves. At this time parents may need to provide a little extra time and comfort before leaving their child to go to work.

When babies have been in out-of-home child care since early infancy, the prevalence of stranger anxiety seems to decrease. Joy, a child care teacher of babies and toddlers, explained how the children in her care have dealt with strangers and new situations differently:

> Most of our children enter our classroom when they are 2 or 3 months old, so they are quite accustomed to a variety of babies, toddlers, and adults. Some of our infants do express stranger anxiety; however, only about 1 or 2 in 10 have these experiences. For example, Jake, who's now 10 months old, had stranger anxiety for about 3 weeks when he was 7 months old. He cried if a new person came into our room and tried to interact with him. He would cry and reach out for his teachers. If the stranger did not interact with him, he was not bothered. But each child expresses stranger anxiety differently. Jake's sister, Amy, when she was in our room 3 years ago, would cry as soon as a stranger entered our room. Interestingly, around 7 or 8 months, some of our babies have a brief period of separation anxiety. For example, Matt (age 10 months) has been clinging to his mother each morning since about 8 months of age. Once I take Matt and get him involved in an activity, he is fine.

Independence and Autonomy

An integral part of social-emotional development involves babies' growing independence and autonomy. Learning independence begins during the first months of life as babies learn to calm themselves. Then around age 5 months, babies become able to begin and end interactions with their caregivers. During toddlerhood, which begins around age 18–20 months, babies' increased mobility propels exploration and increased feelings of independence and autonomy. Toddlers often exert their independence and autonomy by running away from and resisting everyday routine activities. Increased mobility and accompanying acts of independence and autonomy also trigger ambivalence. The toddler wants to move and be separate yet, at the same time, wants the teacher's protection. Children this age tend to push caregivers away and then cling to them a moment later. Saying "no," often even when they do not really mean "no," accompanies this tug and pull. Everyday routines such as dressing and diapering can become a struggle.

Toddlers with strong attachments to their parents and child care teachers have the security to be more independent than do toddlers with anxious attachments. Similarly, toddlers with secure attachments will not become emotionally disorganized during experiences of high arousal, for example, going to the pediatrician or falling down and scraping their knees. If secure toddlers do become disorganized, for example, by crying in fright when a puppy jumps on them, they can readily become calm with adult support. Child care teachers often can anticipate potentially frustrating situations and intervene to prevent a toddler from losing control, such as in the following example:

> *Derrick, a large 17-month-old, rolls around on the rug with Demetrius, a smaller 16-month-old. Derrick wrestles with Demetrius in the same way that Derrick's dad does with him each evening. Derrick's teacher, Joy, gently shows him how to tumble about with Demetrius in a gentler manner. For several moments the two toddlers roll around on the rug together happily.*

Although Joy had not been interacting with these two toddlers, she watched them closely and could anticipate that Derrick's rigorous actions would overwhelm Demetrius.

SOCIAL-EMOTIONAL DEVELOPMENT: 19–36 MONTHS

Young babies need physical connection, such as being held, rocked, or stroked, to feel comfortable and secure. With increasing age, however, toddlers seek less physical contact with their teachers and often can rely on vocalization or mere awareness of the teacher's presence to feel secure. For brief periods of time, they even can leave the vicinity of their teacher, for example, to play in the playground around the corner where teachers other than their own are present. It is as if toddlers can hold onto the emotional connection even when they are separate from their teachers physically.

Around age 20–22 months, toddlers can direct the behavior of their teacher (Kagan, 1989). For example, toddlers frequently request assistance, such as help putting on their shoes or completing a puzzle. When child care teachers engage in pretend play with toddlers, the children often give their teacher directives, such as pointing to where the teacher should sit at the table or giving the teacher a telephone to use. Kagan noted that these behaviors point to the toddlers' expectation that they "can influence the behavior of others" (p. 232).

In the latter half of the second year, toddlers also learn to take the perspective of another person. This new ability allows for empathy. By the end of the second year, toddlers respond to a hurt child as if they are inferring the feelings of the victim. They will hug or kiss the child who is hurt or request assistance from an adult. Research provides evidence that very young children often adjust their conversations when speaking to children younger than themselves because they can imagine how the younger child feels and intuit what the younger child can understand (Lee, 1989).

When toddlers get into conflicts with each other or become distressed, these experiences become opportunities for child care teachers to talk with the toddler about how the toddler is feeling. When young children hear feelings talked about in their everyday life, the verbalization fosters their own perspective-taking ability. That is, toddlers experience this verbalization as caring; and as they feel cared for, they can, in turn, care for others.

By the end of the second year, toddlers can engage in a wider array of play exchanges with their peers. Now they can play a real game of Hide-and-Seek. They are beginning to remember rules and to understand the concept of turn taking. When Derrick (age 17 months) grabs Mimi's push-and-pull toy, Mimi (age 19 months) is able to say loudly "mine." Mimi's teacher then supports Mimi and tells Derrick that she'll make certain he gets a turn in a few moments. By 36 months of age toddlers know that some behaviors, such as biting, hitting, and grabbing, are forbidden. This understanding develops only when toddlers' parents and child care teachers provide clear, firm, and reasonable limits. Two-year-olds continue to have rapid mood shifts and exhibit negativism; at the same time, they are acquiring many new social skills.

By 2 years of age, toddlers spontaneously begin to refer to themselves in speech, such as "I want cookie" or "I do it myself." Kagan suggested that "the child is suddenly aware of a fresh experience. He is aware of what he is doing" (1989, p. 233). Increasingly, young children are aware of their own actions and intentions. Toddlers' secure attachment to their parents and child care teachers and changes in their brain organization make these new abilities possible. Just as brain development influences toddlers' development of independence and social skills, *toddlers' interactions, especially with their teachers, likewise influence their brain development* (Schore, 1994). Effective teachers provide encouragement as well as clear limits for toddlers' increasing mobility and exploration. In addition, they provide clear behavior expectations and recognition as well as support and verbalization of toddlers' feelings. These caregiving interactions provide young children with both a sense of security and a sense of self-worth.

Individual differences in independent actions, emotional tone, fearfulness, anxiety, social skills, and rudimentary self-regulation skills are more notable in toddlerhood than in infancy. The roots of young children's individual differences in their ability to cope with emotionally arousing events lie within the unique patterns of dyadic teacher–infant regulation. These individual differences are related to children's later ability to self-regulate their emotions. Anxious children, for example, react more strongly to their child care teachers' redirection than nonanxious children (Sroufe, 1996). Whether children are able to self-regulate their emotional state, are fearful and anxious, or are skilled socially are all related to both the quality of their early relationships with teachers and the quality of the limits and consequences that their teachers have established for them. *Development always builds on what has occurred previously.* Behaviors never emerge out of a vacuum; instead, behaviors build on prior behaviors and experiences.

The autonomic nervous system also plays a role in children's ability to monitor and modify their emotional reactions by continuously regulating their level of arousal and the accompanying ability to self-regulate. The autonomic nervous system consists of the *sympathetic nervous system,* which energizes us, and the *parasympathetic nervous system,* which helps us return to a balanced state. Teachers can learn to read children's motor actions and level of awareness to interpret the stability of the child's autonomic nervous system. Tight or low muscle tone, a tense face, or frantic movements are all signs of neurological disorganization. Signs of disorganization also include erratic sleep patterns, especially in young babies, inability to self-calm, and a glassy-eyed stare. When a teacher detects signs of disorganization, she may consider that the given task or experience is too overwhelming for the child; she will need to attempt to reduce the demands placed on the child rather than discipline the child for inappropriate behavior (Schore, 1998).

Encouragement versus Praise

Child care teachers can encourage toddlers to explore and attempt new tasks. When teachers encourage young children they can strive to describe the children's actions in concrete terms (e.g., "Demetrius, you put your shoes and socks on!" "Lia, look at all the pretty colors—purple, blue, and yellow—that you drew on your picture"). Encouragement given in the form of concrete descriptions of children's actions helps young children to recognize their own successes, feel good about themselves, and know that they are valued. With encouragement, children learn to do tasks for the sheer pleasure of accomplishing the tasks and the recognition of their increased competence. Encouragement fosters autonomy and an acceptance and valuing of self.

In contrast, when teachers use global evaluative praise, such as "Good boy," "Nice," or "Good job," the children learn that they are pleasing significant adults. Children learn nothing about themselves when praised in this fashion. They do learn that their teacher is pleased that they are obedient. Global praise is an external reward. Children have no understanding of pat phrases such as "Good job" and "Nice," other than that their behavior is pleasing to their teacher. When teachers use these pat phrases repeatedly, the phrases become like slogans. Some children merely tune out these slogans in the same way that, after several days, they might tune out the noise from the construction equipment outside their classroom. Hitz and Driscoll suggested that "no student can always be good or nice or smart. Consequently, in order to avoid negative evaluations, they may tend not to change and try difficult tasks" (1988, p. 7). Some child care teachers develop patterns of praise expression, such as "I like the way Darryl is sitting quietly," or "I like the way Naoko is using her spoon." One liability of this type of praise is that such expressions can instill comparisons and competitiveness. Children may wonder, for example, "Why is my teacher praising Naoko when I'm doing the same thing? Why is she better than me?" Hitz and Driscoll (1988) noted that many teachers use praise to foster self-esteem; however, unwittingly, these teachers' praises can foster dependency instead.

Play

During the second year, symbolic thinking develops and is expressed in toddlers' simple pretend play. Toddlers begin to act out everyday experiences, for example, by washing the doll's hair or pouring and drinking coffee. In this pretend play, they are the "masters" of their feelings, feelings that may be ambivalent or negative in real life, such as when "mommy washes my hair." When child care teachers act as partners in this play, toddlers gain experience in give and take and mutuality; they learn that their actions can influence other people. In addition, pretend play between teacher and toddler gives the toddler a sense of connectedness and affirmation, as in the following example.

> Co-teachers Alicia and Carmeletta are in the gross motor room with eight toddlers. Alicia suggests to the children that they run around the climbers. Alicia and four of the toddlers run around the climbers and a tub of rubber balls. Alicia occasionally calls "Stop!" and she and the toddlers lie down for a moment, then begin running again. Each time they start running the toddlers giggle in delight.

Alicia has initiated a game in which young toddlers can experience shared delight. Often child care teachers can extend the play, for example, by suggesting to a child to cook eggs to go with the pretend coffee. Sroufe described how teachers can use play to shape young children's emotional experiences:

> The teacher in a sense trains the infant in tension management. In the course of playful interaction the infant learns, over time, to maintain behavioral organization in the face of increasingly high levels of tension. As teacher and infant play, tension is escalated and deescalated, to the edge of overstimulation and back again, commonly ending in bursts of positive affect that are so rewarding to the teacher. Episode by episode, day by day, the infant's own capacity to modulate and tolerate tension is developed, and a reservoir of shared positive affect is created. (1996, p. 144)

As Alicia and the toddlers run about, Alicia sees that the running is causing the children to become increasingly excited, and so she directs them all to lie down together. In doing this Alicia creates a pattern of increased arousal in running and decreased arousal in lying down—what Sroufe might describe as an exercise in tension management.

Social Development

Advances in social development are intertwined with advances in emotional development. As discussed previously, emotions develop within the caregiving relationship. At first, newborns have little awareness of their environment. Over time, they develop not only an awareness of their teacher but also an awareness of their own feelings and actions. In toddlerhood, children continue to progress from complete dependency to increasing autonomy and mutuality in relating to their teacher and other people.

Toddlers who have been in out-of-home child care since early infancy have had many experiences of shared delight with other babies and toddlers. Although they may not have the words to express what they are doing, teachers can observe when toddlers are actively observing other babies and toddlers, as well as when they miss their companions. Jake's teacher, Joy, described Jake's closeness to the other children in his program.

Joy: Remember when Jake was 8–9 months old and we'd tell you how fussy he'd become when the older toddlers were napping? It was like he was missing them. In the past 3–4 months our four oldest toddlers have moved to the 2-year-old room. Jake is 12 months old now, and we have only two other toddlers, 18 and 19 months old.

We think Jake is missing the toddlers. The activity level in his group has calmed dramatically, and, Jake, who used to seem to delight in watching the older kids, now seems to more easily become fussy. Even though he didn't interact with these older kids, they were a key part of his day.

Before babies become mobile, the observer can readily see how focused babies are on their older companions. In fact, one of the 7-month-olds in Joy's care can sit contentedly for several moments next to the window, where she can watch the preschoolers play in the yard. As toddlers develop the ability to engage in simple pretend play, as well as language, motor coordination, and mobility, they enjoy brief episodes of play with other toddlers. This first phase of play occurs around 18 months of age and is termed *parallel play*, during which toddlers play side by side. Occasionally they may interact with one another and even imitate each other. But their play is primarily solitary, although they are physically next to a peer. Since the 1950s, child development professionals have regarded parallel play as the primary play model of toddlers. However, an increasing number of children who are in group care, often from the age of early infancy, develop social skills and play patterns that often are more advanced.

Teachers of young toddlers can encourage their social skills, as Alicia does in the following observation:

> Alicia sits on the floor with four toddlers (ages 18–24 months) standing around her. She begins blowing bubbles toward the children. First, the toddlers watch Alicia, then they walk around as they reach up and try to pop the bubbles with their hands. Mimi says, "Bubbles," and Darryl says, "More." As the children reach, Alicia comments, "Reach, reach," and "Pop, pop." She suggests that they can "stomp on the bubbles when they get to the floor." Alicia then stomps on several bubbles, and two of the children join her. These two toddlers then each take a turn blowing the bubble ring to make bubbles, and the other three try to pop the ones their peers have created. Throughout the activity, individual toddlers squeal spontaneously in delight.

Alicia has initiated and supported a simple play activity in which several toddlers can actively participate, respond to each other's actions, and experience shared enjoyment. Other simple play activities teachers can initiate to encourage toddlers playing together include playing "Ring

Around the Rosie" and playing with water, pasta, cornmeal, or other sensory items.

Child care in socialist settings, such as China and Russia during the 1960s and 1970s and kibbutzes in Israel, demonstrated that social skill development in toddlerhood is dependent on clear *adult expectations* (Bettleheim, 1969; Bronfenbrenner, 1970; Chan, 1975; Kessen, 1975; Sidel, 1972). Teachers in these child care centers explicitly encouraged children to help each other, and it was common to see very young children spontaneously assist and comfort one another. As more and more babies and toddlers in the United States are spending from 8 to 10 hours per day in child care, we can expect an increasing amount of shared interaction, even perspective taking, especially if teachers promote these behaviors. When teachers only focus on individual self-expression and achievement, the young children in their care will probably compete for adult attention and not engage in much shared interaction.[6]

Body Image and Sexual Learning

Toddlers' understanding of their bodies and their initial learning about sexuality is integral to their increased mobility, social understanding and skills, and delight in play. Beginning in early infancy, many babies discover they can calm themselves by sucking on their thumbs. Babies discover their hands and feet around 3 months of age and love playing with them. Through these experiences, babies develop new understandings about their bodies. Once babies are mobile, they continue to learn about their bodies as they scoot or crawl about on the floor, "dance" to music, or push nonpedaled vehicles. In these movements, babies and toddlers are gaining an understanding, termed *kinesthetic awareness,* of how their bodies feel in space and in movement. Routine caregiving activities, such as bathing, diapering, and dressing, offer repeated experiences in which babies and toddlers gain increased bodily awareness. Likewise, as teachers hold, rock, and stroke young children, they are influencing the children's awareness of their bodies. Child care teachers and parents are pivotal influences on how much indoor and outdoor space young children have in which to move about as well as on what toys and games young children have to explore, alone and with their caregivers. Babies and toddlers are by nature very curious, and bodily and genital exploration is a natural part of this curiosity. As child care teachers and parents bathe, dress, and diaper babies and young toddlers, these young children are learning about their bodies and their sexuality. In these routine interactions, teachers also are communicating to the young child their own attitudes toward the child's body. All babies touch their genitals and discover that this touching is pleasurable because the nerve endings of genitals are quite sensitive. This touching, which is sometimes termed *masturbation,* is not the same as adult masturbation and is widely accepted as a natural, healthy phase of infancy and toddlerhood. It is important for teachers to understand that the sensations that young children have when touching their genitals are not the same as the intense feelings adults experience during adult sexual stimulation. Toilet learning often increases toddlers' interest in their genitals. Babies and toddlers are most likely to fondle their genitals when they are tired, are going to sleep, or are in a restful activity such as listening to a story. Toddlers sometimes engage in masturbation as a way to self-calm; however, excessive masturbation, like excessive head banging, can be a signal that the toddler is experiencing too much stress.

Gender Identity

Young children observe gender in physical traits such as hair length and dress. Recognition of one's own gender is typically one of the first properties of self that toddlers recognize. Once toddlers recognize their gender, they begin identifying with their same-sex parents; and, by 2 years of age, toddler boys are imitating their father's behavior and girls, their mother's. By 30 months of age, most toddlers know whether other people are men or women, boys or girls. Two- and three-year-olds often enjoy dressing up in clothing that is typically worn by the opposite sex. It is not until children are 4 or 5 years of age that they understand that their gender identity is unchanging, even though they may wear different clothing or change the length of their hair.

SOCIAL-EMOTIONAL DEVELOPMENT: 3–5 YEARS

At around 3 years of age, young children develop the ability to tell stories. (Toddlers can tell very brief stories with adult assistance. Chapter 3 discusses this pattern.) Stern (1991) called this new sense of self the *narrative self*. Now young children can tell stories containing an agent, an intention, a goal, causes, a dramatic line, and so forth. Initially children's stories are about themselves and family happenings.

Stern wrote that the narrative provides the young child "a laboratory in which the child constantly is working on who s/he is, defining, redefining who s/he is and constantly updating" (1991). Interestingly, these stories may be a form of the child's developing ability to self-regulate (Stern, 1985). The ability to self-regulate is poignantly illustrated in the book, *Narratives from the Crib* (Nelson, 1989). Nelson's book reports the results of a study of the monologues of a young toddler, Emily, and the dialogues of Emily and her parents, when Emily was between the ages of 21 and 36 months. In her monologues, Emily often sorts out her everyday life, especially experiences involving routines such as eating, dressing, and sleeping. In the stories she tells to herself, Emily reviews and gains mastery emotionally and intellectually of her feelings about and understanding of these experiences (see Chapter 3 for more information on Nelson's study). Four- and five-year-olds expand their stories to include content that they never have experienced—for example, stories about giants, fairies, or video or television characters. With this new ability, young children delight in a new form of shared storytelling with their parents and child care teachers.

Eloise (age 3 years) and her child care teacher, Pam, illustrate shared storytelling in the following conversation:

> *When Eloise's father brought her to the child care center on the day that this interaction took place, he told Pam that the previous day the family had visited a cousin's farm and that Eloise got to pet a newborn calf.*
>
> *Pam says to Eloise, "Yesterday you and mommy and daddy went to a farm."*
>
> *Eloise replies, "And I petted a baby cow. My hands smelled like a cow." She grimaces, adding, "And the cat climbed the tree. I fed the cat." Then Eloise points to her arm and says, "But then he scratched me."*
>
> *Pam says, "He scratched you on your arm. Cats have claws. You have to pet cats very gently."*

As parents are dropping off their children to child care, they frequently chat with the teacher about events taking place at home. These conversations allow the teachers to initiate conversations with the children and encourage the children to tell stories.

Just as toddlers explore their world through their new motor skills, preschoolers explore through active questioning. Young children are born into a physical environment that includes movement, variety, and change as everyday characteristics. Furthermore, they live in a social environment that has a continual flow of interaction, information, variety, and change. Given their naturally curious state, their physical and social environment propels preschool children into questioning their caregivers repeatedly. As preschoolers ask questions, teachers can affirm this new skill and help to extend the young children's thinking, as in the following example.

> *As they are traveling on a field trip, Mike and the children in his care pass by a church. Greg (age 3 years) asks Mike, "Why do churches have steeples?" Mike replies, "I'm not sure. Why do you think they have steeples, Greg?" Greg replies, "To kill the monsters that fly at night."*

Like most of the children for whom Mike cares, Greg asks many questions. Mike has several options: to ignore Greg, to provide him with quick responses, or to repeat the question to Greg to stimulate Greg's thinking. Often teachers provide simple responses that satisfy the children. Responding to children's curiosity communicates respect and encourages the children to continue to explore. Ignoring preschoolers' questions will motivate the children to eventually cease their questioning, thereby lessening their curiosity and potential intellectual development.

Questioning and storytelling are signs of the preschooler's cognitive advances. These cognitive advances always are intertwined with the young child's social experiences and emotions. When teachers actively listen and/or assist young children in telling stories, their support feels affirming and encourages the young child to continue his or her story-telling and questioning.

Social Development

An important benefit of preschoolers' new symbolic awareness is the possibility for social interactions to blossom among children and their peers and between children and adults. Now peers can become not only momentary companions but friends, and a new quality of child-to-child mutuality develops. For young preschoolers, the central characteristic of friendship is liking another person. "Liking" can take on many characteristics, especially given the developmental levels of the people involved. At first, liking may indicate simple positive feelings stemming from shared activities. With maturity, reciprocity and perspective taking become central. Friendships in child care seem to develop spontaneously without adult facilitation. For 3- to 5-year olds, friends are those children who are fun to be with, not those who have special traits (Damon, 1977). In my case study of Rosehill Day Care Center, of the 50 preschool children enrolled, 10 children were close friends (Klass, 1986). I interviewed each of these children, and their responses mirrored Damon's (1977) research findings. These children either said they liked their friend "because she [or he] plays with me" or "because I like to play with her [or him]."

Although preschoolers have only a primitive understanding of friendships, they do engage in prosocial interactions with their friends, as in the following observation:

> *Nancy and Rachel (both 4 years old) have been friends in child care over the past 10 months and most often choose to play with each other. The girls enjoy looking through picture books together and talking about what they see on each page. They enjoy extended periods of sculpting with play-*

*dough and talk together as they make snakes, cookies, piz-
zas, and other forms. Frequently they engage in role-play
sequences in the housekeeping area. Outdoors they often
swing and climb together. In sum, they engage in shared enjoyment in a variety of activities.*

Child care teachers typically see friendships formed spontaneously as a
positive strand of the children's learning process. Some teachers worry
that friendships between preschoolers can develop into teacher management problems. They are concerned that, for example, young friends
will be more interested in interacting with each other than attending to
their teacher during group periods. It is important that child care teachers understand the developmental value of friendships so that they can
tolerate situations when friends create challenges in the teacher's group
learning processes.

Three-, four-, and five-year-olds in child care have many opportunities to develop prosocial behavior, especially when their teachers value
prosocial behavior and encourage it. For example, a teacher can suggest
that one child rather than the teacher help another child tie his shoe.
Similarly, when teachers observe one child assisting or sharing with another child, they can affirm this behavior by describing it to the first child
positively (e.g., "Joey, you were so good in helping Jennifer figure out
how to finish that difficult puzzle"). Prosocial behavior includes assisting, sharing, and playing cooperatively in joint projects or role play.
Given advances in their cognitive development, preschoolers engage in
increasingly complex fantasy play and role taking. As young children
engage in prosocial activities, their understanding of self in relation to
others is enriched. My activity scan of children playing during early care
(6:30 A.M.–9:00 A.M.) at a child care center illustrates how preschoolers
can enjoy extended periods of shared participation in joint projects:

*Alan and Miguel spend close to 10 minutes hooking to-
gether about two dozen 3-inch plastic monkeys, which they
have hung on the back of a chair. Charisse and Antoine sit
next to each other as they place pegs in all the holes of a
pegboard. Charisse says, "Let's take them all out now." The
two children remove all the pegs; when they finish, Antoine
says enthusiastically, "We did it!" The children then go to
different areas of the room to play.*

*Nancy and Rachel sit side by side in the library area and
look at books together. Ezra and Eddie sit side by side to
work on a puzzle. Next to them is Daniel, who is having difficulty completing his puzzle. Daniel complains, "It just*

won't fit!" Ezra shows Daniel how to complete the puzzle successfully.

The child care teachers were nearby throughout these play sequences, but none seemed to be aware of the children's prosocial activities. At least, they did not affirm the children's behavior directly. In fact, during 6 months of observation at this center, I very rarely saw a teacher explicitly affirm prosocial child behavior. At the same time, however, these teachers were very quick to praise individual children's creative self-expression or independent actions such as self-help skills. The children were quite skilled in initiating play activities; however, with no teacher support, their spontaneous social play sequences were usually brief and surface in quality.

Fear

As the 3-year-olds' world expands, so do their fears. Children this age may begin to be afraid of the dark, worry about monsters and ghosts, or feel tense around loudly barking dogs or noisy fire engines. Young children sometimes imagine ways to address their fears, such as having church steeples kill the nighttime monsters. Teachers need to understand that emerging fears are normal for 3-year-olds, and they should listen to, accept, and respect these fears. They can talk to the children about their fears, and reassure them by letting them know that it is okay to feel afraid. They can prepare the child when a fear-provoking experience is about to occur, such as loud street drilling. Young children may not always understand their teacher, but they will be comforted by knowing that their teacher understands and accepts their fears.

Self-Esteem

Self-esteem is the evaluative component of self-concept. Positive self-esteem is associated with initiative, independence, and competence. When babies and young children have empathically responsive teachers, they develop a sense of personal agency, that is, a sense that their actions can influence another person.[7] As mentioned previously, teachers can enhance young children's sense of competence by descriptively affirming the children's observed behavior, as in the following example:

> Sarah is in her backyard with the four children for whom she cares—Karen (age 5 years), Jennie (age 4 years), Reba (age 3 years), and Kimmy (age 22 months). Sarah watches Kimmy climb onto the swing glider and begin to swing. She says to Kimmy, "We're tough! We can get on there and swing by ourselves, can't we!" Kimmy smiles. Sarah then

> *lifts Kimmy onto the individual swing as she asks, "Re-*
> *member how Karen and Jennie swing their legs back and*
> *forth to go high? Let me get you started." Sarah gives Kimmy*
> *a push and then steps back and watches her. As she watches,*
> *she encourages Kimmy enthusiastically, "You're getting*
> *higher! You're getting there!" Again Kimmy smiles as she*
> *swings.*

As Sarah enthusiastically describes Kimmy's swinging, she is affirming Kimmy's accomplishment for its own sake. When young children frequently hear their behavior affirmed descriptively by their teachers, they develop a sense of self-worth and competence. Teachers have many opportunities to communicate to the children that they are valued and competent.

Sex-Role Learning

Sex roles are the socially defined behaviors, attitudes, rights, and obligations that are part of the role of being boy or girl, male or female. *Sex-role stereotyping* involves rigid assignment of characteristics to people without taking into account their individual qualities—such as women but not men are supposed to cry or women but not men are supposed to wash clothes.[8] Sex roles are defined by one's culture. In the United States, fathers were traditionally expected to behave in certain ways, such as to cut the lawn and fix broken toys; and mothers were expected to behave in certain ways, such as to cook the family dinner and wash the family's clothes. When young children learn sex-role behavior they are learning the behaviors that the culture expects of their gender, such as little boys are loud and little girls are sweet and gentle. Children as young as 2 or 3 years understand sex-role stereotyping in their choice of toys. Most little girls tend to play with dolls, and most little boys tend to play with toy trucks and carpentry tools. Children as young as 2 and 3 also sometimes choose same-sex playmates, although this preference is not nearly as strong as it is at elementary school age.

As more fathers share in household tasks and child rearing, and more mothers work full time, sex-role expectations are changing. Occupations are increasingly open to both women and men; similarly, storybooks and television portrayals are breaking down traditional sex-role stereotyping. With these societal changes, it is more possible for young boys and girls to develop their full potential and not be constricted by old-fashioned sex-role stereotypes. For example, boys are increasingly being expected to learn to express their feelings and develop caregiving skills, and girls are increasingly being expected to be assertive and to solve problems.

Child care teachers can assist young boys and girls to develop to their fullest potential and to know that both sexes can engage in a wide variety of tasks. When female teachers regularly sit in the block corner, they no doubt will attract an increasing amount of little girls to an area that often is dominated by boys. When tables need to be moved, teachers can ask little girls as well as little boys to assist them. Rather than have a male custodian come and help when a light burns out, a female teacher can change the bulb herself.

As teachers strive to provide an environment in which young boys and girls can develop to their fullest potential, they also need to be aware that sex-role behaviors are value-laden and can be sensitive issues for some parents. Teachers always need to be respectful of parents' values and recognize that some parents value certain kinds of sex-role stereotyping more than others.

Moral Self

By 3 years of age the child's moral self has begun to develop. At this age, children have internalized rules about what they can and cannot do, rules that have emerged from their everyday interactions with emotionally available caregivers. Interestingly, many of the emotionally engaging experiences making this possible are stored as procedural knowledge not accessible to the child's consciousness. Procedural knowledge is that information underlying a skill that may not have to be represented in consciousness for a child to express the skill. Expressing emotion in the face, in the voice, or through gesture as well as taking in emotional expression from another person are examples of procedural knowledge at work. Emde, Biringen, Clyman, and Oppenheim (1991) defined *self* as "an organizing mental process and as a regulator of experience (where this includes an individual's sense of continuity, confidence, competence, mastery, and later in age, esteem)." Regulation and the ability to adapt are central to the child's developing moral self. The ability to regulate the frustration between wanting to achieve one's personal needs and desires and adhering to social standards and obligations is one example. These abilities emerge from the baby's everyday experiences with an emotionally available caregiver who responds to the baby consistently.

CONCLUSION

Babies' and young children's social-emotional development is a dynamic, complex process that is integrated with all the other areas of development. A baby or young child's environment and everyday interactions make lasting impressions on his or her development. Of course, caregiving can occur in the absence of this knowledge. But without skillful caregiving, babies and young children can miss out not only on rich experiences but also on the developmental potential that can be achieved most fully in the young years. When child care providers understand babies' and young children's social-emotional development, they can grasp better the meaning of children's behavior and ascertain how to best care for young children. Teachers armed with this knowledge not only will be better able to foster young children's development but also will be able to see, appreciate, and understand more about the children in their care and will find their work to be increasingly enjoyable.

chapter 3

Language and Communication

Each person is born an infant, and every infant is subject from the first breath he draws and the first cry he utters to the attentions and demands of others. . . . There is no miracle in the fact that if a child learns any language he learns the language that those about him speak and teach, especially since his ability to speak that language is a pre-condition of his entering into effective connection with them, making wants known and getting them satisfied.

—*John Dewey (1922, pp. 55–56)*

From the moment babies are born they can initiate contact and respond to their caregiver. But if a child is not allowed to communicate, this ability withers. From the beginning, taken-for-granted, everyday child-rearing interactions form the foundation of caregiver–baby communication. A baby is communicating successfully when a caregiver perceives and responds to the baby's signals. As child care teachers go about everyday, routine activities with very young babies, they have innumerable opportunities to engage them in meaningful communication. As language researcher Kathryn Nelson noted, "The most basic conditions of children's lives are composed of the events of caregiving (feeding, sleeping, changing diapers, bathing, and so on); and in sharing the attention and affection of caregivers" (1990, p. 309). In the following observation, Joy, an out-of-home caregiver, uses the simple routine activity of giving a baby her bottle as an opportunity to communicate with her:

> *Emma (age 9 weeks) has been in Joy's class for 2 weeks. Joy has just given Emma some milk from a bottle. As she holds Emma, she pats her back and says, "We need to get out that burp." Emma burps and then Joy holds Emma facing her as she says, "And we'll help you take more than 1 ounce of formula." Emma smiles, the first smile Joy has seen, and Joy responds, "And you feel okay, don't you?"*

As Joy talks to Emma, she soothes her and helps Emma feel connected. In turn, Emma is able to smile at Joy, a response that triggers Joy's continued talking. From the beginning, this mutuality is central to caregiver–baby communication.

Communication involves sending messages back and forth. We communicate when we let another person know what we think or want. Babies and adults communicate with each other through facial expressions, hand gestures, body posture, and vocalization. As the child develops, language becomes the most important mode of communication; indeed, the ability to use language is the distinct characteristic of our species. Typically developing young children acquire language spontaneously through interactive dialogue.[1] Language is a shared, rule-governed system that people use to express their thoughts symbolically. Language acquisition has three components: the language to be learned, the young child and the abilities that he or she brings to that learning, and the child's social environment (Rice, 1989). Language emerges in the give and take of everyday interaction between baby and caregiver.

Babies develop mental categories, termed *schemas,* from their daily social experience with caregivers; these interactions become the matrix for learning language. How caregivers talk to young children influences the children's own speech. Most effective is when a caregiver's speech matches the content and the emotional tone of the child's prior utterance. Literature on language development terms this immediate matching of content and tone *semantic contingency*. The following observations illustrate how one infant-toddler teacher skillfully matches children's speech content and tone:

> Cory (age 19 months) swishes his hands in the sand as he gleefully says, "Oooooh." Joy replies, "Oooooh, you made hand marks in the sand."
> Carrie (age 23 months) holds up a small plastic rhinoceros as she says to Joy, "Rhino." Joy replies, "This is a rhino. Look at the big horn on his nose."
> Mia (age 21 months) has just arrived and says to Joy, "Mall." Joy replies, "Yesterday did you and mommy go to the mall?" Mia smiles as she nods yes.

This teacher skillfully reads and responds appropriately to the toddlers' communications. Joy not only is motivating children to speak but also is affirming them emotionally.

This chapter explores young children's development of language and communication from birth through age 5 years. The development of language and communication *emerges within the young child's relationships with significant others.* (Table 1 summarizes language and communication development and suggests how caregivers can promote this development in children from birth through age 5.) Although this chapter focuses on language and communication, no one domain functions independently; development is an integrated process. As the chapter sketches the development of language and communication, the reader can see the interplay of all the other developmental domains. As the brain develops, for example, the baby begins smiling and cooing. With brain development and accompanying cognitive growth, babies begin to understand simple speech. With each developmental stride, young children develop new social skills and accompanying patterns of interaction; in turn, their caregivers adapt everyday patterns of interaction to accommodate children's developing skills.

The chapter concludes with a discussion of early literacy. Beginning in the preschool years, early literacy emerges; that is, young children begin to understand that written words are used to communicate with others. The focus of both language and emerging literacy is on meaning and understanding. Very young children develop understanding and the skills of language and emerging literacy through their everyday social interactions, especially the everyday interactions with their caregivers.

Table 1. Development patterns of communication, birth through 5 years, and caregiving practices

Developmental patterns	Caregiving practices
Birth through 4 months	
Watches parents' facial expressions change	Changes facial expression and voice during interactions with baby
Hears differences in sound and speech	Imitates baby's facial gestures and sounds
Has several different cries	Begins and responds to give-and-take vocal play with baby
Makes eye contact with caregiver when caregiver is talking	Sings and talks softly during routine activities
Shows pleasure by smiling and cooing	
4–10 months	
Uses vowels and consonants to babble	Repeats baby's sounds
Laughs and smiles in response to familiar people	Describes what baby and self are doing during routine caregiving
Babbles rhythmically with sentence-like intonation	Plays simple gesture games with baby, for example, Hide-and-Seek with towel
Playfully imitates nonspeech sounds, for example, smacking lips, clicking tongue	Reads simple picture books to infant
Understands regularly used individual words	Sings simple rhymes and songs to baby
Recognizes name and turns toward speaker	Encourages infant to respond to baby's name
Plays gesture games such as Pat-a-cake	
Uses gesturing such as pointing to ask for things	
Understands and responds to "no"	
Enjoys simple picture books	
10–16 months	
Understands simple and short sentences	Continues give-and-take vocal play with baby
Understands simple directions	Identifies baby's body parts and encourages baby to point to them
Enjoys picture books and simple storybooks	Sings simple rhymes, fingerplays, and stories
Points to objects in picture book that caregiver has named	Reads simple storybooks
Imitates gestures like Peek-a-boo	Talks about what baby and self are doing
Points to body parts named by caregiver	Responds to baby's "jargon talk" as though baby is speaking words
Waves bye-bye	Sits with baby during eating times and talks to baby
Says first words	
Checks to see if parent is looking before exploring on own	
Strings sound together in gibberish/ "jargon talk"	

Developmental patterns	Caregiving practices

16–24 months

Has increased understanding of words and simple sentences and directions	Plays simple interactive games like "chase me," telephone talk
Follows simple directions	Has simple give-and-take conversations with toddler during routine care
Enjoys and understands simple songs, rhymes, and fingerplays	Extends toddler's speech
Uses "no" to protest	Sings simple rhymes, fingerplays, and songs
Uses "hi" and "bye-bye" greetings	Reads familiar storybooks
Uses jargon speech with statement, command, and questioning inflections	Has toddler's eye contact before speaking
Refers to self by name	Actively listens and responds to toddler's talk
Names pictures, common objects, body parts, and people	Ask questions that elicit toddler's response
Can understand and follow two-part directions	Encourages and participates in pretend play with toddler
Says two-word sentences to express an idea	Talks to toddler about past shared experience
Uses tuned telegraphic speech	Helps toddler tell story about past experience
Makes simple verbal request	Reads and/or tells stories and sings simple songs and fingerplays

2–5 years

Understands and responds to questions	Has extended daily conversations with child
Asks questions	Actively listens and responds to child's talk
Large increase in vocabulary	Responds to child's questions and invites child to continue talking
Speaks in full sentences	Asks child open-ended questions
Tells simple stories of immediate and past experiences	Encourages and participates in pretend play with child
Enjoys songs, fingerplays, stories, and storybooks	Sings songs and fingerplays with child
Enjoys using language in pretend play, alone and with others	Reads storybooks and tells stories with child
Has extended give-and-take conversations	Provides a variety of writing tools and paper for child to use for drawing and writing
Enjoys drawing and writing	Encourages children to talk with one another
Writes name and recognizes letters	Frequently talks with child about past experiences
Recognizes frequently seen words	Attentively listens to child's stories
Has extended conversations with peers	Labels materials and activity areas
Engages in social role play that involves a lot of language exchange	Uses charts in group time, such as helper charts, activity schedule
Tells stories of past experiences	

LANGUAGE AND COMMUNICATION
DEVELOPMENT: BIRTH TO 7 MONTHS

From birth, babies can communicate their feelings and needs through changes in their face, voice, and body posture. In turn, parents try to match their babies' signals through facial expression, voice intonation, and body cues. When babies experience consistent and responsive caregiving, they soon learn to read their caregivers' signals and to modify their own behavior in response. From the beginning, a volleying of communication goes back and forth between parents and baby, as in a tennis game. Neonates (birth to 4 weeks old) have excellent hearing ability and can recognize their parents' voices and tell the difference between happy, sad, and surprised facial expressions (Field, 1982). Much of the caregiver–baby interaction is face to face.

Neonates are active participants in social interaction. Although the cry dominates the newborn's vocal repertoire, parents quickly learn to decode and respond to their baby's more subtle behavioral cues. Within the first few weeks after birth, parents can discriminate their baby's different cries, signifying, for example, hunger, discomfort, or pain. Soon babies develop vocalizations, cooing sounds that communicate the baby's behavioral-emotional state of arousal, comfort, or discomfort. Parents' responsiveness to their baby's crying and other signals is critical for the development of secure parent–infant attachment. Field's (1982) research indicated that neonates make different facial expressions as early as birth. Studies of these neonatal differences in facial expressions indicate that some neonates are highly expressive, more attentive, and more socially responsive than others (Field, 1982). Not surprisingly, parents have an easier time interacting with expressive babies.

Parents intuitively treat their baby's vocalization as a means of communication, and they respond differently to different vocal signals. Papoušek and Bornstein's review of the research literature indicated that parents across cultures express "typically intuitive didactic caregiving tendencies: contingent rewarding or greeting, encouraging a turn, encouraging imitation, evaluating the infant's state, reassuring of mother's presence, soothing, and discouraging" (1992, p. 243). Their research indicated mothers' astonishing sensitivities and imitative capacities, such as imitation of the pitch, duration, and affective tone of their babies. Mothers of babies as young as 2 months old, when in a room different from their baby, attribute meaning to their baby's vocalizations and match their baby's sounds with parallel emotional intonation. Beyond satisfying the young baby's need for communication, *preverbal communication* also becomes the primary context in which the neonate learns how to, for example, maintain attention, become calm, and initiate an-

other's action. Love and affection, routine caregiving, reciprocal communication of emotion and desire, and regulation of the baby's emotional and physiological state happen all at once within the same interactions. Just as the baby's arms, legs, heart, and lungs are a part of the
same organism, these components of caregiver–infant interaction are a
part of the same whole.

Across cultures, mothers, fathers, and out-of-home caregivers modify their pitch and intonation when speaking to the very young baby.
Melodic patterns of caregiver speech, even with newborns, have emotional communicative functions beyond language learning. Caregivers'
characteristic melodic speech can calm, arouse, elicit, and/or maintain
the young baby's attention, as in the following example.

> *Mary (age 10 weeks) has just awakened from a nap on
> her first day at the child care center. After changing Mary's
> diaper, Carmeletta holds her as she speaks to her in a soft,
> melodic tone. "Mary, you look just like your mommy. She
> had to go back to work today, didn't she?" Mary coos as
> Carmeletta continues, "Really, really, you are telling me a
> story aren't you?"*

Although this is a new adult voice for Mary, Carmeletta's melodic pattern of talking soothes her. Parents and caregivers use melodic speech
patterns to engage babies in social interaction and to enable babies to
experience their own feelings and intentions. Fernald cited research that
points to four common communicative intentions of melodic patterns
of maternal speech, which out-of-home caregivers can apply toward understanding their own use of melodic speech patterns:

1) Attention bid: Mother calls infant's attention to a new toy;
2) Approval: Mother praises infant for retrieving an object;
3) Prohibition: Mother tries to stop infant from touching a forbidden
   object; and
4) Comfort: Mother soothes infant. (1992, p. 265)

The central nervous system controls the newborn's cry, along with the
larynx, pharynx, chest, and upper neck. Around 3 months of age, the
baby's larynx descends and is repositioned in the pharynx; this reposi-
tioning influences changes in the young baby's vocal sounds and allows
a shift to occur from involuntary to voluntary control of crying (Lester
& Boukydis, 1992). Now babies can think about crying to obtain a specific goal. In addition, babies enjoy playing with speech sounds. Three-
month-olds are becoming more active partners in social interaction, with
increased eye contact with caregivers, smiling socially and vocalizing,

and longer periods of cognitive engagement. Much of this interaction occurs during everyday caregiving routines, as in the following example:

> *Karl (age 3 months) awakens from his morning nap, and his child care teacher, Carmeletta, changes Karl's diaper. As she changes his diaper, Carmeletta talks to him softly. She hugs and kisses Karl gently as she lifts him up from the changing table then repeatedly lifts him into the air as she makes melodic sounds. Karl smiles the entire time.*

Babies love looking at faces much more than anything else and will watch their caregiver's facial expressions during dressing, diapering, eating, and bathing. Babies and caregivers learn to read cues from each other's vocalizations, facial expressions, and body movements. At 3 months, the baby's smiling and vocalizing affirms the caregiver's actions and encourages the caregiver to continue the interaction. As their caregivers respond to babies' cues, babies learn that they can influence their caregivers, that their communication with caregivers has meaning.

Between 4 and 6 months of age, babies connect vowel and consonant sounds in a string of sounds called *babbling*. Babies are so delighted with listening to themselves babble that they will practice making sounds without an audience. They also use their speech sounds to get attention and to show interest and enthusiasm. Brief playful exchanges such as the following help babies to feel secure, loved, and connected:

> *Jesse (age 6 months) begins to babble loudly in a rhythmic manner. Joy says to him, "Oh, you are telling me all about it." Jesse smiles. Joy picks up a small plastic telephone and puts it to Jesse's ear as she says, "Say, 'Hi mommy, hi daddy. I'm talking to Joy now.'" Jesse chuckles as he listens to Joy's high-pitched voice. Joy begins talking to a toddler as Jesse begins humming to himself quietly. Joy also begins to hum softly.*

Babies all over the world make the same sounds during their first few months of life; however, by 6 months, babies' sounds match those of their parents and caregivers. Babies have excellent abilities to discriminate sounds. As babies babble, caregivers can imitate these sounds, a response that affirms the baby and helps the baby feel connected and motivated to continue to vocalize. Furthermore, babies learn through these vocal exchanges that their actions have an effect on another person, which is a central component of social-emotional development.

LANGUAGE AND COMMUNICATION DEVELOPMENT: 7–19 MONTHS

Around 7–9 months of age, changes in the brain bring about new communication capacities, and a reorganization of caregiver–baby interaction occurs. The consonant–vowel babbling now has a syllable kind of sound that babies often repeat again and again. This rhythmic babbling can have a rising and falling intonation similar to that of sentences or questions. Babies this age are beginning to use gestures alone or in combination with sounds to ask for objects, to go outdoors, or to be picked up. Caregiver and baby enjoy new dimensions of extended play. Babies can imitate nonspeech sounds such as smacking lips or clicking tongue sounds, and they love to play games such as Peek-a-boo and Pat-a-cake. Adult–child games involving turn taking, such as Peek-a-boo, prepare the way for later turn taking in conversation.

Between 8 and 10 months of age, babies have *receptive language* skills and can understand single words. They recognize their own name, and they can respond to the word *no* when caregivers use it emphatically. Researchers have noted that receptive language ability is a good predictor of babies' long-term language outcomes (Bates, Bretherton, & Snyder, 1988).

Stern (1985) noted that babies between the ages of 8 and 10 months understand that experiences are shareable.[2] In the following observation, Jamie (age 8 months) and her teacher, Kathy, share both attention and emotion. Jamie knows that her teacher understands her experiences and her feelings. Given this understanding, Jamie is motivated to communicate with her teacher.

> *Jamie crawls to pick up a rattle and then sits up. Kathy asks, "Jamie, what is that you have in your hands?"*
> *Jamie holds her rattle toward Kathy as she says, "Di-di."*
> *Kathy repeats, "Di-di."*
> *Jamie laughs, and Kathy chuckles too as she says, "I'm glad you are happy this morning."*

By 9 months of age, babies point at things frequently as a way to ask for things they want, such as pointing at a bottle. They also are beginning to follow simple directions. By 10–12 months of age, babies engage in *social referencing*, a behavior in which babies look toward their caregiver for reassurance that it is okay to move toward a desired goal. These new accomplishments are major strides in the baby's ability to communicate.

Maturation of the cerebral cortex makes these qualitative changes in babies' ability to communicate possible. Babies now can picture their daily routines with their caregivers in their minds, termed *mental schemas.* By 10 months of age, babies have recall memory so that the way in which they experience a new situation is influenced not only by the present but also by their past experiences. Memory is an internal component of cognitive functioning. Memory, however, is not just a distinct cognitive process; it is also a *cognitive activity that is embedded in one's social experiences.* The basic function of memory is to provide guidance for action. Now the baby can use past experiences as the basis for predicting what will happen. With memory, babies can anticipate what is coming next and are able to hide their face when playing Peek-a-boo. Babies can understand commonly used phrases and simple one-step directions such as "Please come here" or "Don't touch." They enjoy vocalizing along with music and often begin using exclamatory speech such as "Ouch!" and "Uh-oh!"

Bruner described the three purposes of communication for 9- to 12-month-old babies as follows:

1) Behavior regulation—signals [babies use] to regulate another person's behavior for purposes of requesting objects or actions, rejecting actions, or protesting another person's behavior (e.g., pointing to request food, pushing bottle away to reject it)

2) Social interaction—signals [babies use] to attract and maintain another's attention to oneself for affiliative purposes, such as greeting, calling, requesting social routines, and requesting comfort (e.g., waving bye-bye, reaching to be comforted)

3) Joint attention—signals [babies use] to direct another person's attention to interesting objects and events, for the purpose of sharing the experience with that person (e.g., showing interesting toys to others, pointing at an object to bring it to someone's attention). Later in development children share information about topics through providing and requesting information through language. (as cited in Prizant, Wetherby, & Roberts, 1993, pp. 262–263)

Cognitive growth and language development tend to appear at the same time and are most strongly related during the early stages of language development. Around 12 months old, babies say their first words, a clear sign of increased ability to think symbolically.[3] Children's first words reflect what they know—that is, the common actions and objects associated in their everyday routines with important people in their lives. Babies differ in the manner in which they learn their first words. Some babies' early words are related to social relationships, such as "hi" and "want"; this style of learning vocabulary is termed an *expressive style.* Other babies use a *referential style*, in which their first words refer to objects, such as "keys" and "ball." Objects that move or the baby can move (e.g., "keys," "bottle," and "ball") are often the first named objects (Nelson, 1973). Nelson discovered that it usually takes 3–4 months for the toddler to add the next 10 words. Receptive language also continues to develop, and around 18 months of age, toddlers can follow one-part directions, such as "Get your shoes" or "Give it to me."

Beginning around 5–6 months of age, babies love looking at picture books; by 9 months of age, they can point to objects that their caregiver names in a picture; and by 12–18 months, they can label the picture themselves. As they identify pictures with their caregiver, babies are mastering the first steps in symbolic thinking. Researchers note that for young babies to understand the representational relationship that exists between a symbol (e.g., a picture of a crib in a book) and its referent (e.g., an actual crib), they need to engage in social interaction and communication with adults (DeLoache, 1996).[4]

Often babies will repeat a new word and thereby increase their vocabulary, as in the following observation.

> *Jesse (age 12 months) is beginning to try to snap together plastic ladders. When he succeeds he says, "Aah." His teacher, Joy, says, "Yeah." Jesse chuckles and puts two more ladders together.*
>
> *Joy says, "You did it."*
>
> *Jesse says, "Lad." Joy replies, "Ladder. That's right. You are making a ladder."*
>
> *Jesse reaches for a tub filled with small plastic animals. He picks up a small turtle and Joy says, "Turtle." Jesse repeats, "Turtle." Joy picks up a small duck and says, "Duck." Jesse repeats, "Duck," and the two continue naming several more animals before Jesse crawls to another part of the room.*

This is the first month that Jesse is able to say words, and he delights in the simple naming game that Joy plays with him. As he and Joy playfully identify animals, he also is learning the turn-taking skills that are essential to conversation.[5] Joy explained that prior to this game, Jesse could say the word "turtle," but this was the first time he named "duck," "tiger," and "lion." With his increasing motor coordination, Jesse is also more able to engage in games with his caregivers, for example, he can clap and roll his hands for Pat-a-cake.

At age 12 months, babies often use *holophrases*, single words used to express a complex of ideas. The 1-year-old may say, "Daddy," for example, to express "Daddy is home"; "Go" to express "I want to go outside"; and "See" to express "See the ball I have in my hand." Sometimes a holophrase can mean more than one thing; for example, "Dog" may mean any four-legged animal. Babies who are beginning to learn words will continue to use gestures to communicate, especially when they are frustrated. In fact, actions such as foot stomping or head banging may indicate that toddlers are frustrated because they cannot communicate what they want.

Between ages 13 and 15 months, babies string sounds together as though they are having a conversation. This stringing together of sounds is often called *jargon talk*. In the following example, Cory (age 14 months) engages in jargon talk with his teacher, Alicia.

> *Cory is washing a doll with a wash cloth. As he wipes the doll, he says, "Da da, ba ba, da da." Alicia says, "Yes, you are washing your baby's face, aren't you?" Cory smiles as he continues to make intonations that sound like sentences. Alicia responds to his jargon talk again, saying, "Your baby loves her bath. I can tell."*

As toddlers play with dolls in the sensory table, Alicia is comfortable to sit next to them and watch them. She is quick to read the language of these children's behavior and to respond to their vocalizations. Cory begins to make jargon talk as though he is talking to himself. Alicia interprets this talk and begins a conversation with him. As Cory and Alicia take turns talking, Cory is sharing his enjoyment with his teacher, and he is learning the basics of conversation. Jargon talk usually disappears by $2^1/_2$ years of age.

The sheer amount of speech that caregivers address toward young children positively influences the children's vocabulary development (Hart & Risley, 1999). Teachers have opportunities throughout the day to stimulate the language development of the babies and toddlers in their classroom. One way of stimulating language development is for the teacher to describe whatever the teacher and the child are doing as they are doing it. This process is called *parallel talk*. In addition, when a baby says a word, the teacher can repeat this word and extend, or add on to, the child's verbalization. In an earlier example of extending toddlers' conversation, Mia said, "Mall," and Joy replied by asking, "Yesterday did you and mommy go to the mall?" Dunham and Dunham (1992) studied individual differences in the tendencies of mothers of 13-month-old babies to describe verbally aspects of the environment occupying their infant's current focus of attention. Results showed that babies' vocabulary development was positively related to this maternal language input.

Between 12 and 18 months of age, social goals control toddlers' use of language. Language during this period emerges primarily as a social tool—to greet, to protest, to gain another's attention, to request something, and so forth. In turn, the toddler's social environment can affirm and validate the toddler's talking. Adult–child interaction during familiar routines such as eating enables the toddler to learn the meaning of words and engage in extended conversation. *In fact, it is essential that child care teachers sit with young children during meals and snacktimes to encourage conversation and a sense of togetherness.* Toddlers who regularly engage in conversations with their caregivers during routines, play sequences, and book reading have the resources from which to develop and expand their vocabulary. In contrast, studies indicate that toddlers whose caregivers have a directive style of speaking to children, consisting of many commands or instructions, have a slower rate of vocabulary acquisition (Rice, 1989).

Studies have shown that toddlers as young as 16 months old can remember not only familiar sequences of events but also completely novel events (Bauer & Mandler, 1990). A critical feature of young children's ability to remember is the conversational style of their caregivers. When caregivers talk about past shared experiences with toddlers, they help the toddlers develop a sense of continuity between the past, present, and future. When caregivers talk about shared experiences with young children, this interaction has an impact on how young children remember those experiences and may even incline young children to recall the experiences themselves. In sum, when caregivers engage in conversations that encourage memory recall, their children have a richer memory of events and are more likely to tell stories about these events. Adults teach toddlers to remember in different ways. Nelson's research indicated that the way in which caregivers engage toddlers in recalling an experience affects what and how the toddlers remember:

> Mothers who engage in memory narratives, elaborating on an experience and asking questions that encourage the child to contribute information to the narrative, tend to have children who are better able to recount an episode than children whose mothers use memory talk only in a pragmatic, reminding mode. (1990, p. 304)

Nelson, Walkenfeld, and Goldstein identified three different kinds of memory:

1. The experienced event may fit a general schema or script for familiar activities, e.g., "going to bed" script.

2. A new or novel event or a salient variation in a standard familiar event may be remembered as a specific episode that has personal meaning. These may be positive or negative, a source of joy, sadness, triumph, or embarrassment.

3. Rather than a whole story, parts of the experience may be retained in semantic memory, that is, as general information or knowledge, e.g., a song learned in pre-school may be retained for many years but the context of learning may not be held in memory. (1997, pp. 17–18)

Out-of-home caregivers can engage in brief conversations with toddlers to help them recall events that they have experienced outside of the program. It is helpful for parents to take a few minutes when dropping off their children to tell their child's teacher about what the family did the previous night or weekend. With this information from parents, teachers are able to engage in brief narratives with toddlers, as in the following observation:

> Joy asks Carrie, *"Did you tell Alicia where you went with mom and dad yesterday?"*
> Carrie answers, *"Zoo."*
> *"And what did you ride?"* asks Joy.
> *"Train."*
> Joy asks, *"You rode the train with mommy and daddy?"*
> Carrie nods yes. Then Joy asks her, *"Did you see a tiger yesterday?"* Carrie nods again.
> *"And what did the tiger say?"* asks Joy.
> Carrie smiles and exclaims, *"Rrroar!"*

As Joy helps Carrie recall her visit to the zoo, she helps Carrie build a sense of the continuity between past and present. Carrie's cognitive development allows her to represent the time and space of past experiences symbolically. Joy and Carrie take turns in creating a story about Carrie's trip to the zoo. Joy organizes the story for Carrie, who can add details at the right moment. Joy extends Carrie's one-word utterances and thus provides an effective language model. Carrie feels secure because she feels a consistency and connection between her time with her parents and her conversation with her teacher. In her conversation with this young toddler, Joy uses simple, concrete vocabulary and simple sentences that are easier for Carrie to understand.

Elements of storytelling and narrative are also often implicit in the play of young children, and the out-of-home caregiver can use children's play as another opportunity to promote children's language and communication skills by helping them to create a narrative.

> Ricky (age 17 months) rides his toy horse and then stands on the horse's back. Jean warns, *"Ricky, that isn't safe. The horsie might fall over, and you would bump your head*

on the chair." Ricky gets off the horse, and as he does the
horse fall over on its side.

Jean questions Ricky, "Is the horsie okay? Did the horsie
get hurt?"

Ricky says, "See."

Jean responds, "You are going to check and see."

Ricky points at the horse's leg and says, "Horsie ouchy."

Jean says, "The horsie's leg has an ouchy."

It is important for the caregiver to provide language that can highlight
some of the story potential in children's play. Jean helps Ricky to develop an imaginary story about his toy horse that Ricky, at 17 months,
is unable to do alone.

LANGUAGE AND COMMUNICATION DEVELOPMENT: 19–36 MONTHS

Toddlers' vocabulary increases rapidly at around 18 months of age and
continues to do so throughout the preschool years. Young children seem
to absorb the meanings of new words as they hear them in conversational interactions. Mothers who speak to children frequently using a
large variety of words have been found to have young children with a
high rate of vocabulary acquisition (Huttenlocker, Haight, Bryk, Seltzer,
& Lynos, 1991).

Toddlers enjoy naming food, items of clothing, body parts, and the
names of people and objects that are a part of their everyday life. They
can understand and follow two-part directions, such as "Get your doll,
and bring it to me." Between 18 and 24 months of age, they begin using
telegraphic speech, that is, two-word sentences to express an idea (e.g.,
"Mommy go," "All gone"). In their zeal to understand and name, they
often ask, "What's that?" Toddlers' telegraphic speech has many functions, for example, making requests ("Go out"), responding to another
person ("Toy mine"), and observing ("Mommy keys"). Often the same
two-word sentence can have different meanings; for example, "Mommy
keys" might mean, "I see mommy has her keys," or "Mommy, give me
the keys."

Child care teachers have innumerable opportunities to reinforce and
extend toddlers' telegraphic speech, as Alicia and her co-teacher,
Carmeletta, are doing in the following interactions:

Cory (age 18 months) runs toward his teacher, Alicia,
exclaiming, "Out, out, out!" Alicia answers, "Outside. We
can go outside in just a few minutes."

> *Mia says to Carmeletta, "Mommy go." Carmeletta says, "Yes, mommy has gone to work, but she'll pick you up after your nap."*
>
> *Demetrius is eating his lunch. He says to Alicia, "More milk." Alicia replies, "You want more milk. You're thirsty today aren't you?"*

Alicia and Carmeletta understand that when they repeat and extend their toddlers' telegraphic speech, they are affirming these young children and encouraging them to continue talking. In fact, these teachers often encourage the toddlers in their care to use telegraphic speech to create a narrative about something they have experienced, as illustrated next.

> *"Bathing suit," says Carrie to Alicia.*
> *Alicia asks "You put on your bathing suit yesterday when you went to the swimming pool?"*
> *Carrie nods yes and adds, "Feed ducks."*
> *Then Alicia asks, "And then you fed the ducks at the park? What did you feed the ducks?"*
> *Carrie says, "Bread."*
> *"Who took you to the park?" asks Alicia.*
> *Carrie says, "Mommy. Mommy swim."*
> *Alicia says, "And mommy went swimming with you," and Carrie nods yes.*

Alicia and Carrie co-construct a story about Carrie's trip to the park with her mother. Alicia helps Carrie organize her understanding of her experience. In responding and questioning, Carrie's teacher helps her to represent her experience symbolically with language.

Working with Toddlers Whose Language Is Delayed

When caregivers work with toddlers whose language is delayed, they can use the toddlers' play experiences to promote language, as in the following example:

> *Vetta, a family caregiver, cares for 26-month-old twins DeVonne and Derrick. The twins live with their teenage mother and extended family (grandmother, cousins, and aunts). DeVonne picks up an orange crayon and begins making lines as he says, "Look."*

> "Look, you made orange lines," responds Vetta.
> DeVonne says, "Orange. I did it."
> Vetta acknowledges, "Yes, you did it. You are making a picture."
> Then Derrick says to Vetta, "Look."
> Vetta answers, "Yes, and you are making round circles."
> DeVonne removes eight crayons from a box and lines them up. Derrick does the same as Vetta says, "You are lining them up pretty, all in a row, aren't you?" The boys smile as they nod yes.

While DeVonne and Derrick play, Vetta is quick to repeat and extend their use of language. When she began caring for these boys 6 months earlier, DeVonne and Derrick did not talk at all. But as she consistently described what she and the boys were doing and expected that they would engage in conversation with her, each child gradually began talking. Vetta's presence and parallel talking affirmed the boys' actions and encouraged them to express themselves verbally. In turn, Vetta learned that behavior follows expectation—that if she expected the twins to talk, in a few weeks they would.

Research on conversations between mothers and their toddlers has indicated that mothers' asking questions that elicit the child's response and responding to the child's speech is the most encouraging mother–child interaction for children's language development (Hoff-Ginsberg, 1991). Vygotsky (1978) asserted that children's learning is primarily a social process that takes place during interactions between children and others in their environment. Caregivers can foster children's language acquisition by challenging them within their *zone of proximal development* (ZPD). Vygotsky used this term to describe "the distance between a child's actual development level as determined by independent problem solving and the level of potential development as determined through problem solving under adult guidance or in collaboration with more capable peers" (1978, p. 86). A young child's actual mental development is what has taken place up to a specific moment, whereas the ZPD is characteristic of the child's mental development in the future. Alicia is probing Carrie's ZPD when she helps Carrie to tell a story that Carrie could not tell *without* Alicia's assistance. Carrie's storytelling experiences with Alicia will enable Carrie to eventually tell stories on her own. Bruner explained how a caregiver—in this case, the mother—fosters a young child's language "on the growing edge of the child's competence":

It is the mother who establishes little "formats" or rituals in which language is used: "book reading," routines with picture books, request patterns, little games, and so on. She plays her part in them with striking regularity. In book reading, for example, she phrases her questions in a regular sequence: (1) Vocative, (2) Query, (3) Label, (4) Confirmation. Or, (1) Oh look, Richard! (2) What's that? (3) It's a fishy. (4) That's right. This sequence provides a scaffold for "teaching" reference. At the start, the infant may understand little. His response to the query may then develop and take the form of a babble. And once that occurs, the mother will hereafter insist on *some* response in that slot of the scaffold. Once the child alters his responding babble to a word-length vocalization, she will again raise the ante and not accept a babble, but only the shorter version. (1986, pp. 76–77)

Research on toddlers' conversations with their mothers indicates that when adult and child focus on something together both the adult and child talk more often and engage in longer conversations. Tomasello and Farrar (1986) videotaped naturalistic interactions between 24 children and their mothers when the children were 15 months old and 21 months old. They found that differences in the ability of mothers and their children to establish and maintain joint attention were related to the child's subsequent language growth. In addition, mothers' attempts to be directive, for example, by repeatedly telling their child what the child should and should not do, was negatively related to the child's developing vocabulary.[6] When out-of-home caregivers can join their babies and toddlers in the same activity as partners, they are promoting these children's language.

Significant strides in language and communication emerge between the ages of 18 and 24 months as toddlers begin to form categories of objects in their minds. "Truck" becomes the name for all large vehicles, "cat" for all small four-legged animals, and so forth. By 2 years of age, changes in brain organization make new communication skills and dimensions of relationships possible. Toddlers now are aware of their own actions and intentions, and they begin to refer to themselves spontaneously in speech, such as in "I want to go out," "I do it myself." With this newfound self-awareness, they repeatedly call attention to what is "mine" and experiment with saying "no" to adult directives. Now toddlers can understand simple phrases, such as "Let's go outdoors and play," without needing a visual cue (e.g., without the teacher pointing to the outdoors). They also can follow sequences in simple stories.[7] They love rhymes, fingerplays, and songs, as is illustrated in the following interaction between Alicia and four young toddlers.

Four toddlers have been playing with sand at the sensory table. Alicia suggests that it's time to put the table away, and she invites them to join her on the rug. Alicia begins singing the fingerplay, "Five Little Monkeys." Mia (age 22 months) does the finger motions with Alicia. Demetrius (age 19 months), Carrie (age 20 months), and Linette (age 17 months) each have one finger in the air as they occasionally say a word from the rhyme.

Alicia then lies down as she begins to sing the song, "Sleeping, Sleeping, All My Birds Are Sleeping." All the toddlers lie down with her as Alicia sings the rest of the song.

Next, Alicia sings the fingerplay, "Bringing Home the Baby Bumble Bee." This song seems to be a favorite; all the children smile as they say, "Bee," or "Home," and Mia is able to do the motions along with Alicia. Everyone laughs when the song ends.

As Alicia sings with the children, they all enjoy sharing in this regularly occurring group experience. The songs are familiar so each child can participate in a manner congruent with his or her particular developmental level—one word for Carrie and Demetrius, appropriate hand motions for Mia. Alicia and her co-teachers distribute the words of favorite fingerplays and songs to parents so children can enjoy these activities at home. On other days, Alicia or one of her co-teachers read the children simple stories, and the children are able to attend to the stories for 10–15 minutes.

From their first vocalizations, children use language primarily to communicate. At the same time, young children frequently use language in "private speech"—talking aloud—to better understand their everyday world and to help them remain focused on the task they are performing. Private speech helps children to sort out their experiences and regulate themselves emotionally and mentally. Adults also have internal monologues that help them plan or reflect on experiences and can involve other people in their lives. Research indicates that toddlers' monologues are different and often more complex than their dialogues with others.

Nelson's (1989) book, *Narratives from the Crib,* described a 15-month study of one child, Emily, when she was between the ages of 21 and 36 months. Nelson focused on Emily's private speech and her dialogues with her parents before bed. Emily's monologues were more varied and rich than were her conversations with her parents. In her monologues, Emily recounted in story form the daily events that had happened or events that her parents told her were going to happen. Sometimes her stories involved imaginary happenings. Often what she chose to talk about to herself was independent of what her parents had talked about with her. Her monologues often were organized around daily routines such as eating, sleeping, and dressing. Emily seemed to be making sense of her everyday experience, even conducting problem solving within these monologues. Infant psychiatrist Daniel Stern explained that Emily was recreating the presence of others in her mind "by activating internal representations of self-with-other" (1989, as cited in Nelson, 1989, p. 315). Stern claimed that the ability to represent others symbolically helps young children self-regulate.

Listening

Another important skill in language learning is listening. Good listening does not just emerge, but, as with talking, young children learn listening skills gradually through their everyday interactions with caregivers. Caregivers who work with young children from homes where there is little everyday give-and-take conversation or where there is a great deal of noise may find that these children have never learned to listen well. Caregivers can help children learn to listen by gaining the child's eye contact before speaking or by distracting the child by suddenly varying their voice tone or singing. Often children can listen and speak more readily when they are involved in simple play sequences that are soothing to them.

By 2½ years of age, most children can understand most adult sentences; descriptive words such as *big, heavy,* and *fast;* and prepositions such as *under, over,* and *behind.* Now toddlers talk in three- and four-word sentences and make simple requests, such as "Tie my shoe." They begin to use plurals and pronouns such as *I, me, mine,* and *you.* In conversation, toddlers as young as 2 years old can change their manner of speaking according to the person to whom they are speaking. A toddler will shout "Mine!" as she grabs a toy from another toddler, but to her mother she might say, "More cookies, please." Studies of children's conversations with young children demonstrate that children 2½–5 years old are skilled at simplifying their language when talking to younger children (Lee, 1989). These patterns provide clear evidence that very young children can take another person's perspective, a pattern that Piaget (1929/1967) did not think possible among preschoolers.

Toddlers first talk about what they know; they rely upon concepts initially as a means of mastering language. Shortly thereafter, they use language to learn new concepts. For example, they learn new meanings through conversing with caregivers. Young children's developing language reflects what they are thinking, and, in turn, language makes thinking possible.

LANGUAGE AND COMMUNICATION
DEVELOPMENT: 3–5 YEARS

By the time children are 3 years old, talking is one of their favorite activities. Young children's sentences are creative, but they also are beginning to incorporate grammatical rules. They begin using plurals, past tenses, and prepositions in a fairly predictable sequence. Because young children tend to overgeneralize, their language also is full of grammatical mistakes; for example, they apply the "-*ed* rule" for past tense faithfully, often with amusing results such as, "falled," "swimmed," and "breaked." Similarly, initial use of questions and negatives follows a predictable sequence, including omission of the auxiliary verb, such as in "When Bobby come home?" or "Daddy no go."

Preschoolers are actively engaged in searching for the answers to what they want to know and understand. Young children's curiosity is reflected in their endless questioning, for example, "What makes the waves move?" "How do you say the day before yesterday?" or "Why does Grandma look sad?" It is important for caregivers to consider how they can best answer young children's questions. Some questions reflect a young child's lack of information, and it can be relatively easy for an adult to fill in the gap by explaining to the child in simple terms how things work. Sometimes, however, a child's question can trigger an emotional topic, and the caregiver can use the question as the setting in which to help the young child understand more about him- or herself, his or her family, or the immediate environment. For example, a child might ask his or her teacher, "Why did Grandpa have to die? I miss him." The teacher can use the child's question to talk about how all living things die. Like flowers and trees, people die, most often when old, but sometimes because they become sick.

The caregiver also may find herself struggling to answer questions (e.g., "Why do stars twinkle?") that either have no simple answer or go beyond the caregiver's field of knowledge. Caregivers can respond to these kinds of questions by letting the child know that, although the child's question is a good one, the caregiver really does not know how to answer it. In many situations, caregivers can stimulate a young child's thinking by inviting the child to think through the answer to the question (e.g., "Why do you think it does that?"). The answers may be delightfully inventive, such as when one child told his teacher that "God must be very angry to make that thunder so loud!" On other occasions, it may suffice for the adult to be an active listener; the adult might restate a child's question, but often a detailed answer really isn't as important as acknowledging that the adult has heard the child.

Now that young children want to talk incessantly, caregivers often have to become mindful about being good listeners. Teaching young children involves many maintenance tasks. It is important for teachers to be wary of using these tasks as opportunities to "escape" from the relentless conversations in which young children engage with significant adults. Paradoxically, when teachers are good listeners, children often are satisfied and are able to engage in extended play without an adult being nearby. Behavior follows expectation for children as well as adults. When caregivers listen actively and take young children's questions seriously, young children develop expectations of these adults' availability. Adult–child question-and-answer sequences become the verbal equivalent of earlier child-rearing interactions, such as hugging, playing Peek-a-boo, or imitating babbling. These interactions provide children with a sense of competence that allows them to continue to feel secure when they are playing separate from their caregiver.

Storytelling

Daily periods of singing, doing fingerplays, or reading or telling stories are integral parts of quality out-of-home care for preschool-age children. These episodes can be rich language-learning opportunities, especially when the children are active participants, as in the following example:

> *Pam and her group of eight 3- and 4-year-old children have just completed singing fingerplay songs. Pam then uses a storyboard as a visual device to tell the children the story of "Hansel and Gretel," a story that is new for these children. "Nibble, nibble, at my house," says Pam. "Who is that nibbling at my house?" Pam invites the children to repeat this phrasing with her, and the children do so. Throughout the rest of the story, Pam continues to invite the children to repeat a portion along with her.*
>
> *Occasionally Pam asks the children a question; for example, "And what do you think Gretel had to do for the old lady?" The children each supply a variety of answers, such as "Wash the dishes" or "Sweep the floor." All children are caught up in the story, and most of them participate verbally.*

Pam has developed a skillful rhythm of telling the story in which she alternates between telling the story and encouraging the children's active participation. These children expect that each day they will actively participate in Pam's group storytelling period. The children know several stories well enough to act them out, such as *The Three Billy Goats Gruff* and *Goldilocks and the Three Bears*. Teachers who are skilled in leading small-group activities in which the children can be active participants are providing experiences that promote children's use of language and their learning of new words and concepts (Linder, 1999). Sharing the storytelling experience with teacher and peers provides positive social benefits for the children as well.

By around 3 years of age, young children not only enjoy listening to stories but also enjoy telling them. Now young children can tell stories containing an agent, an intention, a goal, causes, a dramatic line, and so forth. They often enjoy telling stories that are based on their creative play. They might make up a story about a building they have constructed out of blocks, for example, by calling it an ice cream factory and talking about what kind of ice cream is made inside the "factory."

As mentioned previously, elements of storytelling and narrative are often implicit in young children's creative play. In the following observation, two young preschoolers co-construct a story about their play together:

> *Chunsey and Shalona place small plastic farm animals inside a plastic fence that they have made into a square. Chunsey says to Shalona, "Let's lay them down."*
>
> *Shalona says, "They're taking a nap." As the children lay down their animals, a portion of the fence falls apart.*
>
> *Fixing the fence as he speaks, Chunsey says, "Uh-oh, our farm is breaking."*
>
> *Shalona says, "Now their nap is over."*
>
> *The children stand up all the animals. Chunsey puts a gray, plastic stone-like object on the rug and places a duck on it as he says, "Now he is swimming. It's so hot outside." Shalona picks up a small toy man and puts him on the piece of plastic next to the duck, saying, "I want to go swimming too." She then puts the cow next to the stone and says, "And it's so hot he needs a drink." Chunsey responds, "Now the farmer is going to take the horsies and cows to the field to eat grass." He and Shalona take the horses and cows out of the fenced area and put them on the rug.*

Chunsey and Shalona engage in this role play for about 10 minutes. Their language ability allows them to role-play with the toys symbolically. The children use language to have one object represent another object; for example, the piece of gray plastic represents a pond.[8] Chunsey and Shalona take turns talking as they skillfully listen and then respond to each other.

Kathryn Nelson (1986) and her colleagues explained that stories, which she termed *event knowledge,* are central to the growth of young children's language and thought processes. A key finding of her research is that children as young as 3 years understand the time line of events and can retell familiar stories using the correct time line of events. Event knowledge has significant effects on memory, language acquisition, conversation, and categorization skills. The basis of this event knowledge is the young children's everyday experience, especially the repeated, familiar daily routines with caregivers. The language that young children use to describe event knowledge is more complex and more advanced than language they use in other settings. For example, children use numerous relationship terms in their event descriptions, or stories, which show an understanding of hypothetical relationships, such as "if . . . then" and "when x, then y" as well as an understanding of temporal relations expressed by words such as "before" and "after" (French, 1986; Nelson & Gruendel, 1986).

Storytelling serves many functions for young children. Given the intertwining of language and cognitive development, storytelling strengthens young children's cognition. As children tell stories about past experiences, they begin to understand the continuity of past and present time. When young children tell stories, they are sharing part of their everyday experience with others and establishing an identity as an athlete, as a helper, as a friend—whatever was central to the story's theme. Engle explained that

> Children tell stories as a way of solving emotional, cognitive, and social puzzles and to sort out problems or concerns. Perhaps most important, stories are one of the fundamental ways in which we each create an extended self. The developing child's cumulative repertoire of stories gives her a sense of self across time and situation. When we tell stories about ourselves, we weave together the underlying constant inner self with the many different selves that emerge in context. (1997, p. 8)

Caregivers can provide innumerable experiences that promote children's storytelling. First and foremost, caregivers can engage in extended conversations with children daily. Second, caregivers can encourage children to listen to and participate in story reading and storytelling. Third, caregivers can listen to children attentively to let them know that they are interested in and want to know and understand what the children are talking about. And fourth, caregivers can talk with children about past shared experiences or plan with them future shared experiences.

Caregiving Environment and Activities

Out-of-home caregivers can arrange the environment so that language can flourish. Activity areas can be set up in ways that invite children to interact with each other and the teacher. For example, block areas that contain neatly arranged unit blocks, play people, and vehicles invite children to collaboratively construct together. Similarly, housekeeping areas invite children to engage in role playing together. Each activity area can contain an array of materials that stimulate children to use language as a key element with which to creatively explore, experiment, and problem solve. Teachers also can make use of small-group activities that provide children with a variety of experiences in listening to others, taking turns talking, story reading and telling, as well as singing and fingerplays.

EMERGENT LITERACY

Just as young children learn oral language in a social context, the everyday activities and interactions of caregivers and babies and young children provide the context for emergent literacy. *Emergent literacy* refers to young children's developing understanding of the written word as a means of communicating with others. Holdaway (1979) described the process of learning to speak as one of successive approximation, in which children gradually refine their efforts in speaking. Holdaway argued that the process of learning to read and write is similar to the process of learning to speak; that is, young children's efforts to read and write are acts of successive approximation in which children gradually move from emergent literacy toward conventional literacy (the fluent ability to read and write). Literacy development is part of children's *total communication process,* which includes their active participation in listening, speaking, reading, and writing.

Young children acquire emergent literacy as they learn to communicate their wants, listen to others, and begin to understand how print functions. As discussed previously, young children develop a sense of story, first from being read to and then from their own storytelling. Research indicates that young children's storytelling competence is a strong predictor of literacy (Engle, 1997). Out-of-home caregivers can provide children with a literacy-rich environment of experiences and discussion, books, listening centers, writing paper, and writing implements.

Emergent Literacy: Birth to 18 Months

Between birth and 18 months of age, babies have many experiences that make early literacy possible. Caregivers can recite rhymes, sing songs, and show books to babies during the babies' first several months of life. By 6 months of age, babies love to look at and grasp cloth or vinyl books. (Given babies' continual mouthing, paper and cardboard books often are inappropriate.) By ages 9–12 months, babies can understand many words, point to objects portrayed in a book, and remember past experiences; these are essential elements of early literacy. Babies this age enjoy sitting on their caregivers' laps and looking at books, recognizing pictures, and turning pages. They are beginning to point and will name familiar pictures (e.g., ball, bottle, dog). By age 12 months, most babies can recognize, understand, and relate to familiar objects and activities in their everyday world. They learn that books are entertaining, whether they are looking at them alone or with their caregiver. At this age, babies also love rhymes, fingerplays, and simple songs, and they enjoy repetitive stories such as *Goodnight Moon* (Brown, 1947). They are beginning to perceive meaning in stories. Also important, babies are learning rules for handling books, for example, holding books to face the right direction, learning how to turn pages, and naming objects that the caregiver points to in the pictures. When caregivers provide paper and large crayons, children can begin to scribble. Scribbling allows babies to practice motor control, which leads to writing letterlike forms.

Emergent Literacy: 18–36 Months

Toddlers who are read to frequently begin to understand basic conventions about books, print, and meaning; they begin to pick up, for example, that books have a beginning and an end. Often toddlers can retell favorite brief stories before they are interested in the print. They begin to understand that meaning is conveyed in print and that speech and print are related. Cardboard books are easy for toddlers to turn the pages and look at on their own. As they continue to scribble and draw, toddlers begin labeling their drawings. As their motor development progresses they gain control of their movements and can make intentional shapes such as dots and circles. Although they may not have the intention of making a specific picture, toddlers might name their picture after drawing it.

As caregivers read stories to them aloud, toddlers gradually acquire a concept of story similar to an adult's understanding of story. That is, they come to understand that stories have characters, settings, some action triggering the main character to establish a goal, action by the main character to attain his or her goal, and an ending concerning whether the main character has attained his or her goal. Toddlers develop strategies for deriving meaning from a story as they listen to stories being read aloud. McGee and Richgels discussed how children learn strategies for understanding stories:

One meaning-making strategy children learn is that things in pictures have names and are labeled. A second meaning-making strategy children learn is to draw on their own experiences as a basis for making meaning. Children connect actions in pictures to their own experiences. A third meaning-making strategy children acquire is to draw on information provided in their mothers' or other adults' talk about pictures and text. They learn to listen to what their mothers say about the story as a way of constructing meaning. A fourth meaning-making strategy children learn is to ask questions. A fifth meaning-making strategy children learn is to pay attention to particular components of stories which they have learned can be considered in order to construct a story's meaning. Children learn to use what they know about stories (their concepts of stories) to understand stories. (1990, p. 137)

Young children also become familiar with stories through watching television and videotapes or by listening to their parents or older siblings tell stories about their day's activities. Toddlers often love fingerplays, which often involve a story line, and they can participate in the story with both hand motions and song.

Environmental print plays an increasing role in the beginning literacy experiences of 2-year-olds. Children learn to recognize the meaning of street signs such as *STOP*; fast-food restaurant signs such as *McDonald's*; and lettering on cereal boxes such as *Cheerios* or *Rice Krispies*. When caregivers provide ample materials for drawing and writing (plenty of paper, crayons, pencils, and markers), toddlers continue to experiment with drawing and writing. By around age 3, most children can draw wavy lines or a series of small circles in imitation of adult writing, which indicates that these children have a notion of what writing is. Young children move from scribbling to making representational figures to writing the conventional symbols of written language. Often a letter will be mixed in with scribble writing. Throughout this process, young children are experimenting with both their increasing motor coordination and different forms of writing.

Emergent Literacy: 3–5 Years

Preschoolers learn to recognize and draw circles, squares, and triangles. They notice letters and are able to write their names on their drawings. They regularly read environmental signs, love alphabet books, and enjoy simple board games. Out-of-home caregivers can strive to provide an environment rich in books and writing materials. Bulletin boards can be used to showcase children's drawings and writing, and children's names can be displayed on cubbies for children's coats and belongings. Each day teachers can demonstrate the purposes of writing as they go about their classroom process, such as using a weather chart or a job chart, writing thank-you letters, writing preparation plans for a field trip, or charting a recipe to be cooked during free play. A variety of writing paper, pencils, erasers, felt-tip pens, crayons, and rulers can be made available. Typewriters and computers also can be used if available. In addition, teachers can write down children's dictation, for example, a child's description of a block building or painting or a story about a drawing. The teacher writes down what the child says, and then teacher and child can read it together while the teacher points out the words being read.

Often group time can be the context for children to understand that speaking, listening, writing, and reading are interrelated. During sharing time, individual children can talk about important things happening in their lives; then teachers can write one sentence summarizing each child's news on chart paper and read these sentences aloud to the group.

Young children learn to write by writing, and writing takes time and practice. As young children experiment with writing, they need supportive adults who will provide the tools and guidance needed for writing and the time to use these tools. A writing center with different kinds of paper, pencils, crayons, and felt-tip markers invites young children to practice writing. Beyond developing motor coordination, writing involves learning spatial concepts, such as how to organize writing on a piece of paper. With practice young children will learn to write from left to right, although they may reverse their letters. Most 4-year-olds can write their own names and recognize the names of some of their classmates.

Teachers of preschool children can set up literacy-related items throughout the classroom. A library area with an array of books clearly displayed and comfortable pillows or rocking chairs can be a favorite quiet place for children to gather. Song picture books help young children link oral and printed language (Barclay & Walwer, 1992). The housekeeping area can include paper for making shopping lists, books for reading stories to dolls, cookbooks, and recipe cards. Teachers can label each activity area and place children's names on their cubbies alongside the child's picture. Teachers also can place labels and pictures on material bins and shelves.

Teachers may want to recommend to parents that they read to their children at home each day; however, many parents do not have quality reading materials. Some out-of-home care programs develop a family lending library to promote reading at home (see Brock & Dodd, 1994, for strategies). These libraries can include multicultural books that are inclusive of each family's cultural diversity and that help young children and their parents' to recognize and accept others' cultural differences.

Language and Emergent
Literacy in Multicultural Environments

Many family- and center-based child care environments include children from varied socioeconomic situations and ethnicities. The first language of young children from diverse backgrounds can be a nonmainstream variation of English or a language other than English. Children of diverse backgrounds are often skilled language users; however, their language patterns might vary from mainstream English. When teachers are culturally responsive, they may have to adapt their interactions so that all the young children in their care can actively participate and learn fluent, mainstream English and emergent literacy.

Different Home Cultures May Have
Different Values and Practices of Literacy

When teaching young children of diverse backgrounds, teachers learn that the child's home social context is especially important for both language and emergent literacy. Shirley Brice Heath (1983) described specifically the language patterns of two communities, Trackton and Roadville, a few miles from one another in the Piedmont Carolinas, among whom Heath lived and worked with for nearly a decade. Her work illustrates how different cultures have different values and practices of literacy. Both Trackton, an African American community, and Roadville, a European American community, are working-class communities. Trackton parents do not create reading and writing tasks for their children, nor do they buy special toys or books for their children. Yet Trackton children developed literacy skills through a process of social negotiation that is group oriented, with talk an integral part of literacy events. In contrast, Roadville homes have abundant reading materials, parents read books to their children, give them workbooks and assist them in learning colors, matching shapes and letters, and so forth. Children in Trackton and Roadville talked a lot; yet the children's talking did not transfer well to existing primary-level practices of the school. Each community practiced literacy in a different manner yet neither community's literacy practices matched well with the practices of the children's school literacy.

When teachers are working with young children from different cultural backgrounds, it is important for them to learn how the children interact with their parents at home. Parents from different cultural backgrounds may value and teach literacy in different ways, and teachers need to be respectful of children's home social contexts. Sharing time, for example, when teachers use questions to help young children speak in a literate style, might be a mismatch for a child of a different culture. In one study of sharing time in a class, the author found that the teacher expected the children to center their discussion around a specific topic, such as *water, food,* or *transportation.* But the African American children in the class were more comfortable with a "topic-associating style," in which the children would present episodes linked to a person or theme but with the links left unstated. Because the teacher did not have the cultural knowledge to understand this different style, her comments and questions often cut off any sharing by the African American children.

The starting point for young children's literacy learning lies in *meaningfulness,* that is, knowing the meaning and function of literacy, not learning specific skills in isolation. When teachers infuse children's everyday routines with language and literacy, all children can be active members of the group, regardless of their fluency with the English language. Early education involves repetitive and concrete activities in which each child has many opportunities to hear the same words and phrases and to see words in meaningful ways (e.g., as previously discussed, on helper charts, daily activity schedules, labels on materials and activity areas). Social role play and simple games with rules are rich experiences for young children to expand their language and literacy. Games with simple, repeated rules give children many opportunities to use the same language again and again. Teachers can add appropriate print for social role play, for example, with pretend train tickets, restaurant menus, and so forth.

Daily storytelling and/or storybook reading, along with adult–child verbal interactions incorporating stories, provide a natural, high-interest literacy for young children or children who speak a nonstandard variation of English as well as children for whom English is a second language. Hough and Nurss identified the multiple forms of learning within a story reading activity as follows:

Oral fluency, listening comprehension, vocabulary, concepts, contextual understanding and use of language, story structure, print con-

cepts, sociocultural use of text, oral language/print connections, storytelling, word recognition, science and social studies content, and
creative and written responses to text (1992, p. 150)

Stories can be a rich resource for shared enjoyment among children and
adults. Teachers can use stories in many different ways to foster early
literacy learning, as illustrated in the following suggestions:

- Teachers can read children repetitive stories with predictable and repeated language. Repetitive language allows children with limited
  English proficiency to join in orally with the other children as they
  say repetitive phrases from the story that are meaningful within the
  story's context. Simple, repetitive stories encourage increased vocabulary and broader sentence structure. Some repetitive stories that children seem to really enjoy include *Caps for Sale* by Slobodkina (1940);
  Brown Bear, Brown Bear, What Do You See? by Martin (1967); and *The
  Very Hungry Caterpillar* by Carle (1979).

- Teachers can involve children interactively as the story unfolds. They
  can ask questions, invite the children to predict what will happen
  next, or discuss an illustration, or they can instruct children to join in
  choral responses to the last line of each page.

- Teachers can incorporate prereading and postreading language activities into their daily story reading sessions. Teachers can lead children in a discussion of a story topic before reading the actual story. Or
  teachers can initiate a discussion about what the children think might
  happen in a new story about a familiar topic. After reading a story,
  teachers can lead a discussion about what, in fact, did happen in the
  story or why the characters did what they did. Studies indicate that
  directed listening and thinking activities prior to and after story reading improve young children's comprehension because they focus the
  children's attention on a specific goal (Morrow & O'Conner, 1995).

- Teachers can have children practice retelling stories as an effective
  way of developing their sense of story structure.

- Teachers can read the same story to help young children to increase
  their ability to interpret a story, including the ability to predict outcomes, make associations, and formulate evaluations (Morrow &
  O'Conner, 1995).

- Teachers can retell familiar stories and have children act the stories
  out in dramatic form.

- Teachers can record a child's dictation of a story or a described event.
  As the child and teacher then read what the teacher has written, the

child grasps the link between the child's oral language and written language.

CONCLUSION

Interaction is the soil in which babies' potential to communicate flourishes. Caregivers who are available to children psychologically provide the environment in which the baby flourishes. As babies listen to their caregivers talking to them, they feel accepted, cared for, and connected; in turn, these feelings of security motivate babies' active response to their caregivers. From the beginning, baby and caregiver engage in give-and-take communication, using facial expression, body posture, and crying. The communication process between child and caregiver is inherently mutual. Within the caregiver–baby interaction, babies gain a sense of meaning and purpose. As caregivers respond to babies' cues, babies learn that they can make things happen—that they can influence others.

Language and communication emerge through and within young children's relationships with significant others. Each developmental realm influences the others, and development is an integrated process. As the brain develops, babies gain new communication abilities. In turn, the ever increasing caregiver–baby interaction influences brain development. From birth, within every interaction, both babies and caregivers communicate their feelings to each other. Beyond language learning, babies are immersed in emotional communication, first with caregivers, then with peers and siblings. The process is intrinsically social.

Language and cognitive development are strongly related in the early stages of language and communication. Within daily child-rearing interactions, babies' mental schema are forming; this increased cognitive growth makes strides in communication possible. For example, by 8 months, babies understand that experiences are shareable, and they can point to tell their caregiver what they want. Toddlers quickly learn that language is a powerful social tool—to greet, to get what they want, and so forth. With increasing language skills and memory, toddlers and their caregivers can co-construct stories of their shared past experience. By 3 years, children can tell stories alone. Telling stories is another illustration of the intertwining of language, communication, cognition, and social growth.

The process of emergent literacy is similar to the development of language and communication. Young children learn to understand the meaning of letters and words, to read and to write in successive approximations, just as they learned to talk. Only as active participants in listening, speaking, writing, and reading do young children develop the capacity to understand the written word. As with language development, emergent literacy is social—occurring most often within the young childs everyday interactions with adults and children. It is important for caregivers to adapt their caregiving to accommodate children from diverse cultural backgrounds to promote emergent literacy for all children. Regardless of the caregiving setting, language, communication, and emergent literacy develop within the everyday, taken-for-granted interactions of the caregiver and the young child. These interactions are the core of a relationship in which the developing child experiences acceptance, love, and connection.

chapter 4

Guidance and Discipline

Beyond obedience, is attention fixed on the goal—
   freedom from fear.
Beyond fear—openness to life.
And beyond that—love.

—Dag Hammarskjöld (1966, p. 129)[1]

Guidance and discipline seem to be the number one topics of concern among family- and center-based child caregivers. Since the late 1980s, research has shown that a baby's inclination toward boldness or timidity does not stem from one genetic characteristic alone but rather from a complex interplay of biological and environmental factors. What children experience from moment to moment, especially in their early years, is just as important as their genetic heritage; physiological traits alone do not define a baby's potential (Sameroff & Emde, 1989; Shore, 1997). This new knowledge further confirms the crucial significance of the everyday guidance and discipline of babies and very young children. Patterns established by the caregiver can alter children's innate tendencies. A soft-spoken caregiver who minimizes auditory and tactile stimulation, for example, can lessen a baby's irritability that is caused by his or her sensitivity to sound and touch.

Teachers of babies and young children know that guidance and discipline are key components of successful caregiving. Babies are born without a sense of meaning or purpose. They lack the skills for understanding others and for understanding and accepting themselves. The central theme of this chapter is that the intimate relationships embedded in the everyday routine interactions between a caregiver and young child—feeding, diapering, dressing, talking, singing, and so forth—are the vehicles for guiding babies' and young children's development. How caregivers interact with babies and young children in their moment-to-moment, daily interactions guides how babies and young children will develop.

The newborn is initially a primarily biological entity. Over a period of time, the baby develops consciousness, defined by Greenspan as "a complex combination of perception, intentionality, and selfhood that permits reflection and understanding" (1997, p. 110). The first sign of consciousness is the baby's sense of aliveness, or arousal. The second sign emerges once babies begin to show interest in the people around them. How does a baby's consciousness develop? Babies' capacity to integrate emotions and experience into their consciousness emerges from their emotion-filled interactions with caregivers. These emotional experiences make babies' subsequent interactive experiences meaningful; over time, the baby develops a subjective inner world, which includes feelings such as pleasure and displeasure, as well as an awareness of an outer reality. *The quality of everyday caregiving interactions shapes and strengthens babies' and young children's growing experience of both inner and outer reality.*

Consciousness, then, depends on social interaction and biology. Social interaction affects the physiology of the brain, and the physiology of the brain determines the possibilities of babies' and young children's interactions with caregivers. Nature and nurture, biology and experience, are continuously interacting. As Greenspan explained, "Consciousness develops from this continuous interaction in which biology organizes experience and experience organizes biology" (1997, p. 113).

Discipline is a form of teaching, defined as "training that corrects, molds, or perfects the mental faculties or moral character [or] a control gained by enforcing obedience or order" (*Merriam-Webster's Collegiate Dictionary*, 1995, p. 330). Early education literature on discipline has traditionally emphasized helping the young child to develop self-control. Psychologist and early educator Alice Honig (1985), for example, argued that the first goal of discipline is to teach obedience and that the second goal is to promote the child's self-control, which is only possible when the child has internalized the adult's rules. First, the child learns to follow external control (obedience), and then the child learns to internalize control (self-control). In other words, according to much of the early education literature on discipline, young children adopt their parents' and caregivers' rules of behavior as their own. In this book, the concept of discipline is different. The term *emotional self-regulation* is used here when discussing discipline because emotional self-regulation implies adjusting one's emotional state to meet environmental demands and to achieve a variety of other goals. In contrast, a concept of discipline involving *control* connotes only restraint, that is, stopping an action. Thompson and Calkins identified a range of developmental tasks involved in the regulation of emotion:

> Although strategies of emotional self-regulation originate in the young infant's simple efforts to cope with distress through self soothing, they quickly become integrated into a network of behavioral strategies by which children (and adults) seek to maintain personal well-being, manage their relations with others, behave consistently with their self-image, manage their self-presentation to the social world, and achieve a variety of other goals. (1996, p. 163)

In summary, emotional self-regulation involves the ability to respond emotionally and to adapt one's emotional experience to moment-to-moment situational demands. Each stage and age makes its own demands, builds on earlier achievements, and requires new adaptive behaviors to respond to the environment appropriately.

This chapter discusses how emotional self-regulation develops within the relationship between babies and young children and their parents and out-of-home caregivers. Furthermore, this chapter explains how the structuring and limiting of the young child's everyday experience by caring adults are essential in helping the child control feelings such as anger, greed, and envy, which are as basic to being human as are empathy, love, and compassion. If young children experience being cared for in a loving and consistent fashion, they can learn to care for others.

In out-of-home group care of babies and young children, *group management* also is central to the task of guidance and discipline. Two components of group management are teachers' use of time and space. Does each day have a predictable schedule that balances active and more sedentary experiences? Has the teacher reduced the amount of empty waiting periods during transitions? Are activities clearly structured so that the young children can readily understand both adult expectations and the nature of the task? Does the space allow for both individual and group activities, quiet and more robust activities, accessibility and clarity in the choice of materials? And, most important, is the teacher able both to carefully observe the children and to be accessible so that she promotes development and guides children to prevent trouble before it begins? Teachers who can manage a group of young children successfully allow the children to gain the safety and security that they need to take initiative and engage in activities and interactions with peers and adults.

Providing family- or center-based care for very young children is complex work involving multiple dimensions. A great deal of maintenance and management is always present—putting away toys, cleaning furniture, doing laundry, setting up food and cleaning up after meals and snacks, preparing materials for activities, diapering, helping dress and undress young children, and so forth. Given these multiple maintenance and management tasks, teachers have to be very committed to children's development *if they are going to put the children first and be available to them as much as possible.* Very young children often can be quite compliant and can amuse themselves in an environment rich with toys. Teachers run the risk of becoming preoccupied with maintenance and management tasks and letting the children spend too much time playing on their own. When a child does initiate an interaction, it may feel to a busy teacher like a distraction from keeping things in order. One kindergarten teacher described her first years of teaching as follows: "I still wanted most of all to keep things moving with a minimum of distraction. It did not occur to me that the distractions might be the sounds of children thinking" (Paley, 1986, p. 122). When children are left too much to play by themselves, they may appear to be playing happily, but their play and peer interactions may be of surface quality. Teachers whose main focus is group maintenance may miss opportunities to promote growth and development. When teachers make children their first priority and engage in interacting with them actively, every moment holds the potential for nurturing, development, and learning.

GUIDANCE AND DISCIPLINE: BIRTH TO 7 MONTHS

The important events that help or hurt development are the split-second, ordinary, nonverbal events that occur between baby and caregiver every day. Stern called these interactions *microevents,* which he described as follows: "relatively small and short-lived events, such as what the mother does with her eyes and face at the moment when the infant's smile at her increases in amplitude" (1995, p. 63). Stern noted that microevents consist of microregulations of both the baby's emotion and activation, and he identified four qualities common to microevents:

1. The events are the subjective experience of "real" events.
2. The events are microevents.
3. The events are ordinary, daily, and concrete.
4. The events are repetitive. (1995, pp. 61–63)[2]

   During the first few months of a baby's life, much of what goes on between baby and caregiver involves helping the baby achieve physiological and emotional regulation. Sleeping and eating are two primary tasks of baby and caregiver. During babies' first 3–4 months, the brain has not matured enough to allow for regularity in sleep. By age 3–4 months, however, babies may be taking two to three regular naps throughout the day. By age 6 months, most babies need a morning and afternoon nap, for a total of 2–4 hours. Research has shown that sleep, emotion, and attention are all linked (Dahl, 1996).[3] Naps are very important for optimal learning when babies are awake. Babies who are good sleepers are able to maintain focus and learn. During their first 3–4 months, colicky babies often have irregular sleep patterns and can cry inconsolably. Like adults, babies who are not getting enough sleep tend to be quite irritable.

   At first babies also need to have a regular feeding schedule, and caregivers gradually learn to distinguish which of a baby's cries indicate that the baby is hungry. Feeding is a predictable time in which babies can gain a sense of love and connectedness that fuels their security and sense of self. Holding and loving communication during feeding are as important to babies' well-being as is the food. By 6 months babies are able to eat at regular intervals, usually every 4 hours. Every feeding can be a time for play and communication. All babies deserve to be held for a feeding and *should never* have a propped bottle (drink their milk after the teacher props up the bottle and turns to other tasks). When mothers are nursing, child care settings often make it possible for mothers who work near the center to come to the center and nurse.

   When babies are awake, their caregiver's *emotional availability* is critical for babies to feel secure and for caregivers to be able to respond to babies' signals (i.e., facial expression, vocalization, motor display). As the caregiver responds to the baby's cues, the caregiver's responses invite the baby to continue communicating, and their mutual dance develops. When caregivers are not available emotionally, it can lead the baby to experience developmental problems (Fraiberg, 1980; Sroufe, 1983). Emotional availability makes the caregiver's central role in emotional regulation possible. Sameroff and Emde explained that "affective monitoring in the everyday sense has a dual aspect: it occurs not just within the child but reciprocally between child and caregiver; in other words, monitoring occurs within the relationship experience. Emotions are fundamentally social" (1989, p. 45).

"Goodness of fit" is another important construct in babies' temperament and the baby–caregiver relationship (Thomas & Chess, 1977). Goodness of fit refers to the fit between a baby's capacities, motivation, and temperament and the expectations and responses of the caregiver. The fit between baby and caregiver influences the baby's ability to adapt, self-regulate, and learn. Different caregivers may define a difficult temperament in different ways. For example, an even-tempered 18-month-old son may seem effeminate to his father whereas his mother may think he is a competent, good-natured toddler. Furthermore, different caregiving environments may bring out or inhibit temperamental dispositions. Being in a program with an active group of babies and toddlers may suppress the activity level of a shy baby; whereas a smaller, more quiet group of babies might be a setting in which the same child can express herself more vigorously.

Thomas and Chess (1977) identified inborn patterns termed *temperament*. Babies' different temperaments are seen in how easy they are to soothe and in their level of activity and degree of alertness. Brain research has shown that individual differences exist biologically in babies' central nervous system reactivity and in their ability to learn to self-regulate. Porges (1993, 1997), for example, identified the vagus nerve, which originates in the brain stem, as the nerve that regulates facial expression, cardiac output, and vocal communication. Vagal tone and vagal reactivity underlie neural regulation of emotional states. Babies with greater vagal tone are more reactive and more responsive to their environment and have a greater ability to attend than those with low vagal tone.[4]

Gunnar (1997) found substantive differences in the brain's inner portion, the limbic system, between babies and toddlers who are shy and those who are bold. Babies and young children have different thresholds of fear responses. Babies with lower thresholds are quicker to be afraid. Gunnar's research indicated a high degree of heredity for fear and stress thresholds. The life experiences of babies and young children, however, can affect the tone of their stress/threat system (Gunnar, 1996a, 1996b). When babies and young children are stressed or afraid, they have increased levels of the chemical *cortisol* in their brain. Increased cortisol produces a cascading of response and can damage the hippocampus, the part of the brain that "turns off" the stress response. In a safe environment, however, a low threshold for fear can be limiting because then the young child's ability to explore the environment and learn is inhibited.[5] If a young child's life is constantly stressful, for example, involving recurrent episodes of domestic violence, it is good if the child's stress threshold is low so that the child can be vigilant and prepared for dealing with stress. When attachment is good, the caregiving relationship serves as a buffer for the baby against stress.

In summary, babies have different dispositions in emotional and social behavior that are rooted in their central nervous systems. A baby's temperament affects how the baby approaches and experiences social interactions. Although a baby's disposition is somewhat stable over time, the quality of caregiving can influence a baby's disposition substantively. If a baby is naturally sensitive to touch, for example, the caregiver's gentleness in holding and caring for the baby can prevent frequent irritability.

GUIDANCE AND DISCIPLINE: 7–19 MONTHS

By age 7 months babies can maintain attention and take delight in the intimacy of those who care for them. Now a new form of connectedness emerges as babies begin to respond to social gestures. During the second half of the first year, babies become very interested in exploring their environment. Within this exploration they increasingly engage in mastery behavior, in which babies are motivated to achieve, or master, a specific goal. Behaviors such as crawling to a desired destination or getting a caregiver to follow their directives by pointing, raising their arms, or making other gestures are considered *mastery behaviors* because they are pleasurable in and of themselves. Research indicates that mastery motivation and behaviors are related to subsequent cognitive competence (Zeanah, 1993). Not surprisingly, attachment, caregiver stimulation, and caregiver availability are related to a baby's level of mastery behavior. As babies explore, their caregiver's presence serves as a "beacon of orientation" (Mahler, Pine, & Bergman, 1975). In other words, a baby's relationship with his or her caregiver influences the baby's mastery motivation and behavior. The following vignette illustrates caregiver support of mastery behavior.

Joy and Alicia enter the gross motor room with several toddlers. They sit on a mat, and Jake (age 12 months) walks back and forth between them. The teachers clap as Jake walks first to one and then the other, and Jake chuckles gleefully. A few moments later, Alicia takes Jake's and Ben's (age 14 months) hands, and the three of them walk around the room together. Jake then follows a few other toddlers to the toddler slide. Alicia is standing next to the slide as Jake climbs the four steps. When he reaches the top, Jake leans over and kisses Alicia who returns the kiss. Smacking his lips, Jake slides down the slide.

Joy and Alicia not only are available to Jake but also are celebrating with Jake his new walking skill. Jake is very pleased with his new mastery in walking.

Beginning around age 6 months, babies develop discrete emotions such as anger, fear, and surprise. Emotions, or feelings, are not only psychological states but also physiological sensations. As babies' emotional experiences increase in number and complexity, the growing brain abstracts these experiences into neurological patterns (Greenspan, 1997).

As discussed in Chapter 1, at 6 months of age babies will initiate mutual interactions with their caregivers. Nine-month-olds point and respond when their caregivers point. They resolve uncertainty through *social referencing;* that is, they seek emotional information from their caregiver (e.g., a baby will look back at a caregiver for reassurance while crawling across the room). It is as if babies regulate a sense of security through behaviors that actively maintain their proximity to their caregivers. The caregiver serves as the "holding environment" for the baby (Winnicott, 1965). Caregivers' emotional availability remains critical to babies' developing sense of self. Greenspan explained how a baby's preverbal interaction with a caregiver lays the foundation for the baby's developing sense of morality—good and bad, right and wrong, honesty, and so forth.

> [The baby's] awareness of her own and others' intentions, which take in such basic issues as safety versus danger, acceptance versus rejection, approval versus disapproval, pride and respect versus humiliation, are all initially understood through such exchanges between caregiver and child. (Greenspan, 1997, p. 120)

Caregivers' expectations are already shaping babies' beginning understanding of what is right and what is wrong through their responses to babies' emotional expressions and motor explorations.

Eating and Sleeping

Between 6 and 12 months of age, babies are able to maintain a regular eating and sleeping schedule. Once babies have learned new motor skills like crawling and climbing, however, the surge in development may disrupt their napping schedule, and they may be more resistant to being put in their crib. During these times of developmental growth, a calming activity, such as reading or singing, can assist babies in settling down. Most important are regularity and firmness. It helps always to remember that *learning to fall asleep is an important skill for babies to master.* It is very important for caregivers to avoid putting a baby to sleep in their arms because then the baby will have a harder time learning how to go to sleep on his or her own.

Once babies are 7 months old, they can eat together with other babies in child care, and eating becomes a dual activity—mealtime plus social time. Now babies are able to eat solid food; and, as soon as they develop their pincer grasp (around age 8–10 months), they like to feed themselves with their hands. Exploring food becomes as important as eating it. Eating is an activity in which babies can begin to exercise autonomy. Learning to play with and handle a cup is exciting for babies. Caregivers can allow time for babies to explore their new skills and avoid making mealtimes into a battleground. By 12 months old, babies should be eating finger foods (e.g., cheese and bread cut into small pieces) on their own; and by 16 months old, they should be able to master a small spoon or fork. Feeding oneself is a sign of growing independence. The more toddlers can feed themselves the better.[6]

Group Management

Group management is possible when teachers organize and plan the child care environment so that at the outset young children feel secure. Social, emotional, cognitive, and physical learning are not possible in child care without group management. The critical element in group management is the teacher's relationship with each child. A significant relationship is the key to all of the other critical components of group management.

Teachers can strive to provide children with an organized environment that has clearly defined activity areas and accessible materials, which can be organized and labeled with pictures. Materials can represent varying developmental levels so that each child can succeed well at something without getting frustrated. Materials can be changed so that children do not engage in repetitive activities and are continually challenged to further their development. Similarly, teachers can provide a simple, predictable routine that provides a comfortable rhythm of both quiet and active experiences as well as both individual and group activities. In addition, teachers can organize smooth transitions between activities and give children a warning before moving on to the next activity. Knowing that young children complete tasks at different rates and that clean-up takes different amounts of time for different tasks and different children, teachers can allow flexibility during transitions. In a team-teaching situation, one adult can make herself available to interact with the young children who have completed their clean-up work. During transitions (e.g., taking turns to use the bathroom prior to lunch), teachers might want to involve children in simple songs and fingerplays or storybook reading to avoid idle waiting periods, which often become group management dilemmas.

Last, clear behavior expectations with simple rules that young children can understand and act on with minimal direction are central to effective group management. Over time, young children internalize these rules that control their behavior. The rules can be reinforced consistently by all teachers and posted so that parents know them as well.

In the following observation, teachers enforce the rules to ease a conflict while encouraging the children to learn how to defend themselves:

> *Four toddlers are playing with water, dolls, and washcloths. Blake (age 18 months) takes Cory's (age 15 months) washcloth out of his hands. Cory makes a loud grunting noise. Carmeletta, their teacher, intervenes by saying to Cory, "Cory, use your words. Say 'mine.'" Cory follows his teacher's direction by telling Blake, "Mine!" Blake gives Cory his washcloth back.*

Carmeletta and her co-teachers, Alicia and Joy, have established simple rules for toddlers in their classroom. When redirecting a child, they often help the young toddler follow through with the redirection to make sure the child understands.

> *The toddlers return to their room from the gross motor room. As they walk to the rug area, Blake (age 22 months) pushes Demetrius (age 21 months). Carmeletta intervenes by explaining, "Blake, pushing hurts. You may find another place to play." As she is talking she walks Blake to the other side of the room. Blake whimpers quietly. Carmeletta sits next to him and puts a tub of plastic blocks in front of him. Blake immediately begins stacking the blocks, and Matt (age 20 months) joins in his play.*

Sequences of redirection can be very brief if teachers are specific, firm, and clear. If teachers provide an alternative activity and the toddler does not follow through, teachers can ensure that the toddler goes to another area as a consequence for his or her noncompliance.

> *Jake (age 13 months) plays with three toddlers at the sensory table, which is filled with colored pasta and plastic cups. Jake throws some pasta on the floor. Carmeletta responds, "Jake, we're going to keep it in the table." Jake, however, throws the pasta again. Carmeletta says, "Okay, I guess we're going to be done here." Jake and Carmeletta walk to the rug area, and Jake begins playing with a Pop-n-Pal toy.*

Because his teachers enforce rules for behavior consistently, Jake is learning that he either follows their redirection or there will be a consequence, which often involves moving to another area.

GUIDANCE AND DISCIPLINE: 19–36 MONTHS

As babies begin to move, they experience more and more mastery. Toddlers create their own standards of mastery and know whether they have met their goals. Toddlers now frequently invoke the word *no* to avoid being distracted from their goals (e.g., to put on their own coat to go outdoors). As previously mentioned, caregivers help babies who have not yet learned to talk to begin to gain a sense of what is good and bad. As toddlers' skill levels increase, their goals may be in conflict with those of their caregivers; thus negativism and testing continue. Interestingly, research indicates that parents who deal with their toddler's behavior by controlling the toddler are more likely to have defiant toddlers than those parents who negotiate and reason with their toddlers (Zeanah, 1993). Parents whose primary interaction with their toddlers is to direct and redirect them are most likely to have toddlers who develop a strong resistance to these continual control methods. When a parent explains that hitting hurts or that throwing balls in the house breaks things when the parent is redirecting the toddler, the toddler will be more likely to internalize these rules, for the toddler feels respect.

Encouragement

As toddlers take initiative and strive to reach their goals, caregivers have many opportunities to encourage their explorations. Caregivers can describe toddlers' efforts positively, for example, "You opened the door all by yourself." Descriptive statements help the children recognize their accomplishments. As caregivers encourage toddlers, children begin to recognize their own success and gain a sense of mastery and self-worth. In contrast, when caregivers provide global evaluative comments such as "Good job," toddlers learn that they are pleasing the adult instead of learning to recognize the value of their behavior.

Eating and Sleeping

Given their young age, toddlers continue to need some help during meals and snacktimes, but many teachers may feel it is easier not to eat with the children in their care. Snacks and mealtimes, however, can be wonderful opportunities for toddlers to have an extended shared time with their peers and teachers. When teachers eat with toddlers, eating becomes a relaxed time for talking together about the food, about the day's activities, or about something the toddlers and their families have done together. Most toddlers older than 12 months have learned to use a spoon and fork, although they may still prefer to use their fingers. Deciding how much to eat is a child's task. Given their patterns of negativism, a toddler may refuse to eat the food provided. Caregivers can let the children know clearly that if they choose not to eat, they'll have to wait until the next meal or snack with the rest of the group. Skipping the occasional meal will not hurt a well-nourished child, and missing a meal is a powerful consequence for refusal, so the pattern most likely will disappear quickly.

Some family-based child caregivers and center-based teachers enjoy cooking with toddlers (see Chapter 1). Assisting in food preparation is a good way for toddlers to learn turn-taking skills and take the first steps toward learning social responsibility.

By the later half of the second year, most toddlers take one afternoon nap. Given the high activity level of most toddlers, a simple story after lunch can quiet them so that they can get to sleep. A very small number of 2-year-olds may not fall asleep during this period. These children can quietly look at storybooks on their cot while their peers are napping.

Toilet Learning

Just as it is the child's task to fall asleep, toilet training is also the child's accomplishment. Like eating and sleeping, initially caregiver and child work on the task of toilet training together. Lansky provided the following list of signs of toilet-learning readiness:

- Is aware of the "need to go" and shows it by facial expression or by telling the parent
- Can express and understand one-word statements, such as "wet," "dry," and "go"

- Demonstrates imitative behavior
- Dislikes wet or dirty diapers
- Is able to stay dry for at least 2 hours, or wakes up dry in the morning or after a nap
- Is able to pull pants up and down
- Is anxious to please
- Has a sense of social appropriateness (wet pants can be an embarrassment)
- Tells parent she or he is about to urinate
- Asks to use the potty chair or toilet (1984, p. 9)

Children cannot be ready for toilet learning until their gastrointestinal tracts and central nervous systems are mature enough to allow the children to recognize the sensations that come before urination or a bowel movement. Around the toddler's third birthday, caregivers can look for signs of readiness. Any time before age 4 is normal, and girls often are ready before boys. Children most often gain bowel control prior to bladder control.

Young Children's Fears

As their sense of self and the world expands, experiencing fears is a normal phase for many young children. Typical fears include fear of strange places, loud noises (e.g., fire engines), darkness, Halloween masks, or specific animals. Teachers cannot eliminate young children's fears, but they can listen carefully, respect whatever children tell teachers about their fears, and help them to understand and learn how to deal with their fears. A teacher shows that she respects a toddler's fear of monsters, for example, by explaining to him that monsters are pretend and that she will protect the child when he feels uncomfortable. The teacher can reassure the fearful child that many children his age have fears. Adult overreaction to a child's fear can reinforce the fear. Alternatively, when adults do not overreact to a child's fear, over time the child will cease to be afraid.

Rule Implementation and Conflict Resolution

With their new mobility, toddlers begin to feel independent and autonomous. At the same time, however, their behavior may alternate between demands to be independent and intense periods of clinging dependency. Often toddlers will insist on doing something themselves, such as dressing, even when they do not have the necessary skills to accomplish the tasks alone. In their newly found independence, toddlers often respond to their caregivers negatively, as if they are testing themselves and their caregivers. Most toddlers will say "no" to adult suggestions, and it is important that adults do not treat these exploratory "no" responses as representing what the child really wants. In the following observation, Jeff (age 27 months) is quick to reply "no" to most adult suggestions; but, Sally, his family child caregiver, has learned not to take his quick replies seriously.

> *Jeff and Suzie (both age 3 years) have just finished eating their breakfast with Sally. Sally suggests, "Let's brush our teeth before we go outdoors." As they walk to the bathroom, Jeff chants, "No, no, no, no." Sally imitates in a singing voice, "No, no, no, no." Once in the bathroom, Suzie brushes her teeth first as Sally sits on the toilet with Jeff sitting on her lap. Sally says to Jeff, "Let's watch Suzie. We'll wait. And we can get your toothbrush, and you can help me squeeze a little bit of toothpaste onto the brush." Initially, Jeff is restless, but by the time Sally has the toothpaste, he squeezes the tube for her. Suzie finishes, and without further comment, Jeff stands on the step stool and calmly brushes his teeth. Sally encourages Jeff, saying, "That's good brushing. Here, let's get the back teeth. Now I'll get mine brushed." Sally brushes her teeth while the children watch, and then they all leave the bathroom and go outdoors.*

Sally gives Jeff directives in a positive yet firm manner. Knowing that Jeff is quite young, she remains with him to share in his experience and, at the same time, to make certain that he follows her directive. Jeff has no reason to continue his negativism, for once in the bathroom, his understanding has changed; and, he is, in fact, completely participating in the tooth-brushing process.

Time-Out and Redirection

When a toddler is out-of-control, caregivers can use *time-out*, a brief period during which the child is separated from the group and all attention and asked to sit quietly to calm him- or herself. Time-out ends as soon as the child feels that he or she can manage. Time-out need not be a punishment; rather, it is a strategy to help young children calm themselves. Once the child is calm, caregivers can talk with the child about his or her feelings. The amount of time is not important; in fact, most children can calm themselves in a very few moments.

When a child misbehaves but is not out of control, time-out is not an appropriate caregiver response (see the section on pp. 141–142 called Misbehavior, Challenging Behavior, or Behavioral Disorder? for tips on how to tell the difference). Rather, caregivers can redirect children and, when appropriate, remind them of the rules.

> *Ricky (age 20 months) takes the cowboy hat off Russell's head, and Russell (age 30 months) cries out loudly. Jean tells Ricky, "Russell also wants a turn. Let's give the hat back to Russell." Ricky returns the hat to Russell and picks up a ball, which he throws to Jean.*

When caregivers have simple, consistent rules, toddlers most often are quick to follow adult redirections. Jean has cared for Ricky since he was 2 months old, and Ricky has learned that she is emotionally available to him and that her directives have meaning. It was easy for Ricky to return Russell's hat because Ricky knew that Jean was available to play with him. As noted previously, caregivers also can help toddlers learn how to defend themselves:

> *Blake knocks down Cory's block tower, and Cory complains to his teacher, Vetta. Vetta tells Cory, "Use your words to tell Blake." Cory tells Blake, two times, "I don't like that!" and Blake begins a new activity.*

Previously we saw that in their infant-toddler classroom, Cory had learned to tell Blake, "Mine," when Blake was taking Cory's washcloth. As a 2-year-old, Cory's language skills have expanded to communicate the same message, and the teachers in Cory's 2-year-old class have the same expectations as did his infant–toddler teachers.

Once young children understand their caregivers' expectations, they can adapt their behavior accordingly, as in the following example.

> *Paul (age 27 months) grabs Jesse's small plastic car. Paul's teacher, Maggie, sees this and tells Paul, "Paul, you need to ask Jesse."*
>
> *Paul says to Jesse, "My turn." Jesse gives Paul the car as Maggie says, "Thank you." Jesse then begins making a block tower.*

Jesse and Paul have been attending the center since early infancy; thus, they have learned that turn taking is "what you do." Given the many play options available to Jesse, he had no difficulty giving Paul his car.[7]

Natural and Logical Consequences   In addition to timeout and redirection, teachers can use *natural and logical consequences* to assist children in developing emotional self-regulation. A natural consequence occurs automatically without being arranged artificially by teachers. If a child refuses to eat, the teacher can remove the unfinished food from the table when everyone is finished and allow the child to feel hungry until the next meal or snack is served. The teacher has told the child there will be no more food until the next meal. In time the child will become hungry, a natural consequence of refusing to eat. The teacher's task becomes difficult when the child persistently begs for food before the next meal; however, for the child to learn, it is important for the teacher to maintain her directive. When a consequence does not follow naturally, a teacher can implement a logical consequence to help a child learn self-regulation. For example, a teacher can tell a toddler she will have to leave the sandbox if she continues to throw sand. When the child continues to throw sand, her teacher will remove her from the sandbox.

   Rewards and Punishment   Many parents and teachers think young children respond best to rewards and punishment, as primary tools of discipline. Rewards and punishment, however, have built-in problems and do not enable young children to develop self-regulation. Clinical psychologist Thomas Gordon, founder of Parent Effectiveness Training (PET), identified some common problems in using rewards and punishment. Five common problems with rewards are as follows (Gordon, 1989):

1. To be effective, teachers need to give rewards immediately after the desired behavior occurs, first every time, then intermittently. This process takes a lot of time and is not always possible. For instance, much of young children's behavior is not observed by teachers directly; therefore, teachers cannot reward desired behavior every time it occurs.

2. Children must not be able to acquire rewards on their own if rewards are to be effective. As children get older, however, they often discover ways to satisfy their own needs (e.g., taking a cookie out of the jar by themselves).

3. Teachers often feel that young children may find little pleasure in activities or tasks unless they receive a reward or specific approval from their teacher.

4. Teachers' dependence on rewards thwarts children's intrinsic motivation.

5. The absence of a reward or teacher approval can feel like a punishment if children are looking for them.

Not only do rewards lead to unplanned and undesired outcomes, but punishment likewise leads to several dangers (Gordon, 1989):

1. Punishment works only so long as the punisher is present.

2. Punishment models aggression. Research on parenting has shown that physical punishment can promote aggression rather than prevent it.

3. Teachers have to have remarkable expertise to make punishment work effectively for the following reasons:
   - If a child's behavior is punished once, it should be punished again every time it occurs.
   - For punishment to be effective at all, teachers need to administer it immediately once the undesired behavior has occurred; however, that is not always possible. For example, a child may be punished the first time he or she grabs a toy from another child; however, the next time, no teacher may be in sight.
   - The teacher needs to be rigorous in ensuring that children never receive rewards for the behavior for which they were punished.

4. When teachers punish a child in front of other children, the punished child feels ashamed and embarrassed.

5. When teachers punish young children, the children frequently experience strong underlying emotional messages from the punisher, such as anger and irritation that the children may read as rejection.

This chapter examines ways by which to create a climate where children feel they are understood and cared for and where they can develop inner self-regulation abilities.[8] Rewards and punishments are extrinsic methods that foster obedience, not inner control.

Misbehavior, Challenging Behavior, or Behavioral Disorder?

How does a caregiver see the difference between simple misbehavior, challenging behavior, or behavior that may indicate a disorder? This task is quite difficult because many behaviors of very young children in some settings are common, but they also can be symptomatic of serious disorders. It is common, for example, for toddlers around 18–24 months old to bite another child; it is equally common for young children to grab another child's toy or to hit another child to get what they want. A behavior becomes a problem when it occurs often, in various situations, and with varied peers and adults; in other words, a behavior becomes a problem when it is demonstrating a child's typical pattern. Campbell distinguished challenging behavior from disorder as follows:

> [Challenging behavior is] a pattern of symptoms that has been troublesome for some time, is evident in more than one situation, is rela-

tively severe, and is likely to impede the child's ability to negotiate the important developmental tasks necessary for adaptive functioning in the family and the peer group. Thus, it is not the presence of specific problem behaviors that differentiates "normal" from "abnormal" but their frequency, intensity, chronicity, constellation, and social context. (1990, p. 65)

Young children's behavior problems often are characterized by under-control or overcontrol. Problems classified as undercontrol, often termed *externalized* problems, involve behavior having an impact on others or the environment such as hyperactivity, disruptive behavior, aggression, or tantrums. Problems classified as overcontrol, often termed *internalized* problems, involve expressions of social withdrawal, fearfulness, and/or minimal affect.[9]

Babies act, and their caregivers respond. The response lets the babies understand that their actions have an effect on another person—their actions have meaning. As they interact together, young children and their caregivers create together a world that they share. Together they experience enjoyment in talking, eating, playing, reading, and singing together. As caregivers talk and play with babies and toddlers, the young children's understanding of self emerges. Caregiver and child each experience being accepted, understood, supported, and recognized. These day-to-day consistent interactions give young children a sense of connectedness, a sense of self in relation to others. As noted previously, by 12 months of age babies experience a range of emotions. As babies and toddlers feel angry, fearful, confused, or surprised, their caregiver's response to these emotional expressions helps young children make sense of the world and of the newly felt emotion. The following section explores how caregivers can assist preschool-age children to recognize, express, and constructively channel their emotions, especially negative emotions like fear and anger.

GUIDANCE AND DISCIPLINE: 3–5 YEARS

By 36 months of age, normal children have a history of developing self-regulation, which began when they were first able to put themselves to sleep and calm themselves and continues as they develop increasing knowledge and skill in all developmental domains. Toddlers often lose their self-control; they may bite and hit to get what they want or have a temper tantrum when their caregiver expects them to do something that they do not want to do. By the time they are 3 years old, children who have had consistent positive, reciprocal interactions with emotionally available adults have internalized the rules established by their parents and teachers. They should now be quite skilled at self-regulating, that is, at stopping their impulses to misbehave. Teachers of young children 3–5 years old understand that one of their key roles is to help children learn to self-regulate. It is critical that teachers of preschool-age children understand the full scope of their influence beyond managing a group of children. Teachers need to understand that in every moment of the day, young children can experience care, education, and development; the way in which teachers interact with young children will have an impact on the children's education and development in myriad ways.

Creating a Climate for Social Competence

By 3 years of age, children whose caregiving environments have had a calm, even tempo have developed social competence in their interactions with peers. They are able to be involved in joint projects such as building with blocks, can engage in cooperative pretend play, and enjoy spontaneous conversations together. Children this age are beginning to develop friendships. Ideally, when a problem emerges in their play with another child, the children can work out the problem on their own, as in the following observation:

> *Alex and Abe (both age 3 years) are playing outside. They run to the large sign, the base of which has sand spread over it. Another child, Chunsey (age 3 years) , gives Alex a 3" × 4" piece of cardboard, and Alex tells Abe, "I have a spoon." Abe responds, "I want that. You're not my friend because I want that."*
>
> *Abe tries to grab the cardboard, but Alex throws it over the fence onto the sidewalk. Abe says, "Now neither of us have it."*
>
> *The boys return to the sign, find two sticks in the grass, and use the sticks to push the sand off the base of the sign. They then run about the yard for several moments until they settle in the sandbox where they play together for the remaining 10 minutes of outdoor play.*

Alex and Abe typically choose to play together. Initially they began to argue over who was going to get the cardboard. Alex resolved the issue by tossing the cardboard out of the playground, and the boys then could continue playing together. These two children have enjoyed each other's companionship for more than a year. It is as though their delight in playing together balances their occasional scuffles.

When teachers value their children's extended companionship, they can be flexible and improvise when situations arise that can promote the children's shared enjoyment. During an extended observation of Rosehill

Day Care Center, when I arrived during early care on a Wednesday, I noticed a circle of eight chairs around the breakfast tables. I asked the teacher, Pam, why the chairs were in a circle.

> Pam said, *"Monday, I removed a tablecloth to use it for a road for the children to use to play with small plastic vehicles. I noticed several children had gathered on the chairs and were talking together. I sat with them, and we spontaneously began singing many of the children's favorite songs. I thought, 'This is an interesting variation of early care.' And I chose to leave the chairs for the remainder of the week. And on Tuesday, the same pattern developed; first children sat together and chatted, and then I arrived and we all sang together and did fingerplays."*

Rearranging chairs to form a circle may seem to be a small change in the everyday center environment, but Pam's spontaneous change invited a new form of shared enjoyment for the children and herself. As I observed Pam for several weeks, I often saw that she had this flexibility to improvise use of space, time, or her own action to create a climate for the children to engage in fun activities with each other. For example, in small-group activities, when the children were restless while playing a learning game, Pam was quick to find a high-interest story or song to capture their involvement. When a child was having a difficult day managing, she would encourage the child to "shadow" her and contain his or her lack of control.

Difficulties in Combining Group Management with Children's Education and Development

Each adult learns that everyday life involves some hard times and that aggravation is a part of each person's life. Furthermore, adults learn that they have to accept and cope with painful, difficult situations. Most adults learn to "regroup" and begin again. Young children also deal with disappointments, frustration, and conflict. Parents and out-of-home caregivers can help young children to develop skills in managing these difficulties. Child care teachers can develop specific rules to help children manage; and by 3 years of age, the children can share in developing these rules.

The teachers at Rosehill Day Care Center had a first-choice policy; that is, the first child who chose a toy could choose whether or not to share it with another child. Several teachers explained the rationale behind this rule:

Pam: We have plenty of materials for every child. With this rule, each child has the chance to use materials in her own way.

Barb: The rule protects the kids, and it's an easy way for us to manage fights.

Dana: It seems logical for a child to want to play alone. Children should have the prerogative, even though the material, like Legos, could be shared.

Anne: A child is never urged to share a toy gotten from the shelf because every child needs to possess before she can share.

The Rosehill first-choice policy reinforced the individualistic perspective of these teachers, which I observed in their other interactions with the children. Furthermore, the policy eased potential management difficulties.

Many young children are quite compliant, especially when they are in an ordered environment with consistent expectations. Some teachers develop repetitive directions and redirections or "slogans" that children automatically follow. Here are some typical slogans that early childhood educators use in their management of young children:

- "Use words."
- "I don't like that."
- "Put on your listening ears."
- "I like the way. . . ."
- "Sit on your bottom."

Although children may comply with these slogans, *the dilemma is that their teacher is not addressing the specific experience; nor is the teacher helping the children learn how to resolve the problem embedded in the experience.* The use of global slogans involves management, not learning and development.

Many child care environments in the United States have a large amount of attractive materials with which young children can play. As a result, in some programs, young children are left to play with the materials on their own. At Rosehill, the 2½-hour early care period often involved 3- to 5-year-olds' being on their own. The shelves contained a wide array of age-appropriate toys (e.g., Legos, small blocks, Unifix cubes, puzzles, paper, crayons, markers). In my 6 months of observation, it was not uncommon for more than 20 children to be sitting at the tables as they played, with no adult in the vicinity. The children were often left on their own, as in the following two observations.

> *Early care: Twenty children play with toys at tables in the "big room." Pam cooks scrambled eggs, and Anne chats with her. No adult is in the big room for about 10 minutes.*
> *Early care: The director chats with Pam as both prepare breakfast. With no adult in the "big room," 18 children play with toys at the table as they wait for breakfast.*

During these early care periods, no management difficulties appeared to arise. A low hum of voices and even tempo of activity enveloped the big room. Children were quick to use the program's first-choice policy if another child wanted their toy, so management difficulties surfaced rarely. If observers focused on the children's play, however, they would notice that much of it was surface in quality. Few children had extended involvement with materials. Puzzles often were returned to the shelf uncompleted. Children rarely engaged in joint projects. The block and housekeeping areas always were closed, probably because spontaneous groupings of children there would invite more management difficulties. With no adult to affirm, extend, clarify, or join in their play, the children had learned to be on their own, but their ongoing development was not being fostered.

Value of Television in Out-of-Home Child Care

Across social classes, in rural, suburban, and urban homes, television and video viewing is increasingly taking the place of young children's active learning through play. When teachers of young children know the prevalence as well as the negative implications of young children's viewing of television and videos, they will be cautious about including television in any of their programming, even in early and late care (e.g., before 9:00 A.M. and after 3:30 P.M.). Problems with television and videotapes include the excessive amount of time young children spend watching them as well as the program content. As of 1990, children 3–6 years of age watched an average of 4–6 hours of television each day; for children from low-income families, the hours increased by 50%.

With deregulation of children's commercial television programs in 1984, television shows and toys could be marketed together for the first time. Since 1984, the dominant theme of both television shows and related toys is violence. Within 3 years after deregulation, the number of war toys, such as Transformers and Power Rangers, increased by 600% (Carlsson-Paige & Levin, 1990). Given this pattern, we are seeing changes in young children's play. Early educators report that in much of children's play the children imitate television characters and that this imitation has led to marked increases in violent and aggressive play. Generations of young children have played war games. Previously, however, children chose the content of this war play and used their imagination as they invented the "good and bad guys." Now many children merely *imitate* television characters. As television and videotapes dominate young children's time at home, children are not creatively acting out their everyday experiences in pretend play.

> *Max, 5 years old, is the son of Hank and Stephanie, who have been divorced for 2 years and share custody of Max. They each have demanding, successful careers. Max's parents are enrolled in a parent group that is part of an early intervention program aimed at assisting those parents and child care teachers whose young children are having behavioral difficulties. Hank and Stephanie were approached by the director of their son's child care center because Max does not relate to his peers and seems absorbed in video pretend play.*
>
> > *When at child care, Max often sings softly to himself as he plays alone. All songs are from current popular videos, such as* The Lion King. *When he engages in play, Max is imitating current popular videos. He is interested in relating to the other children only if they are willing to engage in his play. Max's parents report that they each own dozens of children's videos. When living with either his mother or father, Max's primary activity is watching videos.*

Max's story is not an unusual one. Here are some alarming statistics:

- Approximately 99% of homes in the United States have a television, and 57% have more than one (Kulczycki & Toohey, 1997).
- In most homes in the United States, the television is on for an average of 7 hours a day.
- Approximately 90% of out-of-home child care programs have at least one television, and 85% have at least one VCR.
- Saturday morning and after-school cartoons have an average of more than 26 acts of violence every hour (Kulczycki & Toohey, 1997).

- Children in the United States see more than 400 television commercials per week—more than 20,000 per year (Kulczycki & Toohey, 1997).

Given these statistics about television and video viewing in the average American home and the preponderance of violence in children's television, family- and center-based child care teachers can improve their program by being vigilant about television and video viewing. With an ever increasing number of employed parents of very young children, child care teachers surely will use television and videos. Teachers can encourage parents to only use PBS stations for a limited time. Quality child care has no need for television.

Compliance: A Goal Yet a Dilemma

A major theme of this book is that the day-to-day interaction of caregiver and young child enables the young child to develop self-regulation. A key component of this process is the child's internalization of the adult's rules of behavior. Most very young children are quick to internalize these rules and are typically quite compliant. In fact, the reader can visit child care centers in low- and high-income urban areas and see 2-, 3-, and 4-year-olds quietly attending group meetings or quietly sitting at tables as they color or work at a puzzle. In my years in the field, in some of the most depressed urban areas, I have seen young 2- and 3-year-olds sitting in groups chanting the name of the president, the governor of their state, the days of the month and week. I have also seen these young children sitting at tables with their heads on the table. These are definitely compliant 2- and 3-year-olds. But how compliant will they be at age 12? The statistics in these communities indicate that far too many youngsters are getting into a great deal of trouble, both personally and legally (Karr-Morse & Wiley, 1998; Simon & Burns, 1997).

It would be wonderful if research were to show that compliant 2- and 3-year-olds will remain "good" boys and girls as they get older. But no proof is available that compliance at ages 2 and 3 leads to compliance to social norms at 12 and 13. Furthermore, we may be paying a high price for compliance because strict obedience may very well shortchange other developmental needs of young children. Indeed, compliance to teachers' desires may very well be similar to compliance to the gang leader or the prospective lover's expectations. Yes, compliance is a key component for healthy development. But many other aspects of development suffer when compliance is the teacher's main goal. If caregivers aim to nurture the whole child and have in mind long-term goals as well as short-term goals, they will ensure that very young children's activities are developmentally appropriate. Furthermore, caregivers will work to foster children's abilities to attend while encouraging their curiosity, their sense of self and other, and all of the other attributes that contribute to a fully developing young child.

Helping Young Children Learn to Recognize and Manage Anger

Anger is a state of arousal, a feeling that we experience when a goal is blocked and we become frustrated. A key function of anger is to eliminate barriers that block one's intention. What are the stresses in child care that provoke a young child to be angry? Typical stresses of preschoolers that lead to anger include conflict over possessions; physical assault; verbal exchanges, such as a tease or a taunt; rejection; and issues of compliance (Fabes & Eisenberg, 1992).

Young children cannot learn to express their anger appropriately until they first learn to recognize it. Teachers of young children can play a pivotal role in helping children recognize their anger. Talking about feelings helps young children recognize and understand their feelings; when teachers see an angry child, they can talk about the child's feelings (e.g., "I see that you are very angry that you cannot go outside now"). Expressing the child's emotion in words is an important first step toward enabling the child to recognize and understand the emotion. Once a teacher has helped children recognize their feelings of anger, the teacher can encourage them to label their feelings of anger verbally (e.g., "I'm mad that you took my truck"). In group situations, teachers and children can discuss what makes them mad and how they express anger. The Second Step curriculum (n.d.) provides details on how to lead a group discussion on anger. Reading children's books about anger, such as Mayer's (1983) *I Was So Mad* and Noll's (1991) *That Bothered Kate,* also assists young children in understanding this feeling. A safe emotional climate within the classroom is a prerequisite for holding discussions about anger.

Aggression and Conflict Resolution

As young children play with each other, acts of aggression and conflict are natural occurrences.[10] Preschoolers have the verbal and cognitive skills needed for conflict resolution; however, they also need emotional structures to support the negotiation of conflicts. In their day-to-day interactions with young children, teachers can promote the emotional development that is necessary for children to learn to resolve conflicts. Greenspan identified three emotional skills that are needed to resolve conflicts: "the ability to engage empathically with others and imagine oneself in their situation; the ability to picture symbolically one's own and others' intentions; and the ability to tolerate disappointment, which allows gray-area thinking" (1997, p. 237).

When a conflict does emerge, teachers can help children reconstruct the episode by encouraging them to express their feelings and intentions clearly. In situations in which a child is totally out of control, the teacher can state the child's feelings and intentions for him or her. As teachers clarify children's feelings and intentions, young children feel nurtured; nurturance is a prerequisite for caring for another. A child's capacity to understand and resolve differences emerges from within, and this capacity is possible only if the child has experienced care and understanding. For teachers to enter into children's experiences in this manner, they first need to be keen observers. When teachers do not see the actual conflict and must therefore respond to the conflict after its occurrence, they can only implement rules to end the conflict. This type of conflict resolution, where the teacher implements rules without helping children to understand their own and others' feelings and intentions, does not allow for developmental learning beyond obedience. Rule implementation as a means of ending children's arguments is demonstrated next:

> *Pam is preparing materials at the art area. Nearby four boys are playing with Tinker Toys. Another child, Rachel, enters the area wearing a floor-length formal gown. She squats to make a structure out of the Tinker Toys that looks like 10 lollipops on a stand. She then begins chanting, "A dollar ninety-five for one of these lollipops." Brandon takes two and pretends to give her money, then walks away as he pretends to lick the lollipops. Rachel calls to Brandon, "Give one to your kid." (In the meantime, no adults were observing the children's pretend play.)*
>
> *Michael walks about the rug area with his Tinker Toy spaceship as he makes motor sounds. When he comes to Rachel, he takes her lollipops from her, and Rachel yells, "I had it! NO! I had it!" Pam looks up, walks over to the children, and says, "Rachel, with your formal on, you need to be in the housekeeping area." Rachel immediately goes to the housekeeping area, removes the dress, and then goes outdoors. Pam returns to the art area.*

In this observation, Pam's reactive stance ended Rachel and Michael's conflict. Pam has not resolved the children's dispute; instead, she simply has ended it. Nor has Pam used the conflict as an opportunity for these children to understand what happened and why Rachel and Michael were feeling and acting the way they were. Instead, the smooth flow of group management took precedence over fostering children's emotional development.

Hyperactivity, Impulsivity, and Aggression

In the 1990s, early educators across America reported an increasing number of hyperactive, impulsive, and aggressive young children in their classrooms.[11] These patterns are typical of children with attention-deficit/hyperactivity disorder (ADHD). These patterns also can be triggered by anxiety, for example, when young children are experiencing consistent violence, maltreatment, or domestic violence; have no behavioral limits or consequences; or have minimal shared time with their parents.

Attention-Deficit/Hyperactivity Disorder

ADHD is a disability rooted in brain dysfunction. Karr-Morse and Wiley (1997) identified five basic behavioral problems involved in ADHD:

1. Lack of planning and thinking before acting
2. Inability to select what is important from what is not important
3. Easily distracted
4. Inability to maintain attention
5. Difficulty in self-monitoring how one is doing in a task

Following are two case studies describing the behavior problems of two children, Mitchell and Darryl. In both cases, these behavior patterns stemmed from the children's feelings of anxiety. When the children's anxieties were lessened through extra nurturing and attention, both boys began to demonstrate less challenging behavior. In the following description, Mitchell, a young boy who exhibits a great deal of aggressive behavior, is improving his behavior through the loving intervention and extra patience of one of his child care teachers.

> Mitchell, age 4 years, attends St. Paul's Day Care Center, which he began to attend at the age of 2. He is an attractive child who has superb large-muscle coordination. Until the age of 2½, Mitchell lived with his father and three uncles in his paternal grandmother's home. His mother, Sabrina, was stationed at an Army base in another state. When

Mitchell was 2½, his father was killed in a drive-by shoot-ing. Sabrina left the Army and returned home to care for Mitchell. She and Mitchell moved into an apartment in the housing project where Sabrina's mother and two siblings, ages 9 and 11, were living. Mitchell went to his paternal grandmother's home each Sunday. No one had told him that his father had died.

Mitchell's mother provided neither limits nor conse-quences for Mitchell's behavior. She was a full-time student and had two part-time jobs; thus, she did not spend much time with her son.

Mitchell refused to eat at home with his mother; thus, he ate all meals at his maternal grandmother's home. Sabrina's mother cared for him in the evenings while Sabrina attended college and on weekends, when his mother worked. While at his grandmother's, Mitchell watched videos and television with his 9-year-old aunt and 11-year-old uncle. His mother said that he would fall asleep watch-ing television each night between 11:00 and 12:00 P.M.

Mitchell's language was so delayed that adults at St. Paul's could not understand most of what he said. He was unable to participate in group activities. Throughout each day he was preoccupied with violent play. His favorite ac-tivity was banging together small play people. As he played he would hum to himself. If another child approached him, he would engage in unprovoked aggression. Other children either ignored or purposefully kept their distance from Mitchell. When a teacher tried to initiate play with Mitchell, he was unable to attend to the task. If he did not want to do what a teacher had asked, he had a temper tantrum. Teachers reported that when Mitchell wanted affection, he dove into their lap, head first.

When Mitchell began his fourth year at the center, he moved to a new classroom. One of his teachers, Lakrisha, let Mitchell shadow her throughout the day. Lakrisha and Mitchell engaged in a lot of spontaneous giving and receiv-ing of affection. She urged the other adults to avoid asking Mitchell to wait in line to use the bathroom, and she made other accommodations to simplify his day. Whereas previ-ously Mitchell never had initiated conversation, now he fre-quently talked to Lakrisha. Over a couple of months he learned to participate actively in group experiences, as long as he could sit next to Lakrisha. Slowly, he began to play with other children.

In the next case study, Darryl, a young boy with a very different background from Mitchell's, also is experiencing behavior problems related to feelings of anxiety and a lack of loving attention from a parent. Here, too, extra nurturing and attention served to lessen Darryl's challenging behavior.

Four-year-old Darryl attended Maple Hill Child Care Center since he was eight weeks old. Darryl's teachers reported that he was continually hyperactive and impulsive. The only time he remained at a task was during sensory play, such as playing with water or playdough. Teachers had difficulty helping Darryl follow directions and redirections. When they spoke to him, it was as though he had not heard them. He was rarely aggressive, though.

Bethany and Jon Lamb are Darryl's parents. They were both 18 when they had their first child, Andy. A year later their daughter, Amy, was born, and 10 years later Darryl was born. Both parents are successful professionals who each work at demanding jobs with long hours. Jon is an engineer, and Bethany works at a large travel agency. When Darryl's teachers expressed their concerns about Darryl to his parents, Bethany and Jon joined three other parents in an 8-week parenting group that I led.

Bethany reported that her corporation once had 400 employees but now has only 25. With the decrease in employees, Bethany's job was extremely exhausting and stressful. Darryl's siblings Andy and Amy were very involved in after-school activities, and each night Bethany was busy driving them back and forth to acting school, soccer, swim practice, and so forth. The Lambs did not eat dinner together; in fact, the scheduling in this family was almost never consistent, nor were there any regular joint routines. Bethany shared that she spent far more time with her first two children when they were young because then she was only working half time. In turn, both children are more even-tempered than Darryl.

At home Darryl was spending most of his time watching television and videos. His parents noted that he rarely follows their directions or redirections. Yet they were not with Darryl very much, and their lives were so hectic that they never slowed down long enough to focus on Darryl's behavior patterns.

Bethany took a month's leave of absence so that she could spend more time with her son. Rather than return to work after that month, she obtained another position that was less stressful. The family began eating meals together, and Bethany and Jesse developed rules and consequences for Darryl's misbehavior.

When Darryl was in kindergarten, Bethany called me to report on Darryl's progress. Although he seemed to be gaining the ability to remain focused on tasks, he continued to be quite impulsive. When his kindergarten teacher shared her concern with Bethany and Jon, they arranged for Darryl to attend weekly play therapy with a child psychologist whom I had recommended. Bethany reported that Darryl's therapy has triggered significant changes in his ability to manage.

Both Mitchell and Darryl had substantive behavior problems. Each child's behavior patterns are different, and each child lives in a very different family. Mitchell lives in a low-income family headed by a single parent, and Darryl lives in a two-parent, upper middle-income family. Yet each child has the same basis for their difficulties, anxiety stemming from lack of shared time with a parent, a lack of predictability, and few if any limits and consequences.

Teachers who care for children who are consistently hyperactive, impulsive, and/or aggressive can serve as a bridge to help families to recognize their child has a difficulty and then serve as a resource to help the family obtain professional assistance. As an early intervention specialist, I have worked with child care teachers and parents of children with behavior problems. The children's caregivers referred these families to me. Through the early intervention program, parents often were able to recognize that their child was having difficulties, and parents also often realized that they, too, were having difficulties. The early intervention program helped parents first, to recognize difficulties, second, to create new patterns at home and then, when necessary, to seek additional professional assistance. Some of the assistance I recommended to families included play therapy for the child, family therapy, occupational therapy evaluation, sensory integration therapy for children suspected to have regulation disorders, and speech-language evaluations and therapy for children suspected of having receptive language difficulties.

When child care programs serve children from low-income families who have Medicaid, child care teachers can suggest professionals who have gained Medicaid certification to help children and their families. It is also possible for a young child to get needed services at the center from a Medicaid certified professional. As such professionals work with the child, they also can meet with parents and teachers not only to give them information about the child's progress but also to suggest caregiving strategies to assist the child at home and at child care. Making professional services available at a child care program eliminates difficulties in accessibility, which often plague families with low incomes that typically are dealing with a very busy work schedule and poor transportation, and, in some cases, little family and social support.

CONCLUSION

A major theme of this book is that understanding self, other, and the everyday world emerges in babies' and toddler's everyday interactions with their caregivers. Babies act, and their caregivers respond. The response lets the babies understand that their actions have an effect on another person; that is, their actions have meaning. They enjoy interacting together throughout the day—talking, eating, playing, reading, and singing together. As caregivers talk and play with babies and very young children, the young children begin to develop an understanding of self, and the adult's sense of self expands. Both child and caregiver experience feeling accepted, understood, supported, and recognized.

This chapter has discussed factors critical to managing a group of babies and young children. When teachers have clearly arranged the equipment in the room and have a predictable schedule, they can create a warm and calm climate that allows children to interact with peers and adults positively. Teachers' clear rules of behavior and consistent enforcement of these rules allow children to develop emotional self-regulation. When teachers are keen observers, they can enter into children's experiences when conflicts emerge and thereby assist the children in using these conflicts to understand feelings and intentions. In reality, some children may be hyperactive, impulsive, and aggressive, and teachers will need to develop specific strategies for these children who have difficulties with self-regulation.

Out-of-home caregivers can assist babies and young children in learning to regulate their emotions so that they can attend to tasks, adapt to new experiences, and interact positively with adults and other children. Emotions are integral to our social experiences. Emotion regulation is not an independent task; instead, this ability develops when babies and young children are nurtured by emotionally available adults. Each child is born with a different disposition; yet, dispositions also are shaped by children's daily interactions with the adults from whom they are receiving care. The task of guidance and discipline is integral to each moment adults are with babies and young children because development and learning occurs in every moment of very young children's lives.

chapter 5

Play, Learning, and Development

If we examine how the word "play" is used and concentrate
on its so-called metaphorical senses, we find talk of the play of
light, the play of the waves, the play of gears, or parts of
machinery, the interplay of limbs, the play of forces, the play
of knots, even a play on words. In each case what is intended
is to-and-fro movement that is not tied to any goal that would
bring it to an end....The movement of playing has no goal
that brings it to an end; rather, it renews itself in constant
repetition.

—*Hans-Georg Gadamer (1993, p. 103)*[1]

What do we mean when we speak of play? Are we talking about having fun, playing a game, or having a high old time? Are we referring to experiencing lots of laughs and general merriment? Are we talking about a frolic or a caper? No doubt adults will use any of the above synonyms when describing play. *But what does play mean to babies and young children?* As Erikson wrote in 1950, play is young children's primary task. Erikson explained that adults' play is about *recreating;* that is, adults step outside their everyday work world to recreate, to feel restored through play. In contrast young children's play *is* their work, their primary means of acting and interacting (Erikson, 1950). When babies and young children play, we can see in their intense expression that they give no thought to passing time, goals, obligations, responsibilities, or any of the other "shoulds" in life. The play of babies and young children has an endless variety—sheer physical movement and playing with sounds, words, and/or rhythm. All materials—whether sensory materials such as mud, sand, or playdough; constructive materials such as blocks or Legos; dramatic play materials such as dress-up clothes; or balls and other motor materials—can be brought into a child's play world.

Without material props, young children can create a whole pretend world with their minds. But what is the purpose of this play? Children's play serves multiple purposes, including to enjoy exploring, experimenting, and inventing; to rehearse new understandings and skills; to think through and problem solve; to express and master feelings; to imagine and create; and to experience one's own worth in the process. As they play, babies and young children experience mastery and develop competence. Barbara Biber, a seminal early educator, portrayed the power of self-directed play:

> What do play experiences do for child growth? If a child can have a really full, wholesome experience with play, he will be having the most wholesome kind of fun a child can have. His early childhood play may become the basic substance out of which he lays down one of his life patterns: namely, that one not only can *have* fun but can create fun. . . . In dramatic play, children also find a sense of confidence in their own impulses. There are no directions to follow, no rules to stick to. Whatever they do will be good and right. Wherever their impulses lead them, that is the way to follow. This is the freedom children should have in their play, an absence of boundaries and prescriptions that we cannot grant them outside their play lives. (1984, p. 189)

What influences a baby or young child's play? No single, unitary influence can be identified; instead multiple influences interact within an environment. Ecological psychologists term these multiple environmental influences the *environmental press*. A baby's caregiver, the environment, the immediate neighborhood, the parents' support system or lack thereof, the parents' workplace or lack of employment all are part of the environmental press. Garbarino described the elements of an environment and the individuals within it as "mutually shaping systems, each changing over time, each adapting over time in response to changes in the other" (1989, pp. 20–21). Central elements of the environmental press in a child care setting include the setting, the materials and activities, and the babies' caregivers and peers.

Adult caregivers influence when children play as well as how and with whom they play. First, the caregiver provides the space, materials, and activities that invite babies and young children to play. Caregivers can influence children's play in myriad ways. The mere presence and availability of the caregiver can provide a stabilizing effect and help young children feel secure enough to initiate play activities. Caregivers can move in and out of children's play as observers and readers of the language of young children's behavior, influencing their play. The caregiver can try to clarify the meaning of a play sequence (e.g., "Your building is balanced very well") or extend the play by suggesting additional materials, such as small zoo animals, for the block construction or by providing stimulating ideas (e.g., "Who lives in the building?"). A caregiver can be a play partner and enter into the feeling tone of a child's play, providing shared enjoyment and connection for the child.

This chapter follows the developmental progression of babies and young children, from birth through 5 years of age. For each developmental period, the text discusses how babies and young children play; the meaning and purpose of this play; and how the environment, peers, and adults influence the children's play.

PLAY: BIRTH TO 17 MONTHS

Babies are curious by nature and relate to the world through spontaneous exploration. As they interact with their caregiver, whether the activity is feeding, diapering, or other child-rearing activities, babies most often engage in play that is initially exploratory. At birth, babies have a biological readiness for social interaction. Beginning on their first day of life, babies are able to begin and end social interactions by turning toward or away from a caregiver. What a baby finds pleasing and unpleasing governs how the baby interacts. The manner in which caregivers interact with a baby influences both the quality of the baby's play and how much the baby will learn through this play.

Eye Contact and Vocalizations

Babies love to look at people's faces. By age 8 weeks, they can differentiate people and interact differently with their mother, father, and their out-of-home caregiver. At 8 weeks they can vocalize socially, give more direct eye contact, and even smile—behaviors that encourage their caregivers to continue interacting with them. Eight-week-old babies are very interested in their bodies, other people, and small toys such as rattles. They love watching their hands as they turn them over and over in front of their eyes. Mobiles and cradle gyms set on the floor can be a source of great pleasure. When babies are in groups with toddlers, often a young toddler will enjoy moving the cradle gym for a baby or engaging in some other brief playful interaction.

By age 4 months, babies enjoy reaching for toys on mobiles or cradle gyms. Playful exploration is a part of feeding as they smear food over their faces and try to smear it on the highchair tray or on their caregivers. As babies master new vocal sounds they enjoy not only babbling to themselves but also playing vocal games with their caregivers, in which the caregivers playfully repeat the babies' sound. As babies and caregivers play vocal games, this vocalization motivates continued vocalization and provides a feeling a connectedness. They continue to explore their bodies and like to watch their hands and feet as they move them about.

First Toys

By 5 months of age, babies can transfer small objects from one hand to another. Now babies love to hold rattles or other small objects like measuring spoons or keys. Exploration and learning take place primarily through mouthing, touching, and fingering small objects. They bring objects to their mouth, explore them with their lips and tongue, and look at them by bringing them close to their eyes. Now movement becomes important; and although 4-month-olds cannot crawl, they love to roll back and forth and scoot themselves about, either because they enjoy the movement or they wish to obtain an object not quite within reach. By 6 months of age, most babies can creep about on their stomachs.

Each time caregivers engage in routine caregiving tasks, such as diapering and feeding, they can engage babies in playful interaction. Exchanging facial expressions and give-and-take vocalizing, swinging and making exaggerated gestures to capture the baby's attention, and singing are all wonderful ways to interact with a baby. For the very young, caregivers can provide mobiles and cradle gyms. Once babies are old enough to hold small objects, caregivers can provide a variety of small objects and toys, for example, small rattles, measuring spoons, hand-made net balls with a bell attached, lids, rings, and small film canisters. To ensure safety, only those objects that are too big to be swallowed should be given to babies. Babies love to turn these toys and small objects over and over, bang them, and put them in their mouth. This play practice fosters their eye–hand and motor coordination. As babies mouth, touch, and hold their toys, caregivers can describe their actions to them softly.

Play Involving Simple Locomotion

Although 5-month-old babies may not crawl, they like to scoot about on their stomachs. Often a caregiver can place an inviting toy out of the baby's reach to invite the baby to move forward to get the toy, as in the following observation.

> *Ashley's teacher, Alicia, places a wheel toy with three clowns inside on the floor and turns it around and around in front of Ashley (age 5 months). Alicia then places the toy just outside Ashley's reach. Ashley makes movements with her arms as if she were swimming. With effort she finally scoots to the toy so that she can move it.*

Alicia has encouraged Ashley to push herself forward; and, in this movement, Ashley gains success in reaching a new toy. When a toy is out of reach, the baby may initially be frustrated, but simple frustrations can motivate the baby's continued effort and learning as well as help the baby learn to tolerate small frustrations.

Babies this age like containers full of small objects, for example, a plastic sherbet container filled with measuring spoons, film canisters, lids, rattles, and so forth. As babies explore these objects, they will probably put everything into their mouths as their initial means of exploration. Once a baby has emptied the container, the caregiver often can revive the baby's interest simply by putting everything back inside. (Interestingly, when babies have lots of experience with feeling different textures inside their mouths they can more readily make the transfer from milk to different kinds of table foods.)

Interactive Play

By 6–7 months of age, babies can sit up alone, which is a major milestone. As they sit, they can play with toys in front of them. If they fall, they can sit back up again. By 8 months of age, babies can twist around and lean forward or to the side as they are seated. Once children can sit up, creeping or crawling about, their caregivers can provide extended play experience. Babies this age love mirrors; and as they look at themselves, they often try to get a response from their image or to reach out and touch themselves in the mirror.

> *Josh (age 7 months) is seated on the rug with his teacher, Carmeletta, and Cory (age 18 months) nearby. Josh picks up a square metal mirror and looks at himself. Carmeletta says to him, "Is that Josh?" Josh smiles as he touches his face in the mirror. He then points to Cory as Carmeletta says, "Shall we let Cory see himself in the mirror?" Carmeletta shows Cory the mirror as he says, "That's Cory!" and chuckles. Carmeletta then arranges herself, Josh, and Cory so that the children can see all three of their reflections in the mirror. Josh and Cory chuckle as Carmeletta says, "And there's all three of us!"*

Mirrors also are good for adult–child Peek-a-boo games. By 6–7 months, babies like playing motion sequence games such as Pat-a-cake and Peek-a-boo. Playing Peek-a-boo depends on a baby's mastery of object permanence, that is, being able to recognize the continued existence of a person or object when it is out of sight. Bruner and Sherwood discussed the learning involved in Peek-a-boo:

> It is quite plain, then, that complex expectancies are built up in the infant in the course of playing the game, and that these expectancies are characterized by considerable spatio-temporal structuring....the child very soon becomes sensitive to the "rules of the game" as he plays it. That is to say, he expects disappearance and reappearance to be in a certain place, at a certain time, accompanied by a certain vocalization,...the child not only learned procedures, but would have learned them in a way that is characteristic of rule learning, i.e., in a general form, with assignable roles, with permissible substitutions of moves, etc. (Bruner & Sherwood, 1976, p. 277)

The game of Peek-a-boo often varies, and yet babies continue to be able to understand and play the game, which is a sign of increased cognitive ability. Bruner and Sherwood noted that mothers often report that Peek-a-boo is a variation of a game they played with their babies when the babies were younger than 6–7 months old. The authors described this interaction as follows:

> [Mother and child play] a looming game in which the mother approaches the child from a distance of a meter or so, looms toward him almost making face-to-face contact, accompanying the close approach

with a "boo" or a rising intonation. Such looming produces considerable excitement, and when the loom is directly toward the face, a real or incipient avoidance response. (1976, p. 282)

Hiding toys under a small blanket or diaper is also great fun for babies this age and is a parallel game to Peek-a-boo. At 8 months of age, babies can use their thumb and forefinger to pick up small objects with a pincer grasp. Now picking up small objects becomes a game in and of itself. And, of course, everything continues to go into their mouth so it is a good idea for caregivers to ensure that the floor is as clean as possible. Now that babies can explore their world with their fingers, they also point to objects to engage their caregivers in their play. As caregivers hold babies, they will explore caregivers' faces with their thumb and forefinger. Language continues to be a play pastime. Babies not only use syllables such as "da," "ma," or "ba" but also are beginning to string them together into long sequences called *jargon talk*.

Once babies begin to crawl and walk, movement becomes a source of great joy. Babies love climbing in, out, and over just about anything (e.g., climbing into a tub of balls, climbing up steps and going down a toddler slide); pushing a toy lawn mower or vacuum cleaner; or just running about alone or with others. Schore pointed out that "developmental observers have noted that by 1 year-of-age stimulation-seeking exploratory play time may increase to as much as 6 hours of the child's day" (Schore, 1994, pp. 95–96). Schore asserted that "practicing period play experiences are an essential component of a growth-promoting environment....These experiences generate high levels of positive affect that facilitate further [central nervous system] structural growth" (p. 96). Play enhances "behavioral flexibility through an increase in neural interconnectivity" (p. 132). *In other words, play behavior triggers changes in cortical synaptic development.*

If a teacher initiates playing "Ring Around the Rosie," toddlers will play endlessly. In the early 1950s, child developmentalist Lois Barclay Murphy recorded observations of her 14-month-old granddaughter, which captured a toddler's delight in movement:

> She uses many different methods of getting around. She likes to walk and dance, but she creeps upstairs on her hands and knees at times, and in the yard, if she feels insecure on a piece of rough ground, she will use the sit-creep that she used before she could walk. Sometimes she plays kitty or doggie and crawls on all fours, more as a joke than as a method of locomotion. When she hears rhythmic music, she responds whether she is sitting or standing—keeping time with her back, swaying, waving her arms (which seems to be entirely her own idea; I do not know of her seeing anyone waving arms in a dance), jumping, or dancing in a circle on her own. "Being danced" by one of us is one of

the most gleeful things she knows. She loves any kind of rhythmic motion and flows into it with complete freedom.

When she is excited, Colleen bats her hands up and down on her highchair tray or makes jumping movements without getting her feet off the floor—that is, she feels like jumping up and down, but isn't quite secure or agile enough yet to go that far. (1997, pp. 35–36)

It is good to have very young babies who are not able to walk in the same classroom as those who are walking; young babies enjoy watching their older peers move about, and the older babies often enjoy nurturing the younger ones. Teachers can involve young and older babies in simple play sequences, as Joy, a teacher of children ages 8 weeks to 24 months old, demonstrates in the following observation:

> Joy sits in the rug area with three babies. She picks up a 6-inch ring and puts it in front of Casey (age 7 months) as she says, "Peek-a-boo, I see you."
>
> Casey smiles, takes the ring, and puts it in her mouth. Jesse (age 11 months) begins playing with a shape sorter. He picks up a shape as he says, "Bock."
>
> Joy responds, "Block. Can you put it in there?" And she points to the correct hole in the sorter.
>
> Jesse puts the shape into the box as Joy says, "You put it in the box. That's great!" She then puts her finger on another hole, and Jesse correctly places a circle in the hole.
>
> Joy exclaims, "You did it! Let's try the triangle." Jesse again succeeds as he smiles gleefully and bangs together two additional shapes.
>
> Mia (age 14 months) has stacked four plastic ladders together and shows her ladder to Joy. Joy uses her fingers to climb the ladder as she says, "I'm climbing Mia's ladder to the top. I hope I don't fall."

Joy and her co-teachers Alicia and Carmeletta observe and assist the young children in their care and are able to move in and out of the children's play as play partners. These teacher actions not only promote the children's play but also help these very young children to feel secure enough to play alone or next to another child in a purposeful and contented manner for extended periods of time. Children enjoy having their teacher enter into their play. As Joy engages in brief interactions with Casey, Jesse, and Mia, the children experience Joy entering into their experience and feeling tone; and they feel affirmed and connected.

Sensory Play

Carmeletta and Joy use a variety of materials such as water, sand, rice, and beans in the sensory table, which is available for use each day. This type of play is very soothing and fosters fine motor skills and eye–hand coordination. When a group of young children play at a sensory table, they also have the opportunity to refine their social skills. As children dump and pour with funnels and other implements, they learn about measurement and volume, as in the following example:

> *Blake (age 17 months), Mia (age 16 months), and Cory (age 13 months) are playing in water at the sensory table. They have no shirts or blouses on. In the sensory table are dolls and washcloths as well as a few plastic plates. The children have been playing with the water for about 15 minutes. Blake and Mia begin to pour water on their faces and on top of their heads.*
>
> *Carmeletta, who is seated at the sensory table with the children, takes a washcloth and lightly sprinkles water on each child's head. The children laugh happily in response.*
>
> *Later, Cory is playing with sand in the sensory table. Carmeletta sits next to him. Cory covers one hand with sand as Carmeletta says, "Whoa, your hand is missing!"*
>
> *Cory lifts up his hand and laughs. He then buries both hands in the sand as Carmeletta says, "Are both your hands missing?" Cory replies, "Yep."*
>
> *Mia is playing with shaving cream. Carmeletta asks her, "Daddy uses this when he shaves, doesn't he?"*
>
> *Mia answers, "Yes." Carmeletta draws circles in the shaving cream, and Mia makes big circular motions with her hands. Carmeletta then shakes each child's hand as she says, "Ooh, now all of our hands are covered." The toddlers laugh at the sensation of their sticky hands.*

Sensory play in family child care also can offer these rich opportunities. In the next observation, Sally uses a cardboard box on a sheet in her kitchen for children to play with sand, cornmeal, rice, or pasta.

> *Jamie (age 26 months) and Jason (age 34 months) are playing with cornmeal in a box in Sally's kitchen. Sally sits at the table close by. Jamie uses a coffee scoop repeatedly to put cornmeal into a plastic funnel. Jason uses another cof-*

fee scoop to put cornmeal into a plastic margarine tub. Jason dumps his cornmeal into Jamie's funnel and then pours cornmeal from one coffee scoop to another.

Jamie says several times, "I'm going to take a bath," and giggles as he pours cornmeal over his head. Jason does the same as he says, giggling, "I take a bath."

Sally joins in by saying, "You both are taking a bath. You're putting it on your head—right on your nose that time! Does it feel good?" The boys nod yes.

Jamie and Jason have fun with Sally in developmentally appropriate play. Sally descriptively affirms the boys' play as she describes their actions.

Teacher-Initiated Activities

Beyond merely being available, teachers have many opportunities to initiate play activities with babies. In the following observation, Alicia plays with four children ages 8–15 months old. Each child has a cardboard box and either plastic chips, Popsicle sticks, or empty film canisters.[2]

Alicia gives an open cardboard box containing several film canisters to Casey (age 9 months) and Emma (age 8 months). She then gives Marquis (age 13 months) another cardboard box with a hole in its lid and several film canisters. Alicia gives Ben (age 15 months) some Popsicle sticks and a cylinder with a hole in its top.

Ben begins tapping the side of his container with the Popsicle sticks. Alicia says, "Oh, you want to do it that way. Look at the noise you can make." Ben smiles and continues tapping the container. Alicia then puts a few Popsicle sticks in the container and shakes it as she says, "Listen, shake, shake, another sound that is not as loud."

Marquis, who is sitting next to Ben, has put several film canisters in his box. He begins shaking the box. Alicia encourages, "There you go, Marquis. I heard that." Ben then shakes his container, and it is as though Ben and Marquis have a little band. Casey and Emma are chewing on their boxes.

Ben then puts all of his Popsicle sticks into his box. Alicia asks Ben whether he would like to use a different box now, and he nods yes. Alicia gives him a new box and some plastic circles. Ben fills the box with the circles but returns to the Popsicle sticks and canister and begins the task a sec-

ond time. Alicia remarks, "These are your favorite aren't they, Ben?" Ben smiles as he nods yes.

Alicia then begins putting the film canisters into Emma's and Casey's boxes, and the babies begin a repetitive game of filling and dumping. Marquis meanwhile has put all his canisters into the box. Alicia asks him, "Would you like help opening your box?" Marquis nods yes, Alicia partially opens the lid, and Marquis then completes the task and begins the game again.

Alicia plays with these young children and their boxes for 30 minutes. Her presence no doubt allows Ben to remain at his task for a long time. While with these four children, Alicia is able to move in and out of quite a few roles, helping the young babies Emma and Casey play purposefully with their toys, giving Ben alternative materials, helping Cory begin a task, and descriptively affirming all the children's actions. Alicia, Joy, and Carmeletta are quick to take cues from their babies and toddlers during play activities, and they improvise together with the children to create something new.

PLAY: 19–36 MONTHS

Beginning around the age of 18 months, toddlers develop the ability to engage in symbolic thought; that is, they now can transform objects through their imagination to derive meanings different from the original object, person, or setting. This early form of symbolic thinking forms the foundation for later cognitive development and communication. Language develops within toddlers' exploratory play. Chapter 3 discussed the miracle of language and how very young babies and toddlers master language through experience and by trial and error. When toddlers engage in play, they often make grammatical combinations that are more complex than when they talk in practical situations during play (e.g., "If you give me your car, I'll give you my doll"); however, they cannot use the *if . . . then* grammatical form in everyday conversation with adults. Bruner described the interdependent relationships of play, language, and thinking as follows:

> There is a considerable role for playfulness in the child's mastery of the miracle of language. . . . mastered through try-out and experience . . . the mother tongue is most rapidly mastered when situated in play activity. . . . It is not so much instruction either in language or in thinking that permits the child to develop his powerful combinatorial skills, but a decent opportunity to play around with language and to play around with his thinking that turns the trick. (1983, p. 66)

In the following example, family caregiver Sally engages two toddlers in sculpting. It is easy to see the combined play, language, and thinking in this interaction:

> *Two toddlers sit at a table; each has a clump of play-dough. Jamie (age 22 months) fills the compartments of a muffin tin with playdough and puts the muffin tin on the toaster. He then tells Sally and Jason (age 23 months), "Cake done."*
>
> *Sally joins in the pretend play, saying, "Jason's birthday cupcakes are done." Jamie gives Jason the dough from one of the muffin tin compartments. He pretends to take a bite and grimaces. Sally asks, "Does that taste uggy?" Jason nods yes.*
>
> *Jamie rolls the rolling pin on his playdough and then makes small circles as says, "Cookies." Sally turns on the buzzer; the buzzer goes off in about 1 minute. Jamie says, "It's done. Let's eat."*
>
> *Meanwhile, Jason has been making balls and dough strips with the playdough "machine." Jason calls, "Dinner ready!" Sally replies enthusiastically, "Wow, spaghetti and meatballs!" She then gives each boy a "bite" of Jason's "spaghetti and meatballs."*

As Jason and Jamie play with Sally, they begin to develop meaningful language that is integral to their play sequences.

Social Role Play

As with language development, children's cognitive activity is also enhanced when they engage in creative play activities. In symbolic pretend play, the young child's experience is reshaped and assimilated in new ways into the child's memory schemas. Howes et al. (1995) conducted observational research on 840 young children from 10 months to $5^{1}/_{2}$ years old who were enrolled full time in center-based child care programs. The authors found that they could predict children's cognitive level from the children's participation in creative play activities, the security of their attachment to teachers, and teachers' positive interaction with the children. The child-initiated complex play that most often stimulated divergent and creative thinking involved block building and pretend play. Parents and teachers can assist young toddlers in both initiating and moving the pretend play along. Singer (1994) found that pretend play emerges earlier when caregivers actively participate with toddlers in pretend play and make-believe games, as in the following observation:

> *Trevor (age 2½ years) and Rosa (age 3 years) bring the doctor's kit into Sally's living room. Rosa has lifted up her shirt and put a doll on her stomach. Rosa tells her family child caregiver, Sally, "Let's pretend this baby is in my belly, and it's time for it to come out."*
>
> *Sally agrees, then Rosa tells her, "You have to take her out now."*
>
> *Pulling the doll from under Rosa's shirt, Sally announces, "Here comes your baby!" Rosa says, "It's a girl."*
>
> *"Yes, and she's so pretty," adds Sally.*
>
> *Trevor approaches as Rosa says, "Let's wrap her up. Oh, here comes the doctor to check her. It makes the baby cry."*
>
> *Trevor gives the doll a "needle" and then pats her on the back. "Okay, baby. Okay, baby," he says.*
>
> *Sally says, "Trevor, you made the baby feel better. She's not crying anymore. Good work!"*

Sally has cared for Trevor and Rosa for about 2 years. She has a rich array of toys that invite social role play, including a medical kit, dolls, dishes, and dress-up clothing. The children often use these toys to engage in pretend games. Rosa's language ability is more advanced than Trevor's, but they can engage in spontaneous role play as equals. And in play, Rosa stimulates Trevor to express himself verbally. When playing with Sally, these toddlers are able to develop those skills that naturally occur in healthy families.

When young children play, they are immersed in the process and are rarely attached to the results. Because they are focused on the process, they frequently switch their original plan or goal to explore new avenues according to their desires. Children between 18 and 36 months of age discover the joy of social pretend play. Toddlers who have had relatively stable peer groups in out-of-home child care can engage in simple social pretend play with their peers (Howes & Unger, 1989). Vygotsky (1978) explained how the child's individual development occurs within social interactions with peers and adults. As mentioned in Chapter 3, Vygotsky introduced the notion of the zone of proximal development (ZPD), "the distance between the child's actual developmental level as determined by independent problem solving and the level of potential development as determined through problem solving under adult guidance or in collaboration with more capable peers" (p. 86). In other words, adult–child or child–child play can extend a young child's skill and mastery of communication of meaning when their play is slightly in advance of the child's development. A more capable peer or adult can make it possible for the child to do things that the child could not do alone without help. As a result of practice with a peer or adult, the child masters the task. Interactions with more experienced play partners can promote toddlers' social pretend play. Caregivers like Sally can help organize the play sequence and then move in and out when appropriate to maintain the play. In the following vignette, Mattie helps Marva to remain focused on her pretend cooking.

> *Marva (age 25 months) begins playing in the housekeeping area. Using a spoon, she mixes an empty can of stewed tomatoes. As she plays, she talks to herself. Marva's teacher, Mattie, comes to the area and asks, "Marva, what are you doing?"*
>
> *Marva replies, "An ice cream float. You can have some."*
>
> *"Mmm, I love ice cream. Thank you. What kind of ice cream are you using?" asks Mattie. Marva says, "Chocolate...oranges and strawberries."*
>
> *Mattie asks, "Do you need to stir it for a long time?" Mattie responds, "Four minutes."*
>
> *Then Mattie asks, "And then what do you put into it?" Marva says, "Milk."*
>
> *"And when everything is in it, what do you do?" Marva answers, "Put it in the oven. I'm going to make a big doughnut."*
>
> *"And I know you love doughnuts!" exclaims Mattie.*

When children engage in social role play they can practice a variety of ways in which to use language. Marva's teacher asks her questions about Marva's cooking and thus helps Marva to think through her actions and engage in extended conversation. As they talk, Mattie is supporting and moving along Marva's pretend play. When children are younger than 3 years of age, they often need concrete objects to support their pretend play because their pretend play most often involves actions on objects, such as cooking materials, rather than verbal markers typical of older children (e.g., "Let's pretend that..."). Very young children take on familiar roles such as "being" babies, cats, or dogs; whereas older preschoolers are more likely to say, "Let's pretend to be [ship captains or firefighters]"—more distant roles.

Young children may not necessarily be playing out what they actually have experienced. They may instead be playing out the feeling that an experience has left them with because play can be an outlet for their emotions (Biber, 1984). Young children's desires, wishes, hopes, and fears are mirrored in the roles, conversations, and actions that occur within their pretend play.

Some young children's play themes indicate that they are experiencing substantive problems.[3] Curry and Arnard identified some warning signals that might alert a caregiver that a child has some substantive problems:

1) Preoccupation with a single play theme; monotonous, unchanging, repetition of a play theme

2) Highly unusual play themes (which can alert the adult that the child may be portraying a vivid experience uncommon to most children, e.g., jail, a parent's severe illness)

3) Play with a furtive, driven, excited, and explicit sexual quality and content

4) Excessive preoccupation with ordinary objects

5) Play showing a driven intensity, e.g., excessive rigidity in dramatic play, inability to change roles

6) Fluid, fragmentary play by a child older than 3 years of age

7) Inability to distance themselves from a play role and making aggressive attacks on other children by being rather than pretending to be the aggressor

8) Aggression that is annihilative rather than competitive (1995, pp. 6–8)

Role of the Teacher

Beyond interacting with children as they play, the teacher sets the stage for children's play. Whether a program is family or center based, arranging space into activity centers allows for clear organization of equipment and materials, which enables children to move from area to area and make choices. The roots of activity or learning centers stem from the work of 19th-century educator Pestalozzi and 20th-century educator Dewey, who believed that children learn through doing and direct interaction with their peers and environment. Two other critical forerunners of this movement are Montessori, with her carefully prepared environment and sensorimotor tasks, and the open education movement of the 1960s and 1970s (Myers & Maurer, 1987). The environment can be arranged to balance the more noisy activities, such as blocks and dramatic play, with the more quiet activities, such as science and reading. Although children are free to explore the materials, they also need rules, such as only a given number of children may play in the block or housekeeping area at one time. When materials are organized; accessible; and labeled clearly with pictures, words, and/or symbols, the children's response is likely to be purposeful. When children can choose their play activity, their learning is individualized. Greenberg spoke of the power of child choice as follows:

> Motivation cannot be laid on a child; motivation comes from the inside....If a child *chooses* to do it, she or he is making a commitment. Attention is focused. Learning occurs....learning levels can be individualized this way. Choice, complexity, and new challenges at the correct level of difficulty for the individual are essential in stimulating any child's brain....[Another] reason to let them choose what they will do, where in the room, and with whom, is that children learn many democratic skills during the process. (1987, pp. 50–52)

Outdoor Play

Given the long days that young children spend in family- and center-based child care, developmentally appropriate playgrounds are another essential feature of quality programs. The most basic materials to include in playgrounds are natural materials, such as sand, earth, water, plants, and animals such as rabbits and guinea pigs—materials that invite make-believe and construction, forms of play that foster cognitive growth. Structures such as climbers, swings, slides, and sliding poles foster physical development. Outdoor play also can be the context for music and organized games. In games, young children begin learning how to follow rules and how to both compete and cooperate. Teachers and young children can enjoy creating simple gardens, both flower and vegetable. Toddlers who plant and pick lettuce most often become hearty eaters of lettuce or other vegetables they have grown. The process is collaborative and involves social responsibility. Exploration outdoors can be a continuation of much of the indoor curriculum, for example, music, art, science, dramatic play, and block construction.

In outdoor play, movement can be a central activity that fosters development in all areas. As young children move about in the playground, whether on the climber, slide, or in the sandbox, they continually adjust their movements according to the other children playing around them; thus, consideration and cooperation become a part of the play process. As children cooperate in sand play, circle games, or climbing together, their feelings of self-esteem and belonging are enhanced. Often problem solving is part of movement exploration or sand construction. Similarly, creative self-expression is integral to a lot of outdoor play, whether in sand, block construction, or spontaneous social role play. Outdoors, teachers can initiate creative movement, such as acting out movements that depict emotions, occupations, or animals. As children move to different outdoor tasks, they are unleashing creativity and establishing relationships "between thinking and feeling or between mind and body" (Pica, 1997, p. 9).

Guidelines for safety need to be integral to playground use. Following is a recommended outdoor safety checklist. Teachers also can ensure children's safety by walking with them through the playground and talking with them about any potential safety hazards. Teachers can implement simple rules from the start, such as riding vehicles one way only and not throwing sand.

Outdoor Safety Checklist

- A fence (a minimum of 4 feet high) to protect children from potentially hazardous areas (e.g., streets, water)
- Eight to twelve inches of noncompacted sand, pea gravel, shredded wood, or the equivalent material in place under and around all climbing and moving equipment
- Resilient surface, such as firm matting, that is properly maintained (e.g., in place, noncompacted, free of debris)
- Equipment that is sized to the age group using it, with climbing heights limited to the reaching height of the children when standing erect
- No openings that can entrap a child's head
- Swing seats that are constructed of lightweight material with no protruding elements
- Moving parts that are free of defects (no pinching, shearing, or crush points; bearings that are not excessively worn)
- Equipment that is free of sharp edges, protruding elements, broken parts, and toxic substances
- Stationary equipment that is structurally sound, with no bending, warping, breaking, or sinking
- Large equipment that is secured in the ground and concrete footings that are recessed in the ground
- All safety equipment (e.g., guard rails, padded areas, protective covers) in good repair
- Area free of electrical hazards (e.g., unfenced air conditioners, switchboxes)
- Area free of debris (e.g., sanitary hazards, broken glass, rocks)

PLAY: 3–5 YEARS

Children's play activities offer a range of possibilities for learning and development. For example, puzzles and snap-together toys foster eye–hand and fine motor coordination and understanding of spatial relations. Board games enable young children to learn how to take turns, to cooperate, to understand rules, and to win and lose with grace.[4] Activities that allow children to construct and manipulate objects in a goal-oriented way, such as drawing, painting, and block construction, encourage young children to practice their cognitive and motor abilities. Social role play allows children to develop their representational abilities, use language, and enhance their social development as they practice perspective taking and negotiating with their peers.[5]

Research indicates that positive interactions with teachers during these creative, constructive activities influence children's competence. Kontos and Wilcox-Herzog (1997) conducted research that focused on three potential influences on young children's cognitive competence in play: teacher behavior, social context, and activity setting. The researchers observed 114 children, ranging in age from $2^{1}/_{2}$ to 6 years old, during free play. The authors classified children's activities in terms of cognitive "stretch," concentration, and perseverance as follows: *high yield*, such as art and constructive play (e.g., blocks, role play); *moderate yield*, such as manipulative toys (e.g., puzzles, Legos); and *low yield*, such as gross motor play. Findings indicated that cognitive competence during free play was most strongly related to participation in high yield activities. In other words, those play activities in which children create and construct are most strongly related to cognitive competence. Social competence was positively related to peer contact and teacher involvement; whereas teacher presence was a negative predictor of cognitive competence. Pelligrini and Jones (1994) found that teachers' presence provided the support necessary for young 2-year-olds' fantasy play; however, with older children, the teachers' presence seemed to inhibit fantasy play. Reciprocal interactions of peers facilitates play.

As young children continue to engage in social role play, their play increases in complexity. The 2-year-old uses a unit block as a telephone, whereas the 4-year-old uses the same block to make a complex hospital building. Howes, Unger, and Matheson clearly described the progression of play complexity with age:

> Initially, the function of the play is to master the communication of meaning. Once children are able to play pretend with a partner, the content of the play becomes more important and leads to the development of play negotiation skills. Issues of autonomy, control, and compromise underlie the negotiation of social pretend play. The function of pretend play becomes exploring these issues, and once these issues are resolved within social pretend play, the function of the play changes again. Social pretend play becomes an opportunity to explore issues of intimacy and trust. (1992, p. 133)[6]

Both Piaget (1962) and Vygotsky (1962, 1978) found pretend play to be central to young children's developing ability to use symbols. When young children engage in pretend play, they are able to mentally manipulate representations of objects, people, and settings that are stored in their mental schemas. Increasingly, they are able to use less realistic objects and make transformations with blocks, cardboard tubes, playdough, boxes, and so forth. This representational competence is a precursor of school-based literacy learning. Pellegrini and Jones noted that "in both reading and writing, children must learn that words, like fantasy play transformations, are meaningful representations of something else" (1994, p. 33). Singer argued that pretend play

> Is critical for developing in the child a full-fledged theory of mind, an airiness that one can manipulate toys or imaginary playmates and then gradually transform these into more general ideas....I propose, however, that a critical feature of such play is that the child, by manipulating toys that look only partly like real objects, by reshaping the story lines and by acting the parts of the different characters, is setting a firm foundation for developing the rich imagination that can be adaptive in adult life and is clarifying the distinction between reality and fantasy by learning how to manipulate and move into and out of the play role. The floor make-believe of a child, if suitably nurtured, can be a critical step for his or her ultimate mental development. (1994, p. 14)

Findings from Singer and Singer's (1990) studies of 3- and 4-year-olds indicated that the children who engaged more often in pretend play were more persistent, engaged in more cooperative play, and were less likely to be angry or aggressive. As children make believe in their social role playing, they create, learn to think divergently, and learn to solve problems that emerge in the play. This flexibility in thinking enhances children's ability to relate to their peers. Social role play involves developing skills in negotiation, such as choosing individual roles; perspective taking (e.g., seeing how another child understands what being a mother means); and conflict resolution, for typically the children resolve the conflicts because they want to continue their enjoyable playful interaction.

Friendship Patterns

Literature on young children's friendship patterns indicates that those children who have stable friendships engage in sustained and more mature social role play than do their peers (Damon, 1977; Selman, 1980). In my 6-month observational study of Rosehill Day Care Center, the children who engaged in the most frequent and complex social role play were close friends. That is, these children chose to spend most of their free playtime engaged in activities together, as in the following example.

Outside on the playground, Rachel and her best friend Nancy (both age 4 years) are climbing on the climber. Nancy suggests, "You be the dog, and I'll be the big sister." Rachel agrees and Nancy says, "Okay, Furry, you can go outside now." (Rachel climbs off the climber.)

Nancy continues, "I got to go to school now. Stay home with mommy; then I'll pick you up and show you my teachers. Now lay down, Furry." Rachel lies down on the sand under the climber. Nancy says, "I'll get my books," and she picks up two sticks and begins to walk toward the swings until Jessica (age 3 years) approaches her. Jessica asks Nancy, "What am I?" Nancy replies, "Furry." Jessica says, "I want to be the girl cat." And Nancy answers, "Okay, sit, Furry."

Nancy directs her friends, saying, "You [Rachel] are the dog, and you [Jessica] are the cat." Rachel and Jessica begin crawling across the sand area as a dog and a cat. Then all three girls walk about the playground until Nancy says, "Let's go home." As they get close to the climber, Jessica and Rachel begin crawling like a dog and cat again. Nancy says, "Mommy said she was getting home from work late, so I better start dinner." Nancy goes to the bridge on the climber to prepare dinner as Jessica and Rachel crawl about the sand making dog and cat sounds.

This play sequence continues for another 10 minutes. Nancy and Rachel have been favorite companions for about 1 year. They often choose to engage in social role play in the housekeeping area indoors; and, with play equipment, their sequences become quite complex as they negotiate roles and actions. Jessica, a year younger, has discovered Nancy and Rachel's rich play during early and late care (6:30–9:00 A.M. and 3:30–6:00 P.M.); and they readily allow her to join them. When outdoors, Nancy and Rachel can continue their social role play without any props, a skill many of the other children in this center have not yet mastered.

Howes, Matheson, and Wu (1992) compared aspects of social pretend play of four groups of 3- to 5-year-old children who had four different patterns of friendship. The friendship patterns of these children were 1) children who had, over several years, maintained long-term friendships; 2) children who currently were friends; 3) children who had friends but were not paired with them; and 4) children who had no friends. Results indicated qualitative differences in social pretend play among these four groups of children. Children who were friends explored issues of self-disclosure, intimacy, and trust in their pretend play, which were missing from the pretend play of children without friends.

Role of the Teacher

The teacher's role in young children's play and learning can be complex and incorporates multiple forms of interaction:

- To *observe* without direct interaction
- To *support*, for example, providing descriptive affirmation: "You used three colors to paint all over your paper!"
- To *initiate*, for example, inviting three children to play a board game
- To *direct*, for example, orchestrating a tumbling session with eight children indoors
- To *instruct*, for example, teaching the rules of a new board game to three children
- To *extend*, for example, providing toy zoo animals for the children's block construction
- To *help resolve disputes*, for example, suggesting alternative roles when children are arguing
- To *clarify*, for example, talking about the balance, shape, and size of a block construction
- To *be a play partner*, for example, taking on a role in children's pretend play

As mentioned previously, when caregivers enter into children's play as partners, the children feel affirmed and achieve a sense of connectedness.[7] In the following vignette, family caregiver, Sarah, plays with Candace, Mimi, and Josie, whose home environment inhibits the children's active play. At home, there is neither space nor toys for play; and their young mother spends much of her time watching television soap operas while their father is at work. These three sisters live with their young parents in a one and a half–room trailer that is situated next to corn fields.

> *Family child caregiver Sarah, Candace (50 months), Josie (36 months), and Mimi (28 months), are role playing. Candace and Josie wear white medical gowns. A doctor's kit, three dolls, bandages, and chairs arranged as beds surround Sarah, who is seated at the kitchen table.*

Candace gives her doll a shot, and Sarah remarks, "Oh, your baby is sick again." Candace nods yes; then she takes the bandage and wraps it around the doll's arm with Sarah's assistance. Candace explains, "She was swinging too fast and fell."

Mimi brings her doll and another bandage to Sarah, who asks, "Which is sore, her foot or her leg?" Mimi replies, "Her foot." Sarah helps Josie put the bandage around the doll's foot.

Candace lays her doll down as she says, "She is not feeling better."

Sarah answers, "You better give him some aspirin." Candace pretends to give her doll an aspirin from the empty pill bottle.

Sarah asks Candace, "Is this the hospital?" Candace nods yes. Sarah then talks into the toy telephone, "Hello, hello, you want to talk to the nurse?" She then asks the children, "Who is the nurse, and who is the doctor?"

Candace replies that she is the nurse, and Mimi and Josie say that they are doctors.

Sarah hands Candace a doll as she says, "The woman on the phone said her daughter cut her finger with a knife."

Candace answers, "I fix it," as she puts a Band-Aid on the doll's finger.

Mimi brings Sarah the syringe, and Sarah shows her how to pretend to fill it with medicine and then give the doll a shot. Mimi takes the syringe and pretends to give her doll a shot of medicine.

The medical play sequences of Sarah, Candace, Mimi, and Josie lasted for 40 minutes. Going to the doctor and getting shots can be very scary to young children. By role-playing being doctors and nurses, these young children can work through their feelings about going to see doctors and nurses in real life. As Sarah joins these young children's play, she is able to provide support through assisting and extending their play. Practicing a variety of ways to use language is integral to these children's social role play. In the year that Sarah has cared for these children, they each have made large strides in language and communication.

During the course of each day, teachers strive to provide a balance of child-initiated and teacher-initiated play and learning. Some teachers can be too laissez-faire, with the children always playing on their own, without adult guidance or support. Given the rich array of toys in many programs in the United States, children can play for extended times with no adult involvement except for management purposes. Children left to play by themselves, however, miss many opportunities for learning and development. Some teachers can be too directive, and they become intrusive and do not adapt to individual differences or children's interests and needs.

During small-group activities, teachers often initiate and direct children's activities; for example, when each child has a tub of small cubes, the teacher can suggest taking a number of cubes in and out to form different sets. Myers and Maurer described how teachers can instruct in exploratory learning centers:

> Following a teacher-presented experiment in which a cork, a rock, a coin, and a piece of wood are tested to see whether each will sink or float, children may extend the possibilities beyond the initial four items. The presentation thus becomes a model for the children's free exploration. In the presentation, the teacher may want to model attitudes, words, and behaviors she believes are desirable for the children to incorporate in their explorations, but the critical factor is that the children redesign the experiment by extending the set of objects tested. (1987, p. 25)

Often one thinks of free play as being totally child initiated; but as Myers and Maurer illustrated, teachers have opportunities to initiate and instruct not only in group periods but also during free play.

Outdoor Play

Previously, the value of children's having periods of outdoor play each day was emphasized, and the nature of a developmentally appropriate playground was explained. With children between the ages of 3 and 5 years, outdoor play can offer an opportunity for the children to engage in "rough-and-tumble play." Jones identified the movement patterns typical of preschoolers' outdoor play: "running, chasing and fleeing; wrestling, jumping up and down with both feet together . . . beating each other with an object but not hitting" (1976, p. 355). Jones noted that on the surface, this rough-and-tumble play may look very hostile; however, participants' roles change quickly. Moreover, the activity is accompanied by laughter, not by the frowning that is characteristic of hostile behavior. In other words, the rough and tumble does not evolve into real attacks.

Teachers frequently "clump" together during outdoor playtime to chat and do not focus on their children playing on the outdoor equipment. Given their long days with very young children, center-based teachers' desire to chat together and relax is understandable. If for no other reason than safety, however, teachers should continue to observe the children. In addition, they have multiple opportunities to interact with the children and enrich or extend their play, as is illustrated next:

> Six 3- and 4-year-olds are outdoors with their teacher, LaKrisha. Everyone has one foot on a tire sitting on the playground; and they are singing one verse of the song, "If You're Happy and You Know It." After each verse, LaKrisha gives the children a movement directive, such as run around, or stomp your feet, or swing your arms. After several sequences of this spontaneous game, LaKrisha and the children play "Hokey Pokey."

Young children benefit from outdoor play in the morning and afternoon, when weather permits. Often teachers do not enjoy being outdoors when it is between 30 and 50 degrees, but adults and children dressed appropriately can use outdoor play as a wonderful opportunity to engage in play that is not available indoors.

> Ricky (age 36 months) runs to the garage and Nancy (age 37 months) follows him as they both laugh. Family caregiver Jean tells Ricky, "Hide by the tree." Ricky runs to the tree and stands next to it. Nancy also runs to the tree. Both of them run back to the garage and then back again to the tree.
> Jean asks, "Where are you Ricky and Nancy?" Both children giggle and run to the garage. Jean says, "I'm hiding from you. Can you find me?" (She is hiding behind the tree where the children had been hiding.) Ricky and Nancy walk toward the tree trying to be very quiet. As they come to the tree, Jean comes out from behind it and the children follow until they see her. Everyone laughs. The children run to the garage, and the spontaneous sequence of Hide-and-Seek continues.

Ricky and Nancy have been in Jean's care for 2½ years. They are playing in Jean's yard on a chilly February afternoon, but both children are dressed warmly. Jean understands that the children she cares for need a balance of quiet and active play, and outdoors offers the best array of opportunities for active play.[8] In their outdoor play, both the children and their caregiver, Jean, improvise and create new scenarios in which to act. The children not only have an opportunity to engage in rigorous play, but they also experience shared enjoyment with each other and with Jean.

Superhero Play

Because of the many hours that a large number of young children now spend watching television and videos, superhero play has become a fact of life. Given the prevalence of superhero play, teachers are confronted with dilemmas. They may be concerned for the safety of the children and acknowledge the violence implicit in much of the superhero play; banning superhero play, however, may deny them the opportunity to teach their children about safety. Furthermore, children need to master feelings about power, which are depicted in superhero play; role playing being a superhero might assist some young children to express their anger and aggression in a healthy way. Boyd (1997) suggested that superhero play can be seen as a strand of rough-and-tumble play. Both types of play involve fantasy, chasing, and wrestling. Boyd noted that research on rough-and-tumble play suggests that this type of play may be developmentally important for young children. Rough-and-tumble play facilitates forming and maintaining friendships, maintaining and improving one's ranking with peers, and developing social skills (Boyd, 1997). Each teacher can determine his or her comfort level with superhero play. If teaching children younger than 3 years of age, a teacher may choose to ban the play because it provides no constructive purpose. Some teachers may ban superhero play indoors but allow it outdoors, where children have more opportunity to engage in rigorous movement. Because American culture is immersed in violence, each teacher needs to take time to reflect carefully and make a well-considered decision on her or his position regarding superhero play.

CONCLUSION

Learning and development are embedded in the play experiences of babies and young children. Learning and development occur in every moment of the lives of babies and young children, regardless of the activity, environment, or people involved. As babies and young children develop, they gain mastery and develop a sense of competence through play. Teachers can influence not only when children play but also how and with whom they play.

From the beginning, babies and young children are curious and active explorers. Given babies' readiness for social interaction, teachers' interaction influences both the quality of a child's play as well as the learning and development possible in the play. Teachers have endless possibilities for playing creatively with the children in their care—initiating a play sequence, responding to a child's initiation, clarifying and extending a child's play sequence, adding playful interactions in routine caregiving activities, introducing myriad play materials and activities, being a play partner, and so forth. An activity does not have to be "play" explicitly to involve playful interaction. The more keenly a caregiver can observe young children, the more opportunities he or she will see to initiate playful interactions. Beyond interacting with children, teachers also set the stage for children's play. Provision and arrangement of space and materials enable young children to move from area to area, make choices, and engage in extended play activities, activities that promote their development in all areas—emotional, social, language, intellectual, and physical.

chapter 6

Social Environment Problems that Have an Impact on Relationships in the Child Care Setting

This uniqueness transforms the minus of the handicap into the plus of compensation.

—*Oliver T. Sacks (1996, p. xvii)*[1]

Many babies and young children with social environment problems enter family- and center-based caregiving settings, which can result in maladaptive development as well as difficulties in the children's relationships with other children and the caregiver. This chapter discusses the environments that place babies and young children at risk of unhealthy adaptation and create challenges for their out-of-home caregivers. The chapter describes the difficulties of babies and young children living with *psychologically vulnerable families* and closes with a discussion of the resilient child.

When a family is vulnerable psychologically, the children and parents are at risk for having increased *internal* and *external* problems. Internal problems include psychological illness and substance abuse, and external problems include unemployment and inadequate housing. A difficult home environment, however, does not always mean the child will be unhealthy. Thus, it is important for teachers to be dual minded; that is, it is important that teachers not assume or expect that a baby or young child brings problems into the child care program just because of the child's sociocultural environment. Teachers also need to be aware, however, of the potential problems a difficult home environment can create, and they need to be prepared to work with babies and young children who bring problems into the caregiving setting.

Throughout the United States, many families live with high levels of chronic stress. A significant number of these families are coping with more than one stressor, such as low income, parental mental illness, domestic violence, substance abuse, and other difficulties. Given this reality, it is not surprising that many family- and center-based child caregivers are confronted with babies, young children, and parents who have significant problems. Every baby and young child learns to adapt to his or her environment. Healthy development involves adaptation, but some adaptation also can be a limitation. It may be a good thing for a young child living in a violent environment to be fearful. To live a life based on fear, however, seriously inhibits the number of possible trusting relationships a child may have. Jeree Pawl (1997) stated "Babies learn to adapt, but it may mean they never do the tango, only the two-step. And in reality, lots of people never learn to do the tango, only the two-step." A baby's adaptation to a violent home environment may be self-protective for the baby, but this adaptation may severely limit the baby from experiencing his or her full range of potential.

Most early educators would like to ensure that their caregiving environment serves as a protective refuge from the daily stress that some children and their parents face. Prior chapters discuss strategies to address some of the problems children experience such as aggression, hyperactivity, impulsivity, or depression—problems that often emerge when families have multiple stresses. A clearly organized, emotionally safe caregiving environment, for example, can be a protective factor for these babies and young children. Although this book suggests some effective strategies, there are no quick and easy guaranteed techniques with which to address the multiple problems some babies and young children may bring to out-of-home child care.

A focus on inner experience is the most effective tool teachers can bring to their work with babies and young children who have problems. Teachers can focus on the children's feelings and on the teacher's own inner experience—that is, what each of them is feeling inside. When a baby does not respond or when a toddler has a tantrum, teachers can ask themselves, *What is this child feeling? What is the child trying to express?* At the same time, teachers need to consider *how their experiences with children make themselves feel.* How does it feel to be vulnerable? How does it feel to be angry? How does it feel to be helpless? When teachers are aware of how they are feeling, they can use their emotional response as a tool to decide whether and how to intervene. When a parent or a young child makes a teacher angry, the teacher can learn to recognize the anger as a signal that something is wrong. The teacher then can use the energy from her anger to marshal her skills to be patient, nurturing, and respectful in a way that helps the child. A teacher can recognize, for example, that a child's tantrum has gotten in the way of the teacher's running a smooth small-group activity, causing her to feel disorganized and upset. The teacher needs to monitor her anger and strive to support the upset child calmly. As the teacher interacts with a difficult child, she can ask herself the following: Is my inner tension causing me to be sharp with this child, which only serves to increase the child's anxiety and tantrum? When teachers are not aware of their feelings, they let their feelings control them, leading to an increasing feeling of incompetence. When teachers are aware of inner feelings, they can move back and forth from inner experiencing to outer behavior and interaction. Focusing on internal experiences is quite complicated. A teacher who focuses on the internal experience—her own, the children's, and the parents'—possesses multiple, high-level analytic skills, such as the following:

- The teacher respects individual differences concerning internal as well as external experiences. For example, two babies may respond differently to hearing the same sound.
- The teacher strives to understand the uniqueness of every child and every parent.

- The teacher asks herself what kind of impact she is having on a child and what kind of message she is conveying to the child.

- The teacher recognizes that behavior follows expectation, that if the child understands what the teacher expects, the child's behavior can change over time.

- The teacher accepts that changes in a child's or a parent's feelings and behavior take time. The teacher understands likewise that building a trusting relationship with children and parents also takes time.

Babies are born with the ability to establish interpersonal relationships. They seek connection with their caregivers. Children who are vulnerable and at risk also push for connection, although connecting back to them can be difficult. Caregivers serve children as "mirrors, mirrors that tell babies what people think of me, and windows to the world, how other people are feeling and acting" (Pawl, 1997).

Unfortunately, the education of some child care teachers may have focused mainly on activities, scheduling, and lesson planning and not on how teachers can understand their own internal experiences or those of the young children in their care. The task is, then, for child care teachers to learn to read their own and the children's *internal experiences*. Attending to inner experience is a learnable skill. First, the teacher can *pay attention to the baby or young child's facial expression*—the most vivid sign of feeling. Is the baby's facial expression flat? Does the baby look sad? For the very young baby, the teacher can try to identify what the movements of the baby's feet, hands, and torso are saying in response to the teacher's caregiving. Second, a teacher can *watch a child's behavior in different contexts, with different people, and at different times.* With this observational data on the child's inner experience, the teacher can devise strategies that change the child's pattern and open both teacher and child to a closer connection and bond. In what situations, with what people, during what time of the day does this child have the most difficulty? When is the child most at ease? For example, DeVonne was usually the most difficult after a nap, before his parent or a baby sitter picked him up. Because DeVonne's home is very unpredictable and chaotic, he is anxious about leaving his child care center. Once DeVonne's teacher recognized this pattern, she decided to provide extra one-to-one time and soothing activities before he left the center to assist DeVonne in feeling more secure with this transition. Because of the large amount of maintenance work in child care (e.g., ensuring that all toys are clean, preparing food and feeding babies, changing diapers and clothes), the babies or young children can get lost in a teacher's priorities. That is, the children may not be the center of their teacher's attention. It is critical to ask for how many babies the teacher is caring. For children 3 months of age and younger, ZERO TO THREE: National Center for Infants, Toddlers, and Families (Lally et al., 1995) recommended a class size of six to eight children and a one-to-four caregiver–children ratio. The number of caregivers in a baby's life also has an impact on the baby's development. Every baby needs to have *one person aside from a parent who really understands and responds to the baby.* For optimal, healthy development, every baby and young child needs to be the "center of the universe," as Jeree Pawl (1997) explained, "the center of what is going on, not 'dancing around the edges.'" Admittedly, it is much easier for a baby or young child to be a central part of everyday living within the home than within the child care setting. If centers are adequately staffed, however, and if the staff focus on the child and their relationships with the child, every child can be the center of the universe.

When teachers work with young children and parents whose cultural backgrounds are different from their own, one of their first priorities is to develop bridges between themselves and children and their families. How can a teacher of young children affirm and include all children, regardless of cultural or class differences? Here are some practices that early educators have developed to help all young children and their families feel affirmed and included in the child care program:

- Create a welcoming, friendly, "homelike" environment. For example, display pictures of children and their families at a level where children can see them, and laminate the pictures so that children can touch them.

- Make pictures and materials available that reflect the cultural backgrounds of children and their families.

- Maintain a message board that tells parents about the children's day.

- Provide toys and books representing a variety of cultures that are accessible to the children, and store them in the same places so that the children know where to find them. Allow time to greet each family in the morning and to say good-bye to them each afternoon.

- Ensure low child–adult ratios and small group sizes.

- Observe all of the children, and try to understand them as individuals.

- Ensure that a wide variety of materials are available so that each child can experience quiet, peaceful play.

- Individualize the curriculum for each child so that all of the children can be successful.

- Read stories and display pictures depicting cultures represented by the children in the program.
- Invite parents to tell stories and share cultural practices that reflect the lifestyles of their families.
- Talk about and celebrate with the children the holidays of each culture represented within the program.

Regardless of the class, race, or religion of the children and families with whom teachers work, teachers can relate to each child and parent as a unique individual, different from every other individual. Knowing that each child and family may have different attitudes, values, and behaviors, teachers can strive to understand their experiences and lifestyles. The more teachers understand themselves and their own cultural patterns, the more they can understand and work with others. As they work with children and families from different cultures, teachers can attend to the nonverbal as well as the verbal communication and strive to focus on strengths rather than that which seems atypical to them.

FAMILIES THAT ARE PSYCHOLOGICALLY VULNERABLE

This section addresses the issues and concerns of families that are psychologically vulnerable and the effect of such a family situation on the children involved. In particular, the following family issues are discussed: marital discord and divorce, mothers' mental illness, parental substance abuse, community and domestic violence, and child maltreatment.

Marital Discord and Divorce

Family relationships are the first context of development. As discussed in Chapter 1, a baby and young child's relationship with parents becomes internalized as the child develops. As the parent–baby relationship matures, the baby continues to acquire internalized memories that help to stabilize the relationship itself. Reiss clarified this dynamic as follows:

> The pivotal concept in this perspective is that not only are the coherence, stability, and substance of the relationship represented by these internalized structures, but the stability and coherence of the relationship itself may be located and conserved through time by such structures. In sum, this perspective, although it considers a range of mechanisms, highlights internal representations as a source of stability in relationships. (1989, p. 192)

Given the pivotal impact of parent–child relationships on the child's developing self, parental stress and even absence can lead to young children's having problems.

As a result of long-term social, economic, and demographic changes in American society, the American family has changed dramatically. Since the mid-1980s, the divorce rate in America has been approximately 50%. Yet approximately 70% of divorced adults in the United States seek to remarry (Carter, 1988). The uncomplicated family as depicted on television programs from the 1950s, such as *Ozzie and Harriet* and *Father Knows Best*, is a myth.

Child care teachers inevitably work with families experiencing marital discord, separation, or divorce. Children from intact families with chronic marital discord frequently have more behavioral problems than children from separated but conflict-free families (Pellegrini & Notarius, 1988). Parents immersed in marital discord may be less emotionally available to their young children. Belsky, Woodworth, and Crnic (1996) examined the consequences of troubled family interaction. The researchers observed 64 families rearing their firstborn sons in the child's second year of life and again in the child's third year of life. The children's externalizing problem behavior (e.g., anger, aggression, non-compliance, hyperactivity) at 3 years was related to the chronicity of troubled family interaction. The authors found that "it is not 'troubled' family interaction at any particular time during the toddler years that principally fosters the development of problematic child behavior, especially of the externalizing variety, but rather the chronicity of such experience" (p. 480).

Divorce is a transitional process, not a legal relationship, and young children are an integral part of the process. Every divorce involves stress and many changes for each family member, some expected and others not expected. Family systems theory posits that the behavior of each family member affects the behavior of every other family member (Kerr & Bowen, 1988). Separation and divorce lead to disruptions in each individual's relationships with family members. A family is like a mobile; move one piece, and the entire mobile moves.

Babies and young children are bound to suffer when their parents separate and/or divorce. Even when marital discord occurs in the original family, young children dream of having their parents together with them again. Very young children especially have difficulty understanding their parents' separation and divorce. When one parent leaves, a young child might wonder, "If one can leave me, will the other also?" or "Will the parent who left still love me?" Very young children do not have a clear understanding of fantasy and reality or the ability to differentiate clearly between self and other. Thus, a young child might feel somewhat responsible for his or her parents' separation and divorce, wondering, "Did the parent leave because he (or she) doesn't love me?"

A young child whose parents are having marital difficulty or are separated may regress and, for example, resume bed wetting, have sleep difficulties, suddenly be intolerant of frustration, or cling to adults. Teachers can help by offering a listening ear, reliability, support, and nurturing. They can reassure children that they are not to blame for their parents' difficulties. And they can protect the children from their fear of desertion. Reading picture books about divorce also can help young children gain an understanding of their pain.

McHale and Rasmussen's (1998) longitudinal research provided evidence that young children's adjustment problems can be traced back to subtle indices of family stress from 3 years previous. The authors observed 37 couples at play with their 8- to 11-month-old babies. Preschool teachers then rated child behavior 3 years later. Relationships during the play sessions indicated high levels of hostility and competitiveness, low family harmony, and high parenting discrepancies. Greater hostility and competitiveness and low family harmony forecasted child aggression, and parenting discrepancies seen in the original observation predicted greater child anxiety as rated by teachers. In other words, 4-year-olds had behavior problems that reflected disturbed family relationships.

Mothers' Mental Illness

Constantino defined *mental illness* as "the relative inability (assuming physical health and a reasonable living environment) to experience fulfillment (or happiness) in self, in work, and in love" (1993, p. 3). Babies and young children can be at risk if either of their parents has mental illness. This section, however, focuses on mothers' mental illness because the vast majority of research focuses on the mental illness of mothers, who are usually primary caregivers. A mother's mental illness does not necessarily lead to inappropriate parenting and resulting child difficulties. For some mothers, the bond with their child may be the most stable part of their life. Yet the task of child rearing can be more difficult for a mother dealing with mental illness. In the second half of the 20th century, research has indicated that child rearing by a parent with mental illness may create developmental risks for the child through both genetic and environmental factors (Constantino, 1993).[2] Risks should not be surprising because when a mother is emotionally unavailable, she probably is also physically unavailable. For example, the preverbal interaction between baby and mother often taken for granted in routine caregiving may not exist:

> A depressed mother may be acutely aware of her baby's developmental needs, but may not have the energy to maintain an active and stimulating interaction with him or her. A psychotic father may recognize his children's need for structure but may not be able to maintain consistent limits in dealing with their behavior. A personality disordered

parent may be very invested in a child, but may have difficulty distinguishing his or her own needs from those of the child. A parent with an anxiety disorder may be too internally focused to be emotionally available to his or her children. Through complicated chains of events, all of these situations can result ultimately in frustration, in intense dissatisfaction with the role of being a parent, and in a consequent disruption of the emotional connection between a parent and a child. (Constantino, 1993, p. 4)

Depression is the most common mental illness among mothers of young children. Symptoms of depression include a negative mood, loss of pleasure, low energy, apathy, problems with sleep and appetite, and negative views of self. Women are twice as likely to be at risk for depression as men are. Women are susceptible to developing depression immediately after the birth of a child; depression during this time is termed *postpartum depression*. Postpartum depression occurs in 10%–20% of women. Factors beyond pregnancy and childbirth may contribute to postpartum depression, such as problems with the marriage or other strains such as inadequate social supports, economic strains, or having a child with a difficult temperament (Goodman & Radke-Yarrow, 1993).

How does depression affect parent–child interaction? Depressed mothers express very little positive and a great deal of negative emotion. Often their young babies develop emotional and behavioral regulation by repeatedly using their mothers' facial expression; that is, many babies of depressed mothers have a depressed affect themselves. Research indicates that depressed mothers' parenting often is impaired in ways that may be problematic for their children's development (Berkowitz & Senter, 1987; Dodge, 1990; Murray, 1992; Seifer & Dickstein, 1993). Rutter summarized the literature that describes depressed mothers' difficulties in interacting with their young children as follows (1990):

- The mother's depressed mood may lead to her baby mirroring this depressed affect (Field, Healy, Goldstein, & Guthertz, 1990; Zahn-Waxler, Ianotti, Cummings, & Denham, 1990).

- A depressed mother may be less aware of and slower to respond to her child's cues and needs (Bettes, 1988; Cox, Puckering, Pound, & Mills, 1987; Stein, Bucher, Gath, Day, Bond, & Cooper, 1989).

- Depressed mothers may inappropriately use their baby as a source of comfort (Radke-Yarrow, Richters, & Wilson, 1988).

- Depression can impair a mother's ability to discipline her child appropriately (Davenport, Zahn-Waxler, Adland, & Mayfield, 1984).

- Depression often is associated with family discord (Gottlieb & Hooley, 1988), and this marital conflict may impinge adversely on young children (Rutter & Quinton, 1984).

Research shows that early caregiving experiences influence the growth of brain interconnections and the maturation of the frontolimbic system of the brain, which regulates psychological states and ability to cope with stress (Schore, 1997). This research points to the risk of children of depressed mothers having a predisposition for psychiatric disorders. Jones, Field, Fox, Lundy, and Davalos (1997) studied the brain activity of babies whose mothers were depressed and babies whose mothers were not depressed. They found that even in babies as young as 1 month of age, an EEG activation indicated that babies of depressed mothers exhibited greater frontal lobe EEG asymmetry as compared with the other babies. This asymmetry, the authors observed, was related to more frequent negative facial expressions, less activity, and more erratic sleep. In addition, Seifer and Dickstein's (1993) research indicated that parental mental illness can be related to negative child outcomes, such as children's cognitive deficits, delinquency, or poor social adaptation.

Daniel Stern (1995) described four ways that babies have adjusted to living with an emotionally unavailable mother. Each of these methods of adapting continues to develop over time. That is, the pattern or style of relating to the world and to the self that begins in the first few months between the depressed mother and her baby may remain the baby's pattern and style throughout the rest of the child's life. These four styles of adapting to life with an emotionally unavailable mother are listed next:

- Some babies learn to "turn on their mother," and sometimes they are successful in reaching their emotionally unavailable mother. Stern described these babies as a "spark plug," for they can stimulate their mother. The baby becomes an "antidepressor" (p. 102). Sometimes the baby's vocalizing, smiling, and gesturing works, and the mother is momentarily reanimated even though she is depressed. This infrequent response is good reinforcement for the baby's behavior. These babies often develop into charmers who are skilled in capturing people's attention.

- When the mother is not responsive, some babies turn away, become curious, and seek stimulation elsewhere. These babies develop their own ability to stimulate themselves with external objects and events.

- Some mothers are aware that they are not responding to their baby enough, and thus they make a huge effort to overcompensate in bursts. Stern suspected that babies can discriminate these forced interactions from an easy flow; yet they are so eager for relationship that they adjust their behavior accordingly. Although the desires of both baby and mother are very real, "a false interaction between a false mother and a false baby occurs" (p. 104).

- Some babies, in their desire to be with the mother, identify and imitate the mother's depression. These babies have low levels of activity and negative or minimal facial expressivity.

Gail, a Mother with Depression, and Her Daughter, Nancy

Gail and her family live in a rural town of 3,000. Gail, a 26-year-old mother of 11-month-old Nancy, and wife of Gary, a short-distance truck driver, has joined the Therapeutic Family Child Care Project. Gail is the eleventh child of a mother who committed suicide when Gail was 10 years old. From the time she was an adolescent, Gail has suffered from severe depression; she has been hospitalized at least once a year and takes several medications. Prior to Gail's enrollment in the project, Gary had cooked all of the family's dinners. Nancy was in the playpen alone 100% of the time she was awake.

When family caregiver, Jean, began caring for 11-month-old Nancy, Nancy had no verbalizations and little if any affect. Jean cared for Nancy 4½ days a week, and Gail also came to Jean's home 1 morning a week. When Nancy was 5 years old, Gail began working as a nurse's aide at a nursing home; and Jean cared for Nancy in the afternoons after kindergarten.

Sometimes when Jean returned Nancy to her home, she would teach Gail to bake brownies and cook simple meals. At Jean's home, Nancy and the three other toddlers for whom Jean cared always cooked simple items together such as biscuits or muffins. After 1 year in Jean's care, Nancy was spontaneously talking and was emotionally expressive. In fact, by the time she was 3 years old, her behavior showed that she possessed a quick intellect. After 3 years in the project, Gail continued to see her psychiatrist regularly, continued to take her medication, and had no more hospitalizations.

Ten years after Nancy and Gail left the project, I interviewed Jean. She stated that she sees Nancy a couple times a year and that Nancy seems to be a spontaneous, happy teenager. Jean also reported that she frequently sees Gary and Gail in town; and upon meeting, they exchange friendly brief conversations. Gail continues to work at the nursing home.

Parental Substance Abuse

Many babies prenatally exposed to substances are likely to experience ongoing parental substance abuse. When teachers work with babies and young children of parents who are potential if not actual substance abusers, it is important to understand the different effects of different substances. For example, crack cocaine users tend to be jumpy and full of vitality; whereas alcohol abusers are more likely to be listless, with little energy (Jones-Harden, 1997). This section discusses the effects of drug abuse (e.g., abuse of cocaine, marijuana, heroin, other street and prescription drugs) and then alcohol abuse on the person abusing the drug and on the person's child.

Given the surge of cocaine use since the mid-1980s, much of the research on babies who have been exposed prenatally to street and prescription drugs has been studies of cocaine-exposed babies (Mayes, Bornstein, Chawarsk, Haynes, & Granger, 1996; Myers, Olson, & Kaltenbach, 1992; Zuckerman & Brown, 1993). This research provides no consistent pattern of anomalies in prenatally exposed babies. At present, it is not certain what effects prenatal substance abuse have on the developing fetus because the study of the effects of street and prescription drugs is quite complex. First, it is difficult to know for certain that a drug is responsible for a child's maladaptive behavior or development. Second, most cocaine-using mothers are polydrug users; that is, they also use alcohol, cigarettes, marijuana, and other street or prescription drugs. Third, some children have psychological disturbances or live in a maladaptive environment and deal with such issues as domestic violence, unemployment, or lack of social support. In other words, prenatally exposed babies, including those whose parents are still using drugs, have multiple risks—the drug exposure plus parental and family dysfunction.

Many babies exposed to drugs in the womb are born premature; it is not yet known whether prematurity, low birth weight, or prenatal drug exposure triggers the problems these babies often face. Findings on this issue are mixed (Behnke & Eyler, 1994; Lester & Tronick, 1994). Some studies portray no differences between drug-exposed and non–drug-exposed babies. Other studies of babies exposed to drugs prenatally indicate that they are at risk of having low birth weights and being premature. Whether this finding is due to drug exposure or the mother's other multiple stressors is an unanswered question. Because studies of babies exposed to drugs have involved only families with low incomes, issues related to low income can be confused with the effects of drugs like cocaine when these studies are read (Myers et al., 1992).

Zuckerman and Brown (1993) noted that prenatal effects of drugs often can be seen in the central nervous system development of the fetus, for these substances cross the placenta and the blood–brain barrier. Mayes et al. (1996) investigated the relationship between cocaine exposure and babies' regulation of arousal in response to novelty. Thirty-six babies exposed to cocaine prenatally and twenty-seven babies with no exposure participated in the study at 3 months of age. The researchers measured the babies' behavioral state, emotional expressiveness, and attention to regulation of arousal. Compared with the group of babies with no prenatal drug exposure, babies exposed prenatally were more likely to cry and express negative emotions on novel stimulus presentation. The consequences of prenatal drug exposure depend on many factors, such as the type of drug, the timing and dose of exposure, emotional state, maternal mental illness, or other unhealthy habits or environmental stressors. For example, Zuckerman and Brown (1993) noted that many babies exposed to drugs prenatally have difficulty in regulating arousal, and such babies may not elicit adequate caregiving. That is, their mothers may be less likely to respond to the babies' cues for food or stimulation. Immediately after delivery, exposed babies have behavioral abnormalities detected in Brazelton's Neonatal Behavior Assessment Scales (1973), such as increased irritability, low responsiveness to visual stimuli, decreased consolability, tremors, and low muscle tone (Zuckerman & Brown, 1993).

Norinne: Living Amidst Drug Abuse

Norinne, 32 months old, entered Redbud Child Care Center on her second birthday. Norinne's mother is addicted to cocaine and lives in a home where there is a steady traffic of drug dealers. Norinne's health record at the center shows no evidence of prenatal drug exposure. Currently, Norinne and her 4-year-old sister, Cassie, live with their father, Sheldon; his girlfriend; and her three children. Ordinarily, Sheldon drops off and picks up all five children. Sheldon reports that at home, Norinne rarely eats. However, Harriet, her teacher, reports that at school she eats as though she is unable to get enough to eat. About once or twice a month Norinne's mother brings her to the center. On these days, Norinne repeatedly asks for her mother.

Harriet reports that often Norinne has no facial expression and seems depressed. Her speech is clear, but she rarely talks. She relates to her peers only with unprovoked aggression. She frequently has urine accidents and puts everything into her mouth. Each day she spends long periods of time playing in the water table. Whenever possible, Norinne clings to her older sister, Cassie. She is quite aggressive with dolls, as in the following observation:

> *Norinne enters the housekeeping area and picks up a doll. She says, "Sleepy baby." Then she rigorously hits the doll's stomach, saying, "I'm going to hit your butt!" Norinne's teacher, Harriet, enters the area and talks to her softly. They then leave the area, with Norinne carrying her doll, and Harriet begins to read Norinne a story.*

Harriet reports that the one time that Norinne is emotionally expressive is when she is alone and playing with the dolls. On most occasions she is expressing anger and aggression.

Norinne has lived in an environment of drug use and drug dealers. Her caregivers do not know if she has experienced or witnessed violence. Norinne's chaotic home life during her first year with her mother has caused her a great deal of anxiety, which often is externalized into aggressive behavior, as Norinne demonstrates with her dolls. To address Norinne's high level of anxiety, Harriet has water play available; and Norinne plays with water quietly each day for about 20 minutes. Harriet also ensures that she gives Norinne focused one-to-one time each day, often reading her a storybook.

Similar to children exposed to street and prescription drugs prenatally, babies and children exposed to alcohol prenatally frequently live in environments of chronic stress caused by factors other than alcohol, for example, low income, parental unemployment, parental mental illness, and so forth. These children also are likely to experience ongoing parental substance abuse.

Extensive research has demonstrated that prenatal exposure to alcohol causes serious maladaptation in development. *Fetal alcohol syndrome* (FAS) is the term used to describe disabilities due to prenatal alcohol exposure. Because much of babies' neurological development occurs after birth, however, *children with FAS can make progress when receiving competent caregiving and adequate nutrition* (Zuckerman & Brown, 1993).

Developmental delays or disabilities caused by prenatal alcohol exposure involve the growth and proper formation of the fetus's brain and body. The central nervous system and brain are especially sensitive to effects of prenatal alcohol exposure. Characteristics of babies and young children with FAS include facial features such as thin upper lip, short nose, flat midface, and flattening of the jaw; low muscle tone; and central nervous system dysfunction, typically mental retardation, hyperactivity, impulsivity, and/or seizures (Streissguth, 1997). Olson, Burgess, and Streissguth described preschool children with FAS as follows:

> [The children are] often alert, talkative, and friendly. They have been described as typically short and skinny, with butterfly movements, but a generally vigorous appearance. These children may have severe temper tantrums and difficulty making transitions. More than half show hyperactivity and many are oversensitive to touch and other stimulation. Attentional deficits, fine motor difficulties and developmental delays also are seen. (1992, p. 25)

Although much of the research focuses on maternal alcohol abuse, paternal alcohol abuse also has a significant impact on families. Eiden and Leonard (1996) studied 55 mothers and babies ages 12–24 months old and found that paternal alcoholism has an impact on both family functioning and the mother–child relationship as early as infancy. Fathers' alcoholism was linked to maternal depression, marital dissatisfaction, and poor mother–baby attachment. Wives of alcoholics had more depressive symptoms and less marital satisfaction compared with wives of nonalcoholic husbands. Sixty-seven percent of babies whose fathers were heavy drinkers had insecure attachment with their mothers.

Brianna: A Mother Abusing Alcohol

Brianna is a 20-year-old mother of two preschoolers, 3 and 4 years old. During the day, her children are cared for by Kassandra, a therapeutic family child caregiver. After Brianna spends one morning at Kassandra's home with her children, Kassandra writes the following in her journal:

> Brianna told me that her children need to improve their speech. Throughout the morning, she was quite open about her drinking habits. She says she is trying to "cut down" somewhat. But then she goes on to say that her idea of having a restful day is to get drunk and then have the children take naps with her while she passes out. She seems unable to grasp the concept that her children might get up and hurt themselves while she is sleeping. Rather, she insists that they always just keep sleeping, so it is okay for her. All morning, Brianna's 3-year-old son, Isaiah, wanted to sit on my lap.

Kassandra reports that on some days, the children are ready when she comes to take them to her home. On other days, their mother is sleeping, and the 4-year-old is cooking eggs and toast for their breakfast. Some days when she arrives, mother and children are all asleep together.

The reciprocal interaction between babies' and their social environment influences the developmental outcome of babies and young children exposed to drugs and alcohol. Competent out-of-home caregiving can serve as early intervention that can make a substantial difference. High levels of stress trigger high cortisol levels in the brain, which can cause cell death in the brain and reduce the number of dendrites (connections) among brain neurons. Excessive cortisol damages the prefrontal cortex, which controls attention, emotions, and skills like perspective taking. The newborn's brain, however, has a significant capacity for adaptation, what brain researchers term *plasticity*. High-quality caregiving can protect the developing brain from the negative impact of stress hormones and buffer the brain's stress systems (Gunnar, 1996a). Thus, biological vulnerability may be compensated for by competent caregiving. The most optimal environment would be a therapeutic child care environment; however, given today's funding realities, many of these children are mainstreamed into traditional out-of-home caregiving programs.

Teachers may suspect that parents who abuse substances may have weak parenting skills and need a great deal of support. Once teachers are able to develop a trusting relationship with a parent, they may have the opportunity to help a parent utilize community resources for treatment and other needed assistance. Knowledge of accessible substance abuse treatment centers is a first prerequisite for teachers and directors to serve as a resource for parents. In reality, many of these families need comprehensive, multidisciplinary intervention to assist them with their chronic problems. Thus, if the resources are available, teachers might want to consider making referrals to agencies that can provide the help these families need. Were a teacher to suspect that a child is in danger in the home, the teacher would need to be vigilant in checking the child for signs of maltreatment as well as informing her administrator about this concern. Every early educator is required by law to report evidence of child maltreatment.

Community and Domestic Violence

The United States has the highest incidence of violence of any industrialized nation in the world. The murder rate in the United States is 5 times that of England and 10 times that of Spain (Wallach, 1993). In 1993, 22 per 100,000 males ages 15–24 years in the United States were homicide victims; whereas all other Western industrialized nations had 5 homicides or fewer per 100,000 for males 15–24 years of age (Osofsky, 1993). With both the high incidence of violence on television and the increased frequency of homicides in our nation, it is reasonable to speak of violence as being part of the inner psyche of each American citizen. As researcher Cicchetti and clinician Lynch noted, "Violence, in fact, is becoming a defining characteristic of American society" (1993, p. 96). In urban, low-income neighborhoods, violence is epidemic. Young children are both victims and witnesses of episodes of community and domestic violence (Richters & Martinez, 1993). Karr-Morse and Wiley provided data on incarceration in America in 1997:

> If our present rates of incarcerating continue, one out of every twenty babies born in the United States today will spend some part of their adult lives in state or federal prison. An African-American male has a greater than one in four chance of going to prison in his lifetime, while a Hispanic male has a one in six chance of serving time....And our prison population has exploded. California, for example, is now spending more on its criminal justice system than on higher education. (1997, p. 8)

Child development experts believe that children in America today may be the most fearful in history (Children's Defense Fund, 1994). This sense of fear is most prevalent in some urban, low-income neighborhoods, where drive-by shootings, gang conflicts, and drug dealing are daily occurrences. Child psychologist James Garbarino (1993) warned, "Children are growing up in a much more socially toxic environment than ever before. They live in a world in which chronic danger displaces the fundamental safety that children need."

Adults also are fearful. Several years ago, for example, when colleagues learned that I was driving 1,000 miles alone, they insisted that I borrow their car telephone so that I would be safe. The popularity of television programs about violent incidents, such as *America's Most Wanted* or *Cops* seems to play into this adult fear.

Many adults think that babies and young children who witness violence are too young to understand what happened and that they will not remember the violent event. Clear evidence shows, however, that babies, toddlers, and older children *do not forget* traumatic events.

> The ability to re-see or, occasionally but less frequently, to re-feel a terrible event or series of events is an important common characteristic of almost all externally generated disorders of childhood. Re-seeing is so important that it sometimes occurs even when the original experience was not at all visual. Visualizations are most strongly stimulated by reminders of the traumatic event, but they occasionally come up entirely unbidden....Even those who were babies or toddlers at the time

of their ordeals and thus were unable to lay down, store, or retrieve full verbal memories of their traumas, tend to play out, to draw, or to re-see highly visualized elements from their old experiences. (Terr, 1991, p. 12)

In addition to remembering a visual picture of a traumatic event, children can recall the verbal aspect of traumatic experiences that occurred when the children were as young as 2 1/2 years of age (Sugar, 1992). An additional concern for children younger than 6 years is their confusion of fantasy and reality. This confusion can put them at even greater risk of having specific fears, nightmares, and disturbing fantasies.

When young children live in an environment that has unpredictable, frequent occurrences of violence, they are unable to gain feelings of either safety or security—two essential milestones of early development. These experiences have a significant impact on the children's development in the present and will continue to do so in the future (Terr, 1991; Zeanah & Burk, 1984). Researchers and clinicians have provided poignant descriptions of how young children's exposure to violence leads to social-emotional problems that can be lasting (Osofsky, 1993; Pynoos & Eth, 1986; Terr, 1991; Wallace, 1993; Zeanah, 1993). Studies provide convincing evidence that community violence increases the risk of family disruption and parental stress, thereby increasing the probability of child maltreatment (Cicchetti & Lynch, 1993; Richters & Martinez, 1993). The younger the child, the greater the threat to healthy development when he or she is exposed to violence. Osofsky (1993) identified behaviors associated with young children's exposure to violence, including the following:

- Reexperiencing the traumatic event—often in the form of nightmares and in repetitive play sequences
- Trauma-specific fears, for example, fear of the dark, strangers, being alone, specific animals, vehicles
- Sleep disturbances
- Enuresis (bed wetting)
- Low tolerance of frustration, aggression, and impulsivity
- Selective inattention
- Lack of curiosity and lack of pleasure in exploring
- Depression and perpetual mourning
- Lack of a sense of trust and security
- Avoidance of intimacy
- Sensitized, hyperaroused state

These symptoms overlap with those of posttraumatic stress disorder (PTSD). In fact, studies of young children exposed to violence point to clear associations between the exposure and the occurrence of PTSD (Garbarino, 1992; Osofsky, 1993; Terr, 1991; Zeanah, 1993). If experiences with violence are chronic, young children may develop a permanent pattern of hyperarousal or numbing, which can become the precursor to learning and behavior problems. With prolonged stress, the brain's chemical profile can be altered by changes in hormone levels, which affect information processing and can lead to maladaptive behavior (Karr-Morse & Wiley, 1997). Zeanah and Scheering identified parent factors that seem most closely related to PTSD symptomatology in young children:

1) mothers' and fathers' own symptoms of PTSD

2) levels of general parental psychopathology

3) the presence and/or extent of denial concerning the child's symptomatology

4) changes in family functioning that may have a powerful indirect effect on the baby's functioning and development (1996, p. 13)

Research shows that prolonged and frequent periods of stress can have lasting effects on alteration of a child's brain from the third trimester of pregnancy to 24 months of age. Damage is greatest for those areas of the brain that control emotion regulation. With no interactive repair, the child's stress state occurs for long periods at a time. Stressful experiences trigger biochemical changes and permanent alteration of cortical receptors in the brain and structural impairment of the orbital frontal cortex, changes that inhibit optimal brain development. The earlier the trauma, the more severe the effect (Schore, 1998).

Many individual differences exist in how a small child experiences a traumatic event. Young children's caregivers differ in the quality and amount of soothing they provide after a trauma has occurred. The amount of distress experienced may depend upon how children perceive their caregiver's affect (Drell, Siegel, & Gaenbauer, 1993). Babies and young children also have different sensory sensitivities; these sensitivities influence how a child responds to.an event. Osofsky (1996) identified factors that can influence young children's response to traumatic events:

- *Intensity* Witnessing someone pushing another person is likely to result in a less severe traumatic response than witnessing a shooting.

- *Proximity to the event* The research of Pynoos (1985) and others on sniper attacks in school yards suggests that a child who is a firsthand witness to a violent event is likely to be much more strongly affected than a child who is shielded from full sight of the violence or only hears about the event.

- *Familiarity* with the victim, perpetrator, or both, strongly increases the intensity of a child's response to witnessing violence.
- *The developmental status* of the child will affect his or her response and capacity to cope with the impact of violence.
- *Chronicity of exposure to violence*   It is likely that experiencing violence repeatedly over the years may be devastating to the social and emotional development of young children, who learn, from what they see, that violence is a usual and acceptable way to respond to other people.

It is critical for teachers of young children to be aware of the effects of violence, to be able to note signs of these effects in children, and to have knowledge of how they can work with children at risk. The list of symptoms of PTSD described previously can be helpful in this task. Specific strategies for working with these children include the following:

- Teachers can provide a calm, safe, nurturing environment for the children who have witnessed or experienced violence.
- Teachers can ensure that each child under their care has a loving, trusting relationship with them.
- Teachers can focus on inner experiences, or feelings, their own and those of the children.

When child care teachers work closely with parents, they can learn to be aware of signs of physical adult abuse, such as bruises or swelling on any part of the body. It also is important for teachers to recognize their own feelings when working with these parents. Teachers' personal attitudes and feelings, such as impatience with a mother who chooses to continue living with her abusing partner, can obstruct teachers' ability to be caring and supportive of the parent.

Maurice: Living Amidst Violence

Maurice, age 4 years, lives with his single mother who abuses alcohol and other drugs. Maurice was prenatally exposed to drugs. An array of adults come in and out of Maurice's home, with violence frequently erupting. The last time his teacher made a home visit, adults were throwing bricks at each other.
Maurice's teachers report that during eating times, he seems to fear that he will not get enough food and eats as much

as possible. He engages in unprovoked aggression throughout the day. He is unable to participate in any group activity and has nightmares when sleeping during naptime. In the classroom or during gross motor play, Maurice is able to maintain focus in an activity only if his teacher, Jerri, is at his side; otherwise he either runs about or engages in unprovoked aggression. Maurice can function appropriately when Jerri is able to "shadow" him. This shadowing seems to contain his excessive anxiety and resulting lack of self control.

The child care center is working with the school district to have Maurice evaluated for placement in special education for the following year. Jerri also is assisting Maurice's mother in arranging for a psychiatric evaluation to determine whether medication could help him.

Child Maltreatment

Children younger than 3 years of age are most at risk of abuse and neglect; in fact, the majority of deaths by child maltreatment occur among children younger than 3 years of age (Mrazek, 1993). Statistics from *Kids Count: Data on the Well-Being of Children in Large Cities* (The Annie E. Casey Foundation, 1997) show that in the 1980s the United States made no progress in seven of the nine measures of well-being of children. The seven measures showing a lack of progress are as follows:

- Low birth weight
- The violent death rate of teens ages 15–19
- Percentage of births to single teen mothers
- Juvenile custody rate
- Not finishing high school
- Percentage of children living in poverty
- Percentage of children in single-parent families

Child maltreatment includes neglect, physical abuse, sexual abuse, and emotional abuse. The most frequent forms of abuse are neglect (45%), physical abuse (15%), and sexual abuse (16%). Behavior patterns of very young children that most often spark maltreatment are incessant crying and negativism as well as wetting and soiling. External signs of physical abuse are bruises, lacerations, scars, and burns (Mrazek, 1993). Young children often experience multiple forms of abuse, for example, physical and sexual abuse often occur together. Mrazek identified the following factors that are highly correlated with child maltreatment:

- Negative maternal attitude toward pregnancy
- High level of perceived social stress
- Low socioeconomic status
- Lack of financial resources
- Parents' low intelligence
- Parents' criminal record
- History of parents' own . . . maltreatment [as a child] (p. 162)

Egeland and Sroufe (1981) conducted a prospective, longitudinal investigation of 270 children from birth through 5 years. Their study provided lucid documentation of the progressive decline in functioning of maltreated children, with the greatest decline among those children raised by psychologically unavailable mothers. Because maltreatment most often occurs along with other risk factors, maltreatment affects different children differently.

Studies have indicated that babies who have been maltreated consistently have a greater percentage of insecure attachments than do babies who have not been maltreated (Toth, Cicchetti, Macfie, & Emde, 1997). Many young children with a history of maltreatment develop not only negative representational models of their attachment figures but also negative representations of themselves. Moreover, these young children often distance themselves from their actual emotional experience. Toth et al. clarified that "maltreated children often act compulsively compliant with their caregivers (e.g., ignore their own needs in order to care for and please the parent and display insincere positive affect)" (p. 783).[3]

When maltreatment is chronic, young children develop brain pattern changes as well as changes in behavior similar to those mentioned previously among children exposed to violence. Some maltreated children respond to anxiety by being hypersensitive; others dissociate. Karr-Morse and Wiley summarized that "instead of providing the foundation for self-control, for empathy, and for focused cognitive learning, abuse in earliest life undermines all three" (1997, p. 164).

Karr-Morse and Wiley's book, *Ghosts from the Nursery*, clearly articulates how maltreatment from gestation through the second year of life is a precursor to the growing epidemic of violence by children in the United States:

> The last three decades have provided us with research that brings to light a range of more subtle toxins profoundly influencing our children's earliest development: chronic stress or neglect, which affects the

development of the fetal or early infant brain; early child abuse and neglect, which undermine focused learning; chronic parental depression; neglect or lack of stimulation necessary for normal brain development; early loss of primary relationships or breaks in caregiving....

Through the interplay of the developing brain with the environment during the nine months of gestation and the first two years after birth, the core of an individual's ability to think, feel, and relate to others is formed. Violent behavior often begins to take root during those thirty-three months as the result of chronic stress, such as domestic or child abuse, or through neglect, including preingestion of toxins. . . . Maltreatment of a baby may lead to the permanent loss or impairment of key protective factors—such as intelligence, trust, and empathy—that enable many children to survive and even overcome difficult family circumstances and later traumas. (1997, p. 15)

Sexual abuse of children can range from excessive exposure to pornography to living in sexually explicit environments to physical acts of abuse, such as fondling, oral copulation, vaginal intercourse, or sodomy. Sexual abuse can result in children's having thoughts pervaded with sexuality; engaging in inappropriate sexual behavior, such as excessive masturbation; disturbing toileting patterns (e.g., sniffing underwear, wearing soiled underpants); repeatedly stuffing the toilet until it overflows; or molesting other children (Gil & Johnson, 1993).

Charetta: A Victim of Sexual Abuse

Charetta, age 3, is the only daughter of 33-year-old Keona. When Charetta was 8 months old Keona divorced Charetta's father, Joe, who is a self-employed plumber. Keona worked as an executive secretary for a large corporation in the heart of a city. She and Charetta lived in a comfortable home in the suburbs. Charetta's father, Joe, has returned home to live with his parents and four adult brothers, three of whom use and sell drugs.

Keona and Joe are one of five couples who attended a parenting group. Joe stated that Charetta is "the apple of my eye, my reason for living." On some days, before Keona picks up her daughter from the child care center, Joe takes Charetta for an hour or so in the afternoon, then returns her to the center. On Sunday, Joe takes Charetta to his mother's home to be with him.

During the first week of the parenting sessions, Charetta's teacher, Jean, told me that Charetta was masturbating persistently throughout the day. Jean, Keona, and I met together to discuss Charetta's masturbation. Keona commented that she too had noticed Charetta's increasing masturbation.

Keona arranged for Joe to have visits with her daughter only when she, too, was present. With help from Charetta's child care director, she also arranged for Charetta to have one year of weekly play therapy with a child psychiatrist. Charetta's masturbation ceased. At 7 years old, she is a bright, high-achieving second grader.

When a teacher suspects that a child in her or his care has been physically or sexually abused, the first step is to have a confidential conversation with the child's parent. Then the teacher can assist the parent in obtaining a medical evaluation of the child and psychotherapy to help heal the child. In most families where child maltreatment occurs, family therapy can assist family members in healing and the family in becoming whole. Once a teacher's suspects that a young child is being maltreated, he or she is mandated to report the maltreatment to the state child protection agency.

THE RESILIENT CHILD

Most of this chapter has addressed the environmental problems that are part of many babies' and young children's lives. But young children are not necessarily always victims of their fate. The literature (e.g., Werner & Smith, 1992; Wolin & Wolin, 1993) has described children living in the midst of chronic stress and deprivation who have been able to overcome this deprivation and maintain healthy development because they are resilient. Each family suffering from psychological vulnerability will be different from other families suffering similar difficulties. Each child responds to family difficulties in his or her unique way; and, in fact, some children are resilient enough that their family difficulties do not substantively damage their development.

Cicchetti and Rogosch defined resilience as "the individual's capacity for adapting successfully and functioning competently despite experiencing chronic stress or adversity, or following exposure to prolonged or severe trauma" (1997, p. 797). Resilience is not a static condition but, rather, a state of dynamic transaction between oneself and another. Wolin and Wolin identified seven strengths that they see as part of the selfhood of resilient children (1993, pp. 5–6):

Insight: The habit of asking tough questions and giving honest answers

Independence: Drawing boundaries between yourself and troubled parents; keeping emotional and physical distance while satisfying the demands of your conscience

Relationships: Intimate and fulfilling ties to other people that balance a mature regard for your own needs with empathy and the capacity to give to someone else

Initiative: Taking charge of problems; exerting control; a taste for stretching and testing yourself in demanding tasks

Creativity: Imposing order, beauty, and purpose on the chaos of your troubling experiences and painful feelings

Humor: Finding the comic in the tragic

Morality: An informed conscience that extends your wish for a good personal life to all of humankind

Each troubled family is unique; similarly, each resilient child does not have all seven of these strengths. Karr-Morse and Wiley (1997) discussed two protective factors that resilient children often have. First, they have "effortful control; that is, they are able to choose one behavior while inhibiting another; thus they are able to focus on important information in school. Second, they have an affiliative or social personality and can generate relationships."

Cicchetti and Rogosch (1997) conducted a longitudinal study of 213 6- to 11-year-olds who attended a week-long summer day camp, 133 of whom had been maltreated. Maltreated children exhibited greater deficits than nonmaltreated children across the 3 consecutive years of assessment. Those maltreated children who were resilient had stable characteristics of self-reliance and self-confidence, along with interpersonal reserve and positive future expectations for the self.

Resilient children often figure out how to locate allies outside their families, and child care teachers can serve as needed allies for children from troubled families. Resilient children often have the capacity to see themselves as separate from their troubled parents and to intuit that their family is not what it is supposed to be. When child care teachers are loving, predictable, and available, these teachers can be models to help young children learn that there is a different way to relate than the way that they experience at home. The classic longitudinal study of children of Kauai, Hawaii (Werner, Bierman, & French, 1971), indicated that the best predictors of school success of children at age 10 were caregiving practices of warmth, low physical punishment, responsiveness, verbalness, and encouragement to develop.[4] These are all traits that every out-of-home caregiver can and should provide to all the children in their care.

When teachers recognize that a baby's or young child's daily life at home is immersed in stress and adversity, they can ensure that they give this baby or young child loving care and a sense of safety and security. In their interactions, they can provide a trusting predictable relationship. Many of these children live in homes in which they have no control over events. The teachers can ensure that these children experience a sense of efficacy by being quick to respond to the children's initiatives and by providing opportunities for the children to make choices.

CONCLUSION

Every baby has the right to interact routinely and consistently with an admiring, supporting, and loving caregiver in a relationship that provides security and intimacy. Unfortunately, tens of thousands of babies and young children are at risk for not realizing their full humanity given their families' extreme deprivations. The framework for each of the chapters in this book is that development occurs through and within relationship. *The critical issue is how does the caregiver interact with the child and contribute to the healthy development of the child.* As Elshtain noted,

> Familial ties and models of childrearing are essential to establish the minimal foundation of human social existence....The family's status as a moral imperative derives from its universal, pan-cultural existence in all known past and present societies. (1981, pp. 326–327)

Margaret Mead's daughter, Mary Catherine Bateson, poetically described the self: "The self in relationship is necessarily fluid, held in a vessel of many strands, like the baskets closely woven by some Native American tribes, caulked tightly enough to hold water" (1994, p. 63). But what happens when babies and young children live in very troubled families? Young children in these families are at risk of failing to achieve a strong sense of self and optimal development because their relationship with a primary caregiver is not strong enough to contain them and nurture them. Longitudinal studies such as those completed by Schweinhart and Weikart (1998) have provided convincing evidence that high-quality, full-day, out-of-home child care can protect young children at risk. Ramey, Campbell, and Blair's (1998) Abecedarian Project, for example, studied 111 children randomly assigned at birth to either early intervention or no early intervention. These children were followed from birth to 15 years of age. The intervention group attended high-quality, full-day child care each day, 52 weeks per year. The early education curriculum focused on cognitive and fine motor development, social and self-development, and motor and language development at an individualized pace. From 18 months to 15 years, substantial differences in all areas of development were observed between the children who had received intervention and those children who had not (Ramey, 1998).

Child care providers have reached a period of accountability. Lisbeth Schorr (1997), who has studied programs supporting children and families across the nation, noted that essential attributes of work with families at risk involve supportive relationships, intensive engagement, consistency, perseverance, and flexibility. Out-of-home caregivers can and do make a difference in the lives of children from troubled families by providing them with the love and nurturing they need to develop into full human beings.

chapter 7

Personal History, Professional Competence

The person, understood as a character in a story, is not an entity distinct from his or her "experiences." It is the identity of the story that makes the identity of the character.

—*Paul Ricœur (1992, pp. 147–148)*

Effective teaching is an art and a craft that is learned on the job. A teacher's knowledge is like a musician's; thinking and doing are interwoven, and the skill is learned in the doing. Musicians improve their skill by reflecting on how they play and by having mentors to guide them. Like musicians, teachers improve their practice through self-reflection, and they gain increased skill and knowledge through mentoring that is directly related to their practice. No perfect solutions to problems or strategies for success exist in teaching; instead, teachers develop knowledge and skill through reflecting on their lived experience with co-teachers, young children, and the children's parents.

This chapter explores how the personal and professional histories of early educators are a core element in their professional competence. Teachers' commitment, values, decision making, and patterns of interaction are rooted in their unique, interwoven personal and professional histories. Literature on educators' personal life histories points to how life experiences are the roots for teachers' sense of self-identity and their way of seeing and valuing the world (Butt, Raymond, McCure, & Yamagishi, 1992; Clandinin & Connelly, 1994; Goodson, 1992; Nias, 1989; Smith, Klein, Prunty, & Dwyer, 1986).

To explore how an early educator's personal life is connected to her childhood and current personal life as an adult, this chapter presents life history interviews that I conducted with family caregivers, center-based caregivers, and center administrators. The center-based teachers and directors work at accredited centers and are members of the Child Day Care Association (CDCA),[1] which provides 15 weeks of developmentally appropriate practice (DAP) classes for all new teachers and six full-day observation/consultations to member agencies each year.[2] As director of two early intervention programs and one professional development program, I have worked with these early educators at various times over the years. Some of the vignettes used in previous chapters stem from my prior work with them. Each of these women is a talented early educator, bringing unique strengths to her work with babies and young children.

The early educators presented in this chapter represent the diversity in the field. They are in different stages of their life and range in age from 27 to 68 years old. The women discussed here are single and married, with kids of their own and without. Two teachers had been married within a year of my interviews with them; another teacher had been married 48 years and had six grandchildren. They live in families with low- or middle-income levels and in urban, suburban, and rural communities. Seven of the eighteen early educators I interviewed for this book are African American. These caregivers serve a diverse array of children and families.

In discussing the use of narrative and storytelling, Bruner (1986) pointed out that no separation occurs among the person, the setting, and the action or event. In the life histories presented here, the setting, events, and each individual person create unique patterns, although common themes can be found in all of their lives and in their work with young children. These diverse caregivers share assumptions and beliefs about young children, about what they are doing with young children, and about the meaning and purpose of their work.

In the interviews, the women began by telling me how they became involved in early education, then they traced their career paths and shared both the meaning of their work and which experiences helped them to grow in their work as child care professionals.[3] They then described their childhood and current personal histories. These personal and professional histories are not meant to be used either as case studies or as blueprints; they are meant, however, to help readers reflect on their own personal and professional development. In thinking about how these educators reflected on their histories and integrated them into their work, readers can apply this process in their own personal and professional lives.

As a way of introducing the commonalities in the work of these early educators, this chapter begins by looking closely at the life histories of Sarah, a family caregiver working with rural families, and Nettie, a teacher at a suburban child care center. After sharing the personal stories of these two women in depth, the chapter discusses common themes that arose from all of the interviews that I conducted with these early educators.

SARAH: A FAMILY CAREGIVER
FOR YOUNG CHILDREN AT RISK

Sarah lives in Fordham, a rural community of 3,000. She is one of the family caregivers in the Therapeutic Child Care (TCC) project, an intervention program that I had directed for babies and young children at risk of maltreatment. TCC met for $2^1/_2$ hours each month for training, and I visited each home every 4–6 weeks to complete a verbatim observation.

I first interviewed Sarah in 1987. When I returned for a second interview 11 years later, Sarah was 57 years old. Sarah had been one of the most gifted caregivers I had worked with, and I was eager to catch up on her life during the past 10 years. I was shocked and saddened to learn that both Sarah and her husband, Jim, had had very difficult times during the past year. Eight months prior to this second interview, Sarah and

Jim had added an 18-foot room to their small home and purchased $6,000 worth of equipment from a child care facility that had closed for Sarah to use in her work with children. Shortly thereafter, both Sarah and Jim became seriously ill. Jim had repeated dizzy spells and was diagnosed as having diabetes. Then 2 months later, Sarah had congestive heart failure. Jim sold his bait shop and started collecting disability checks, and Sarah ended her 15 years of family child care.

I had not seen Sarah in 10 years. We sat under the large maple trees in her back yard with Annie, her 15-year-old adopted daughter. Flora, her 18-year-old adopted daughter, was swinging nearby. Sarah used this second interview to talk about her child care experience retrospectively. I was sad that she could no longer do what I had seen her do so well, but Sarah is a positive person. She used the interview to celebrate what counted most in her life.

I had looked forward to my monthly visits with Sarah and the children in her care because her home had always been full of life and laughter. Sarah was a wonderful play partner, and she participated in a wide array of activities with the kids ranging from role playing nurses and doctors or mommies and daddies, to doing creative art activities with a gigantic range of "beautiful junk," to building block towers, to playing outdoors. Sarah's large yard was shaded with three gigantic maple trees and contained swings, a plastic swimming pool, and a large sandbox. Sarah involved the children in story reading, singing, and doing fingerplays each day. Sarah's husband, Jim, and her elementary-age daughter, Cindy, were integrally involved in Sarah's work. Jim owned a bait shop one block from their small five-room home, and he joined Sarah and the children each day for an extended midday meal.

Integrating Work and Family Life

When it came to young children, Sarah and Jim always had a "porous" family; that is, their family extended to include the young children in Sarah's child care program. After she started doing child care full time, Sarah would have children in her home during the day, in the evenings, and often even on weekends. For many children, Sarah was a second mother.

Sarah: I remember [the] first kids. Once when I gave them lunch meat, they told me, "We eat that all the time at home. Can't we have something hot?" And I never had lunch meat sandwiches with them again. And they would say, "Let's all go to McDonald's." And I would take them, and they'd each have their Happy Meal. Their parents never had any money. I figured if I make money, I can spend money putting it back to them. And it all pays off right here [points to her heart].

[In the] spring of 1987 we adopted Flora and Annie [two preschool-age girls who had been Sarah and Jim's foster children and who had a prior history of maltreatment]....Once we adopted Flora and Annie, we built them a room and they became our family.

I've had dozens of kids [in my care] and, of course, their moms too. I had little kids whose dad was in the penitentiary for putting a contract out on his wife. And then the mom was put in jail. And I just got right in the car and got the kids. You know I had to go get them. I said they're guests in my home so they cannot get me in trouble for having them over 12 hours because they're guests.

When I went to full-time babysitting, [doing] the therapeutic and private care, I cared for kids on the weekends, holidays— kids, from 6 in the morning until sometimes 2 A.M. I love the kids. When they hug you, they just melt into you—every one of them. They're family. They are just family. Their parents are even family too, although they can be hard to get along with. I don't regret a moment of it.

Sarah and Jim have found their place in the world; they have found meaning through their love and care of very young children. Caregiving became a family affair because Jim was also actively involved with the children.

Sarah: Jim just loves kids. We take the kids with us everywhere. When we go to the cabin by the river, the kids come with us. When Jim sits down, a kid will crawl up beside him and just practically melt right into his side.

I tell the kids, "Anytime you want a hug, come here. I need hugs too." We just hug. I think it's important for little kids. I mean people have needs and if it's just a hug, well, give it to them. And everybody feels better afterwards.

Caregiving Provides Meaning in One's Life

Sarah seemed to identify with the young children in her care, and her caregiving seemed to be therapeutic for her. Her own mother was repeatedly abusive to Sarah as a young child but was not abusive to any of Sarah's siblings. Despite this abuse, her mother was a giving woman who opened her home to many other people. And Sarah saw her caregiving as parallel to her mother's pattern of taking in people, although she is explicit about not repeating the abuse. Sarah described her childhood as follows:

Sarah: I always thought if other kids have to grow up thinking their mama doesn't love them, well, maybe I can make up for some of the stuff that I missed. And you know what? I think it helps me too, in my heart and soul I guess. Because these little kids, boy, can they love you. When they wrap their arms around you, it's just like a piece of butter melting into your soul, I guess you'd say. It…makes me feel like a part of my life that was missing isn't missing. I really enjoy kids. I think because mom always gave people a home, maybe that stuck with me—giving people a home.

As Sarah went on to describe her mother's life, it was apparent that her mother cared for and loved young children because, like Sarah, she had experienced deprivation as a young child. Sarah continued the cycle of loving as she cared for and loved young children even though her own mother was unable to give her unconditional love. Her caregiving seemed to compensate for her own childhood maltreatment as she identified with these young children, many of whom also had been maltreated.

Sarah also shared how her father provided the love denied by her abusive mother. With her father, Sarah could react appropriately to the hurt, humiliation, and coercion and thus integrate her childhood abuse into her personality rather than repress her feelings. Miller noted, "A child can only experience his feelings when there is somebody who is there who accepts him fully, understands, and supports him" (1982, p. 10). Sarah's father was not strong enough to confront his wife about her abuse of Sarah, but he did give Sarah unconditional love; support; and a caring, listening ear into which Sarah could pour out her feelings of pain and confusion instead of repressing them. With her father, Sarah was able to experience and develop her own emotions and understand herself as an individual. Thus Sarah was able to be an emotionally healthy adult who could provide high-quality out-of-home caregiving to children at risk.

Sarah: My mother always kept me in the house up in my room away from her. Any time I would open my mouth to my mother, I got smacked. So in kindergarten . . . they had me in therapy because I would not open my mouth to anyone. As a child I was so afraid of my mom. I'd just try and always go off to myself.

When I was little, I was always with my dad. He would tell me, "God sent me an angel to love, and I just picked her up off the ground." Dad tried to make up for the affection mom didn't show. I can't ever remember her even showing any affection to me. He was such a hard-working old guy. Everybody else had a tractor, and he had a team of mules. He was working all the time. And I can remember coming in and sitting in his chair with these bib overalls on. He would be sleeping, and I would have a comb and curlers and would curl his hair. Mom would spank me for that. He would tell her, "Mary, leave her alone. That's what puts me to sleep." He didn't have hardly any hair. Bald spot here and two little wigs there. But I'd curl it. I don't know why, just to be close to my dad, I guess.

As a teen, Sarah married and had two daughters. Although this marriage ended in divorce, Sarah and her current husband, Jim, have had a full life together. A central bond in their relationship is their love of children and their commitment to caring for those children most in need.

Sarah: I got married young and had two daughters. Then my husband was in a very serious accident and suffered brain damage. Then he started drinking. He was nuttier than a fruit cake, so I took my daughters and I moved . . . to get away from him. That's when I met Jim, and we became close friends. Jim helped me through a lot. He was divorced and had two daughters. I got a divorce, and Jim and I got married. We started out as friends, and I think we're still friends. . . .

I think I've learned a lot about myself and my cause in life. I've tried to figure it out, with having kids around me. I find out something about myself with the kids. Being around and watching kids, I don't care if they are little bitty, they are people. They have feelings and they know more than what you think they know. And I've just learned a lot with kids, trying to figure them out, why they're doing what they're doing and all. It's just a fulfillment to me. I enjoy it so much.

After the interview, Sarah showed me the new room that she and Jim had made for the children in her care. In the room were long shelves with wooden unit blocks and other developmentally appropriate toys that Sarah had bought from a child care facility. As we walked out of her home Sarah said to me, "You know, Carol, I found my niche. . . . There's nothing I would have rather done in my life than care for children."

NETTIE: CAREGIVER FOR 2-YEAR-OLDS

Nettie is 39 years old and single. Whereas Sarah worked in a rural context with a specific population of very low-income families, Nettie teaches 2-year-olds in a small, suburban, industry-sponsored child care center for lower- and middle-income families. I had worked with Nettie during the 6 years when I did early intervention with parents and child care teachers of children with behavior problems, and I interviewed her 2 years after that.

Nettie's Childhood and Upbringing

Nettie grew up in a large, close family in which her mother and father provided unconditional love and nurturance. Nettie's parents continue to be her role models. As a child, much of Nettie's and her siblings' daily lives centered on their father, who remains a beacon for Nettie. Her comments about work are laced with her father's teachings, which continue to guide her. She is single and lives with her mother. Her life is full— she is close to her mother and siblings and enjoys teaching 2-year-olds.

Nettie: My parents were great role models. They always seemed to be so relaxed and didn't let things bother them. I thought we were the most precious people in their lives—the way they treated us. We were just jewels to them. . . .

I'm from a family of nine children, and I have a twin brother. We are numbers seven and eight with one younger brother. . . . My father worked at a lumber yard, and mom was a full-time homemaker. And mom and dad were active in the church, where we went every Sunday. Dad had a strong belief in God. He'd say a prayer before he'd eat anything, wherever he was. He was always thankful.

My father was a fun person. He was easy to get along with. He always stressed teaching us to treat each other with kindness. He didn't believe in spanking us. Rather, he talked, and the way he talked we would feel worse. Every day he had a story, maybe two or three times a day. And all of his stories had a moral. He didn't have an education, but we thought he was the smartest person in the world. . . .

I always thought we were the poorest on our block because we never took vacations like the other kids. And the other kids had the latest clothes. But everyone always ended up at our house, even to eat with us. Dad would go to the farmers' market and buy four watermelons at a time. Then on the front porch he'd cut them, and all the kids in the neighborhood had watermelon with us. Dad told the other kids stories too. He was daddy to everyone, and mom was mama.

All my brothers and sisters live in the area, and they and their kids are always coming to see mom and me. They ask me about their kids, you know, wanting me to give them advice. We're all real close, hugging each other [often]. Dad died 4 years ago of pancreatic cancer, and mom continues to miss him. She doesn't laugh like she used to. When dad was sick, all his grandkids were visiting every day. He was everyone's favorite.

Like Sarah, Nettie is a gifted play partner with young children. Most often I found her on the floor singing, reading, or building with the children or at a table surrounded with messy art materials. Inevitably a child would be on her lap or snuggled nearby. Nettie's voice had a soft, melodic tone, and her classroom activities had a calm, even tempo that seemed to match her easy, relaxed manner.

Nettie: I graduated from high school in 1978. Before that, I always had a love for children and knew from the beginning I wanted to spend my life working with children. After high school, I took child development courses at Foster Community College and in high school I also took child development classes. I got my A.A. degree in child care, worked at Mulberry Park Day Care Center for 3 years, and then went to Anderson Center for Maltreated Children until I came here 10 years ago. Lillian, our director, asked me to come when she got her position here. Lillian has been a role model. And she keeps on encouraging me to go back to school. She even cut out an article for me regarding scholarships. Lillian has been very supportive.

I asked Nettie what challenges she faced as a teacher. She explained how, growing up in a large family, she was accustomed to everyone participating in family chores, in a process in which no one focused on whether each person was contributing an equal amount of time and work. In contrast, Nettie's co-teacher was accustomed to "measuring out" tasks.

Nettie: With Melinda, my co-teacher, the biggest thing that gets in my way is the work is so divided. If today is my day to put the cots out but I have a child who needs a diaper change, my co-worker will not change the diapers. If my co-teacher is doing snacks, I change diapers in the morning, and she does it in the afternoon. [Whenever] a child has a poopy diaper, I'll change it; but not everyone thinks that way.

Nettie began teaching young children 19 years before our interview. As we talked, Nettie reflected on her growth as a teacher:

Nettie: Over the years, I think I have changed [by] being more regarding. That is, I'm beyond my family, and I don't work like at home;
and I have to realize I'm in the world now, and things are different, so I'm more flexible. I finally realized I could relax. And I
learned I'm not responsible for others' feelings. Before if a worker
left a cup of coffee on the table, I would feel it was my responsibility to move it so that nobody got mad.

Although Nettie finds fulfillment in her work, she knows that many of her friends earn far more money than she does. She is satisfied, however, because she knows she is making a contribution. When she was younger, her friends did convince her to try another occupation.

Nettie: About 12 years ago, my friends from high school always were
telling me, "Why don't you get a real job with real money?" So I
did quit working at Anderson Center and got a job in a law office.
And I did make a lot more money, but I hated my job and wanted
to return to the kids. And my dad told me, "Do what will make
you happy, not what makes your friends happy." So I wrote a resume and asked Anderson Center if I could return. They said yes,
and as fast as I could, I returned. And I'll never leave kids again.

There's no other work that Nettie would want to do. Like Sarah, she's "found her niche."

Both Sarah and Nettie define who they are and the meaning of their lives in terms of their work with children. This question of meaningful-ness and identity is a central construct embedded in the personal and professional lives of each early educator whom I interviewed. As teach-ers they feel at peace within their place in the world; they are able to love and nurture babies and small children, so the babies can, in turn, feel trust in others and themselves. As discussed in Chapter 1, trust is the primary achievement of the baby's first year. This trust emerges through the baby's attachment relationship with his or her caregivers. The care-giver who has a sense of trust in her world and herself can provide the baby with the daily interactions needed for the baby to develop this trust. In the following sections, I discuss how these early educators whom I interviewed defined meaningfulness in their life and sculpted their unique identity.

MEANINGFULNESS AND PERSONAL IDENTITY

Whether consciously or unconsciously, each person defines meaning-fulness, how the world works, and their place in it—that is, their identity. Each early educator whom I interviewed spoke about her work with children as being central to both her understanding of how to make meaning in the world and her sense of identity. Sarah, for example, explained how caring for young children in need is how she has defined her place in the world. When interviewing Suzanne, a 68-year-old director of a suburban child care center, I learned that the meaning of her work is tied to her early parenting and feelings of helplessness in this role. She is committed to giving parents what she herself had lacked as a young parent.

Suzanne: When I was 19 with my first child and didn't know anything, I was overwhelmed with the responsibility of this little person. I used to think, "How come I never got education in parent-ing?" I read everything I could. I talked to my babies, read, and sang to them.

Then I accidentally began teaching nursery school. My hus-band lost his business, and we knew I had to go to work. My fourth child was the age for nursery school, and I was asked to be a teacher by his school's director. I started teaching, read everything I could find, and took a course in child develop-ment. I learned a lot and in reading always felt reinforced in what I was doing. . . .

I became assistant director of this nursery school and em-braced my new career. I was at this school for 14 years; and, before I left, I began a toddler–parent program. I then spent 4 years at Anderson Center for Maltreated Children and learned a lot. I've been at Rosehill for 12 years, director for 8.

What keeps me going is the knowledge that children need intelligent care with an understanding of child development— social, emotional, physical, and moral. We make a difference in these children's lives. I believe if a child is treated with love and respect, it is going to make a difference. . . .

Parents are very important at our center. Teachers spend lots of time talking to them at the beginning and end of the day. Parents in the infant-toddler rooms meet together for supper once a month. And before their child goes to the 2-year-old room, they visit this room. We try and make our center have the quality of a nurturing family for everyone.

Family always has been central in Suzanne's life. Her work is meaning-ful to her because she knows she is helping young families have the support, knowledge, and confidence that she lacked as a very young mother of four children. Likewise, when Nettie thinks of the meaningfulness of her work, she thinks very concretely of helping young children and their parents—what she loves most in life. And she sees her work as a continuation of the love and nurturance her parents have given to her.

Nettie: When I get home most days, I ask myself, "Did I help anyone to-day?" For example, today, Sammy came in with his dad and immediately had a tantrum. He was screaming and crying, and his dad just looked lost. He couldn't do anything with him. So I told his dad that I would give Sammy extra lap time and lots of hugs. And then a little later I'd call him so he'd know Sammy was okay. My mom and dad always did those kind of things for us. I know I'm making a difference like they did.

Religion and Meaningfulness

For many of the women I interviewed, religion is a dominant theme in their lives and central to their caregiving. When describing events, thoughts, or feelings in their lives, they often take a religious perspective. The children they care for are seen as "blessings," they put their problems "in His hands," and their good fortune is a "miracle from God."

These women's religious perspectives provide a definition of self. Some caregivers see their work as a religious calling. Caregiving is where they are supposed to be in terms of their relation with God. More than half of the family caregivers, teachers, and administrators whom I interviewed are active members in a local church or synagogue. They gain a feeling of selfhood through their acceptance within a community, which gives them a reference community for their daily life. Charlene, a family caregiver who works in a large, metropolitan area in an intervention program for children at risk of maltreatment, explained how she views her work as an expression of her religious life.

Charlene: When I was growing up, church was our lives. . . . My mom told me one time, "Dad and I realized we couldn't give you much; but we could give you your faith." You know, I think she's right. And my work in the day is my ministry. . . .

There came a place in my life where I wanted to do more and to give to others. When this project came up, I knew that this was what I was supposed to do. I just feel really centered on the job because I drew closer to my religion and to God. I have to go to daily mass and have daily prayer meditation

> because it's a very real, hard, difficult job. To be able to leave those kids and not walk off with them. I couldn't do it without knowing that God is in the middle of all this and taking care.

The caregivers I interviewed are able to find meaning in the simplest acts of physical and emotional caregiving. They can do so because their lives are unified by their religious faith.

Self-Identity

Who people perceive themselves to be is as important as what they are able to do. When early educators I interviewed described their understanding of self and the experiences that they find most meaningful in their lives, they defined themselves in terms of mothering, caring, and loving. Dilthey (1910/1961) explained that an *awareness of meaning* characterizes human life and provides the unifying framework of a person's life. And, meaning emerges through relationships within a person's life.

Relationships are at the core of meaning in these caregivers' lives. And, unlike Sarah, many of these caregivers began life with an exceptionally close relationship with their mothers and remained close throughout their childhood, adolescence, and adulthood. Sally and Jean, both family caregivers in rural communities, described their close relationships with their mothers.

Sally: As far as I can remember, my mom has been just a tower of strength, and very loving. And she did creative, fun things for us when we were kids. She played with us and encouraged whatever we did.

Jean: I was the 11th of 13 kids, so my mom was busy running the house. I mean, she cooked, did the dishes, washed and hung up the clothes—this is before automatic clothes washers and dryers. But mom was always there and easy to talk to. Now, she's one of my best friends. We talk about my boys, and she loves to talk about when my brothers and sisters and I were little.

Noddings (1984) described dimensions of caring that help to clarify these women's understanding of self. Noddings described the core of caring as follows: "Caring involves stepping out of one's own personal frame of reference into the other's. To care is to act not by fixed rule but by affection and regard" (p. 24).

Jean, a family caregiver in a rural area, and Alicia, a teacher in a suburban child care center serving primarily middle- and upper–middle-income families, described themselves as follows:

Jean: I see myself as a good mother in that I put [the] kids [in my care] before me. I'm either doing something with them or doing the laundry or something, but often they help me with these things too. When they're up, they are my first priority rather than having a good time. In reality, I am having a good time when I can watch them, see what they're going through. I think I'm pretty good at taking a perspective—"What does Randy think of this and what's he going to enjoy?" And for me to do something that the kids really like to do and to watch them have a good time is great! And just to be there for them. I think of myself as a mother first, somebody who always is putting somebody else first—children most of the time . . . but others too. I see myself in relationship with other people.

Alicia: Some days I do go home wishing I had more patience that day. But then I'll apologize to Joy [a co-teacher] for being such a bad teacher that day, and she's like, "What are you talking about?" But I know that I wasn't there; I wasn't fully there. Might have been my bad day . . . and no one else might have noticed, but I did.

Patience is unbelievably needed day in and day out. These little children are not here to make your life miserable. They don't cry and they don't have tantrums and they don't hurt other children to make you angry. It's always something underlying for them. If they cannot be at home, just make sure they are somewhere that is just as beneficial.

It amazes me what kind of effect you can have on a young child if you put the time and effort into getting to know that child and making that child feel comfortable. It's unbelievable. They trust you. And sometimes, you know, it's overwhelming. They depend on me and Joy so much.

Alicia can step outside her own reality to take the perspective of the children in her care. She observes, reacts, and responds, and she is receptive to children's needs, interests, and abilities.

Age, Life Stage, and Experience

The age and life stage of early educators help to explain differences in their approach to their work. Sarah was in her early 40s when she joined TCC, and she made child care her full-time employment. For Sarah and Nettie, work with young children is the source of their life's commitment. Other women find that family child care is a perfect fit during a stage of their lives when they are beginning a family. Sally was 23 years old and pregnant with her first child when she began working in TCC. She lived in a rural town of 400, where her husband was a pastor. Her child care income helped subsidize her husband's low income. Three years later, Sally and her husband moved to another state so he could begin graduate school. At that time, Sally taught preschool. Once her husband received his doctorate and a university appointment, Sally became a full-time homemaker and active volunteer in her family's church.

Family Support of the Caregiver's Work

Family child caregivers have chosen to be both full-time homemakers and gain employment in their home. Once they begin caregiving at home, this work inevitably changes their daily family routine, and caregiving most often becomes incorporated into the private domain of the family.

Caregivers' husbands often support their work; in fact, family caregivers' husbands and children are typically involved in some aspect of the child care process. Often, caregivers' families chip in when a caregiver has other commitments to attend to. Sally and Charlene described how their husbands have embraced their work.

Sally: The project has really stretched our family, which has been good. My husband was leery at first. He was scared for me. But he loves Jeff [a child in Sally's care] like his own son and would take him in a second if we could. And it's been great for Joey [Sally's 1-year-old son] because it's so positive for him to have other children around. At first I thought I would want to keep my first baby all to myself. But I soon learned to trade in that solitude for Joey's interaction with other children.

Charlene: My child care enriched our family. It's been especially good for my husband, Bob, who does shift work and can be actively involved in caregiving every other week....When Bob is home, he cooks breakfast for the kids while I'm picking them up. He loves woodworking; so he has made the kids toy shelves, a sandbox, a cradle for the 6-week-old, and simple toys like little cars and trucks. And for my son, David, one of the neatest things is he said, "Mom, you're probably the best thing that ever happened to these kids."

In rural communities, some husbands eat their midday meal with their wives and the children for whom they care. Often these husbands give their wives a brief respite from their caregiving responsibilities:

Jean: My husband always enjoys Nancy a lot because Nancy gets real excited whenever he comes home for dinner. He comes home when we're about halfway through with dinner, and he eats an apple or orange or something to sit with the kids. And while I do the dishes, he reads them a story.

Sally and Jean also described how their own children spoke about the other children in the caregiving arrangement as though they were their siblings. Both women take all the children with them everywhere—on brief errands, to the park, or to other recreational places.

During summer months, when caregivers' own children are out of school, the child care children often join them on family outings to the zoo, to a local park, to a farm, and so forth. Caregivers with children older than 8 years sometimes "hire" their own children to assist in child care during the summer.

Sarah: During the summer, Annie, my 9-year-old daughter, and her friend are both on the "payroll." They are my "assistants" and earn $2.00 a day. They play with the kids and help make breakfast and lunch. And I think the things that they are learning are invaluable.

Those caregivers who work with families with little or no income speak of how their own children have developed an increased awareness of poverty and a compassion for the other children.

Jean: Will is 10 years old and, as the third child, always seemed a bit spoiled. But he has been so giving with these kids. And he gets so upset if he thinks they are being neglected at their home. With the one child that finally was put in foster care, he kept asking, "Can't we keep her? She can share my room." It has helped him not to be selfish.

Not surprisingly, some caregivers' children, especially those who are the youngest of families with three or more children, initially saw the other children in their homes as intrusions; and caregivers reported that at first their own children were more problematic than the child care children. Caregivers' youngest children often were fussy and demanding when needing to share their mother's time and toys with the child care children. In each case, this pattern dissipated within a few months.

The family caregivers and their families have extended themselves to include other children within their daily family routine, and they speak of this extension as enriching their family life. Interestingly, many center-based teachers and directors also do not seem to have the traditional separation of work and home, personal and professional life. When I asked the center-based teachers and directors with whom they talked about their work, and from whom do they receive support, a significant proportion spoke of their own families. Teachers Nettie and Alicia, as well as center directors Rebecca and Suzanne, are illustrative of those early educators who regularly share stories of their child care work with their family members.

Nettie: I always am talking about the kids to my mother, my brothers and sisters who often drop by—even to my neighbors. And my brothers and sisters often ask me for advice about their own children for it seems that in my family I'm "the expert."

Alicia: I'm just thankful I have Mark, my fiancé, soon to be my husband. When I first started seeing Mark he really made me mad. He'd say, "I don't know why your job is so hard. You babysit all day." So I decided from that day on to tell him everything important that happens to me during the day. And now he's so funny because if somebody else says, "She just babysits," he's quick to say no and explain what I do.

Rebecca: I talk with my husband. We have no children, but we both have worked all our married life with children and families in a low-income social service–type field. We are able to bounce [ideas] off each other, even though we work with [children of] different ages.

Suzanne: You know, Hank and I have been married for 50 years now. And 49 years ago, we struggled as young parents who had minimal knowledge of young children or support. As parents we always worked together. And to this day, Hank seems to enjoy hearing about the children and their parents. So he's one of the people with whom I often share my work. . . . It's not always easy for me to go to other people because I'm supposed to be able to handle all these things, right? I'm the director.

The center-based child care staff whom I interviewed enjoy talking about work with family members and feel supported by them as they share stories about their day. For some, their work seems an extension of their childhood. For example, Sarah sees her work mirroring that of her mother, and Nettie sees her love of children as parallel to her parents. The family caregivers in rural sites especially had family members become integrally involved in their caregiving. Although each woman expresses this differently, none saw her caregiving work as being separate from her personal family life.

PROMOTING PROFESSIONAL GROWTH

For those early educators who choose to work with young children and their families as a life career path, it is important to consider what experiences have helped them to grow and develop skills and knowledge as early educators. Early educators change in countless ways over the tenure of their career. Carl Rogers noted that effective teachers do not rest on "answers provided in the past, but must put [their] trust in the processes by which new problems are met" (1969, p. 303). Rogers described a self-reflective teacher as a person "who is open to the experience which is going on within herself" (p. 251). Some changes stem from aging and life-cycle processes, such as parenting and "empty nest" periods. Other changes involve professional growth and development, and it is important to ask what can promote this development. This section examines how to support and promote the professional development of child care providers.

Professional Development

The early educators whom I interviewed spoke of changes they have experienced over the years and what influences have promoted these changes.

Alicia: I learn most from the other teachers. I see how everybody (since we're all outside together) deals with all the children. And it really makes me take a look at myself and kind of compare what they do with what I do or don't do. This really helps me change or helps me to be proud of what I do. And we have our teachers' personal growth counseling group that meets every 6 months. And we sit there and talk, listening and learning about how people deal with children. It really helps me grow. I know a few teachers that have really affected me in just the way they deal with the children, and that's how I want to be. And Robin, my supervisor, has helped me a lot. She is always so supportive and makes me feel confident enough to make decisions. . . . she is experienced enough to know how to handle lots of problems.

Joy: Seeing other teachers and how they handle matters helps me. I also learn by just trial and error, on my own. But also, Stuart [the in-service facilitator] is special. He speaks with all the teachers several times a year, in the evening; and he's made a big impact on me. He especially has helped me focus on respecting each child and parent.

And talking with Robin, our infant-toddler coordinator, having her as my mentor and supervisor is invaluable. She observes me, and I feel free to come to her to talk about problems. She gives suggestions about how I could handle a situation, how I could have done it differently. She's been an inspiration to me. And I always feel at ease going to her for help.

Alicia and Joy are self-reflective teachers. They see their relationships with other teachers as opportunities for observing and reflecting on how others teach. Alicia and Joy are fortunate to have an experienced infant-toddler coordinator who provides ongoing mentoring and supervision.

Chapter 2 explored how all learning occurs within the context of relationships, which are at the core of teaching babies and young children. Teaching is a craft that involves emotion as well as intellect. Teachers' craft improves through their active reflection on their practice, reflection that helps them see the meaning of their actions and experience. Joy and Alicia's supervisor, Robin, provides regular collaborative supervision that promotes their continued professional development. She provides a safe setting in which to reflect collaboratively with them on their teaching and on their successes and failures. During these conversations, Joy and Alicia are able to gain feedback from an experienced practitioner.[4] The teachers' relationship with Robin involves parallel processes; that is, the relationship affects how Joy and Alicia relate to their co-teachers and to parents, which, in turn, influences how their co-teachers and children's parents relate to the children. Relationship enriches relationship.

Unfortunately, the budgetary constraints of many child care centers prevent them from having coordinators who provide supervision. Some programs have built in collaborative peer mentoring and supervision by setting aside a substantial block of time for case presentation as a part of each staff meeting (Norman-March, 1996). Staff meetings can include a collaborative process of reflection on practice when the meetings have a psychological climate of safety, and teachers embrace mutual trust and feel free to express both positive and negative feelings.[5] Meetings can become a context for peer mentoring, in which teachers can share with and support each other. They can also voice differences of perception and interpretation. Supervision by a coordinator or by peers is very different from the supervision model based on monitoring and evaluation that is common in traditional educational settings.

Joy and Alicia have college degrees in early education, and they work in a center that can afford to hire program coordinators plus facilitators of professional development. The center where Nettie and Rosa, one of Nettie's co-teachers, work has no program coordinator and few if any professional development sessions. These women attend workshops each year to gain their 12 hours of in-service requirement for center licensure, and they have taken a few college courses.[6] Rosa is halfway through gaining her bachelor's degree. The influences on her teaching integrate traditional professional development paths more so than the other women with whom she works.

Rosa: I'm 49 years old, and I have been teaching since I was 26. And I think what has helped me improve has been seminars like those that were a part of the project which you directed—those monthly meetings [with other teachers]. But also the project's monthly on-site visits helped. And I read a lot, especially since I've returned to school. In college, the physical sciences like biology and geology have been very helpful. From them I have many new ideas of what to teach my children.

Most family caregivers have had minimal traditional education focused on professional development. But each family caregiver whom I interviewed described how she is learning and growing in her work. Jean and Sally expressed themes similar to those identified by center-based teachers.

Jean: I loved our meetings with all the caregivers twice a month. I learned a lot then. Not only from the topic you were discussing but especially from hearing stories the other women told in handling situations. But I also see the connection between the way my mom raised me and my 12 siblings, and how I try to raise my own kids and the day care kids; it's all the same.

Sally: What helps me the most is understanding the background of each child, where he is coming from, his family background. I want to provide for each child's needs, but they aren't always academic. Often it is emotional, as far as loving and nurturing.

    And I learn a lot from the parents, who often give me feedback. You know, we're like a family. When the children go to public schools, their mother often calls me to tell me how they are doing.

Several family caregivers like Jean and Sally explained how their most significant learning takes place in the doing, through direct experience with young children and problem solving within that experience.

Early Educators' Professional Support Systems

As I talked with family caregivers and center-based teachers and directors, they spoke of their need for relationships in which their thoughts and feelings *could be heard*. Some of the teachers have close personal relationships with their co-teachers, with whom they process their work and gain support.

> **Joy:** I talk about my work mostly with my co-teachers—on a day-to-day basis, an hour-to-hour basis. I remember Alicia telling me, "You are really a good personal friend as well as my co-teacher," and I feel that way about her. Initially, Alicia and I taught together for about 16 months before Carmeletta joined us. Though we worked very hard during those months, we enjoyed working together so much and became so close that we worried about having a third teacher join us.

Joy and Alicia have created a classroom climate in which each can be herself while enjoying her work with babies and toddlers and where each can interact with her co-teacher spontaneously. Chapter 2 discusses more fully the dimensions of team teaching.

Center directors, in contrast, work mostly on independent, solitary tasks. Rebecca and Suzanne direct programs large enough to have program coordinators and secretarial help and/or bookkeepers. Tiffany, director of an urban child care center, in contrast, is in charge of programs that have no secretary, bookkeeper, or program coordinator, and she has to perform all these roles herself. The combination of the complexity of the tasks and the isolated nature of the work requires her to have a strong support system. Rebecca described the CDCA directors' monthly breakfast meetings, which are facilitated by a child psychoanalyst and sponsored by CDCA as a significant reference group and means of professional support.

> **Rebecca:** The monthly CDCA breakfast meetings give me lots of support. About 8, 10, or 12 directors get together, and there always is a topic we have chosen.[7] Sometimes we stay on it and sometimes not. Basically it provides trusting relationships. We can share something and know that we're not the only ones. Everyone else has had that. As a director, I think it is very easy to get caught in pulling yourself in too many places at one time. And that's not good for you, the staff, or the families you serve. And CDCA provides support, to me and to my staff. A child specialist spends 6 days a year observing and consulting with

us. And if I have a question or problem, I know I can call a CDCA staff person and discuss it with her.

What Keeps Early Educators Going?

With the exception of two young family caregivers with small children whom I interviewed, these women have chosen early education as their life's career path. They are in a field that has had a 45% turnover rate since the late 1980s. In fact, as I listened to these women, I wondered how they avoided burnout. (For tips on stress management and avoiding burnout, see Bernstein, 1999.) Rebecca has worked in church-sponsored settlement house child care programs for 26 years. She shared how she has learned to take care of herself to avoid professional burnout. She spoke clearly about pathways of support and of the need to create outside escapes and to do things for herself, which have assisted her to remain committed to her often difficult and demanding work with families of low income.

Rebecca: This field will never give you satisfaction monetarily or even emotionally because it is a draining field. We come in giving a lot of emotional support, and I don't think we understand the real drain that our emotional support to children is. And so as we grow in this field, we have to understand that we have to have outside escapes, and outside support so that we don't take everything home. I finally learned that sometimes I need to do [something] for myself, which may not look like it's for myself. I try to make sure that I come to work in peak condition. And I think that's very important because if I'm not at peak, it's hard for me to support the staff. When I started people told me 10 years is the burnout time in a city. This is my 26th year, and I wouldn't work anywhere else.

Rebecca explained why she remains so committed to her work:

Rebecca: I don't do this because of any great service need. I do it because so much is given back to me. My work also has helped me grow in my life. So it's really a reciprocal relationship, yet one that I do have to balance because it can eat you up.

Tiffany is 33 years old. She has worked in the field since she graduated from college, and she has been director of an urban child care center for 3 years.

Tiffany: I'm not in this for the money because I know I'm never going to make more than about $30,000 a year, probably. But you know, I just have a love for the field and love for what I do. Just like my mother always loved being a foster mother—for 30 years now. And my mother, she has been an excellent role model for me.

I used to be very shy and kind of withdrawn. But over the years, I have just noticed with myself, how easy it is for me to talk about early childhood. . . . When I have to give a presentation it just amazes me that I am able to do that. But if I have to talk about anything other than early childhood education, I am just like a turtle in its shell.

Pam has worked at Rosehill Day Care Center for 24 years, first as a teacher, then as program coordinator. She learned that even though she loves her work, sometimes she does feel that she's had enough. But she knows this feeling will pass.

Pam: In reality, I don't avoid burnout, but I experience it. And I accept that that's just a part of life and will end. In truth, I don't know what else I could do. The bottom line is the kids, who are in situations where they can't be with their parents and are in a place where they are valued, respected, and feel good about themselves. . . . That's what we can provide for the kids.

Just like family caregiver, Sarah, and center-based teacher, Nettie, the administrators I interviewed have found their "place in the world" through their work with young children and their families.

What Is Needed for Quality Caregiving?

The question of quality caregiving is a key concern for each administrator. Each of the early educators I interviewed was quite skilled in working with babies and small children. When interviewing directors Rebecca and Suzanne, I asked what they look for when hiring a teacher and what skills and/or knowledge they would like their teachers to gain.

Rebecca: I'm looking for an eagerness to learn, an ability to show warmth, and a very strong ability to withstand frustration. When you are new in the field, what happens is that you become totally frustrated and often times the only power you have is to fall back on inappropriate practices your parents used when raising you. So I require a lot of ability to handle frustration. I also look for motivated teachers who will stay in the field. Our staff retention right now is approximately 9 years.

Carol: What would you like to provide for your teachers to broaden their perspective, knowledge, and skills? What do you think is missing most?

Rebecca: I guess what is missing most is a real understanding of how children think. We often put how we as adults think onto children, even some of my best teachers might do this sometimes, forgetting that children are still developing how they think.

It's also really important to develop relationship-building skills. I have a favorite saying about our program, that what we primarily do is to help develop healthy individuals—when the teacher is meeting with the mom who's had a hard day and tries perhaps to ease her burden a little bit, or when the child, who is normally a happy child, is having a difficult day. The teacher's relationship [with a child] has to help the child grow and begin developing coping techniques. And we teachers need also a lot of coping techniques.

Suzanne: What I think our teachers need most is an understanding of how children develop.[8] I don't think they know that, and I'm talking primarily about emotional development. Sure they know about physical development, when they crawl, they walk, and so on. But what happens when I have four kids and each of them is totally different?

Center directors such as Suzanne mentioned a desire for their teachers to gain more child development knowledge. Child development knowledge does provide guidance for both thinking about and working with children,[9] although it is only one piece of the puzzle. Suzanne touched on the need for teachers to have a greater understanding of relationships, an essential of effective early education. An understanding of child development and skill in relating to young children to promote that development are remarkably high-level attributes. Although center directors want to ensure that their teachers are grounded in child development and possess skills in relating to young children and adults, they know they are in a tough position because teachers often earn low wages. This minimal compensation gives little incentive to seek continued professional development.

CONCLUSION

As I thought about my interviews with these early educators, I saw that several of their life patterns reflect the principles discussed in Chapter 1. First, these women's development occurs within relationships. For example, both Jean and Nettie spoke poignantly of how their families were their anchors when they were children. Rebecca described how her first mentor has become a beacon and close friend for the past 26 years. Joy and Alicia talked about how their infant-toddler coordinator has been an invaluable guide in their growth and development.

Second, these early educators have experienced mutuality in their work relationships, which promotes their professional development. For example, Rebecca and Suzanne spoke of their monthly directors' breakfast group as being the setting for child care directors to learn from one another. Joy and Alicia each described how their team teaching provides remarkable affirmation as well as professional growth.

And, third, the lives of these women are intertwined with their social environments. For example, in rural sites, the family caregivers' husbands and their own children are very involved in their caregiving. For some family caregivers, teachers, and directors, their religious life intertwines with their caregiving, gives meaning to this caregiving, and fills their work with a deep sense of fulfillment. Also, many of the teachers come to view their relationships with other teachers as being like those of a family.

I have conducted repeated observations with all but two of the women I have interviewed for this book. I observed their talents and commitment, and I have asked myself what keeps these women going. Several factors seem central. First, each woman cares for babies or young children in a comfortable, supportive work environment. Second, in addition to their CDCA membership, all center-based interviewees received regular professional development throughout the year. The family caregivers received monthly or semimonthly 1/2-day training plus monthly observation and consultation in their homes. Third, and probably most important, each woman has received acceptance, acknowledgment, and affirmation from family members and colleagues. Several see their work as part of their religious ministry, and all see caregiving as a part of their identity. Most believe that they are making a significant contribution. They are expressing themselves creatively. It was clear that, although they make minimal money, they feel that their lives are fulfilled—a sense that many workers in our society do not share.

Are these early educators the *exception in our society?* If these women are so fulfilled, why are so many out-of-home caregivers providing low-quality child care that does not meet the developmental needs of children? *Why is there so little support for out-of-home child care in the United States?* To answer this question we can look at several cultural values. The first answer is that our economy is profit based and most often focused on short-term benefits. For example, industries pollute because developing pollution control is expensive in the short term. Industries often fail to focus, however, on the long-term impact of pollution. So, too, it is difficult for many to accept the reality that there is no short-term profit motive to high-quality child care. High-quality child care is quite expensive. The long-term benefits of high-quality child care, however, mean that we will have citizens who are able to contribute to our society. The second answer is that, since the early 1900s, our society's ideology has been about maternal child rearing. Although in 1994, 34% of mothers with children younger than 3 years of age and 63.3% of mothers with 3- to 5-year-old children were employed (Galinsky, 1994), the ideology of maternal child rearing continues to reign. The third answer is that in America the women's movement of the 1960s and 1970s initially demeaned mothering (Elshtain, 1981). To be a liberated woman meant to compete in the workplace. In contrast, the European women's movement embraced motherhood, and all Western nations except the United States support universally accessible out-of-home child care (Elshtain, 1981). Although the women's movement did have an impact on women's employment, its omission of out-of-home child care ironically reinforced our society's maternal child-rearing ideology.

What can we do to provide high-quality care to young children and effective professional development to their teachers? Given the limited governmental support of out-of-home child care in the United States, this is a gargantuan question. The dismal quality of most of our nation's out-of-home child care means that we need substantive public and professional policy discussion if we are going to ensure that our young children receive quality care. Quality care, however, is in the best interest of young children and their families and in the interest of our society as we move into the 21st century. Many at-risk young children in our nation are experiencing poor-quality care; however, poor-quality care is happening up and down the socioeconomic scale (Whitebrook, Howes, Phillips, & Pemberton, 1989).

We are fortunate that some of our children do receive high-quality child care, even if their teachers are underpaid. Why do many teachers then continue to remain in the field? Their work is a central part of their identity, and those like Nettie who have left the field for other work often feel incomplete and wind up returning. In their work with young children, caregivers and teachers have myriad opportunities to express themselves creatively. And, as so many of the women I interviewed expressed, they know their work is making a difference in the lives of young children.

We are fortunate that so many talented caregivers devote their lives to promoting the development of young children. They deserve our support just as the children deserve our care. Let us continue to strive toward doing the best we can to ensure optimal quality child care for the nation's children.

Endnotes

CHAPTER 1

1. Young children with disorders on the continuum of autism, such as pervasive developmental disorder, Asperger syndrome, or autism, have great communication and relationship difficulties. For decades medical professionals
have had a bleak prognosis for young children diagnosed with autistic disorders. Stanley I. Greenspan (1992) and his associates, however, have demonstrated success in helping these children learn skills in spontaneous communication and relationship. Greenspan most often begins working with a
child younger than 2¹/₂ years. The child receives intensive occupational therapy, speech-language therapy, and play therapy, and the child's parents receive regular parental coaching. Studies whose aim was to teach elementary
school–age children with autism skills in pretend play and how to understand other people's mental states have not had significant success (Hadwin,
Baron-Cohen, Howlin, & Hill, 1996). In the Hadwin et al. study, results indicated no significant improvement in children's spontaneous pretend play,
which suggested that imagination deficiencies are a central aspect of autistic disorders. Although children with autism could succeed in tasks assessing another person's emotional response, they could not generalize this skill,
which indicated that they learned rules without genuine understanding.
2. In *The Young Child as a Person: Toward the Development of a Healthy Conscience*
(1980), the Snyders spoke of the adult verbalization of children's feelings in
a conflict situation, feelings of both the aggressor and the child being at-
tacked, as central to young children's experience of caring and the foundation of conscience development. Once a young child experiences understanding and caring, the child can care deeply and understand others, key
aspects of conscience. The Snyders gave many clear illustrations how, when
children engage in conflict, teachers can enter into the children's experience,
reconstruct this experience, and state clearly the children's feelings and intentions.
3. Across disciplines, the use of storytelling and dialogue has been recognized
as a significant way to give meaning to our experiences and as a vehicle to
work collaboratively. Jerome Bruner discussed how we come to understand
others as we come to understand how they construct meaning in their narratives (1986, pp. 44–78). Narratives are central in some of the therapy literature (e.g., Anderson, 1992; White & Epston, 1990). Anderson wrote that
when we talk, we are not only informing others but also forming ourselves:
"The act of talking certainly involves giving information to others, but it is
something more, namely constitution of self during the self's way of ex-

pressing her or himself" (p. 166). Educators use storytelling and dialogue as valuable vehicles to foster school change and reform (Wallace, 1993). In still another field, an area of study termed *story theology* has called attention to the narrative quality of the Old and New Testament (Bausch, 1984; Tilley, 1985).

CHAPTER 2

1. Cicchetti and Rogosch (1996) made clear that diversity can always exist in both process and outcome. In any individual, there are multiple contributors to outcomes and myriad pathways, including change that can lead to an outcome. Different conditions and different psychological processes can lead to the same outcome.
2. With advances in neuroimaging, neurophysiologists can study physiological and biochemical processes in the developing brain noninvasively. They have learned that the brain does not follow a linear course during its development. Rather, brain development involves phases during which an exuberance of neuronal populations is followed by phases during which elimination, or *pruning,* of excessively produced cells and connections takes place. Furthermore, various brain regions develop at different times. For example, rapid neuronal development occurs in the brain stem during the neonatal period, and between ages 2 and 3 months, the visual and auditory brain regions undergo rapid neuronal development. This neurological development allows for the remarkable developmental leap babies make by 3 months, when they begin smiling, have longer attention spans, and engage more actively in their environment (Chugani, 1998).
3. Significant developmental changes in the first 3 years of life indicate qualitative changes in the baby and young child's brain and social-emotional behavior. Developmental theorists, however, question the notion of phases or stages of development as depicted by Erikson, Freud, and Piaget. Researchers view issues defined by such stage theories (e.g., orality, anality, trust, mistrust) as issues for the life span rather than critical issues of a developmental stage in life (Stern, 1995).
4. Extended conversations with Alicia and her co-teachers indicated that Mark has touch and noise sensitivities. Greenspan (1992) discussed these biologically based sensitivities, which he termed *regulation disorders.* Some babies' and toddlers' sensory systems are overreactive or underreactive, causing sensitivities in vision, touch, sight, hearing, or kinesthetics (movement). Caregivers often have difficulties soothing young children with these sensitivities. Caregivers may need assistance in adjusting their interaction style to accommodate a young child's learning style and sensitivities, for example, by learning to speak softly and shield the child from loud noises. Occupational therapists who have sensory integration certification can identify specific regulation difficulties. These therapists can provide sensory integration therapy that can help desensitize the young child's sensitivities.
5. Gunnar's research provided evidence of neural plasticity (1996a, 1996b, 1997). Not only does the brain underlie competence but prenatal and postnatal experiences also influence brain development. Gunnar studied babies at 15 months of age, and followed them at 17, 19, and 21 months of age. The research indicated that quality of attachment is related to whether stress activates biochemical reactions in the brain. Quality of attachment was related

to fearful responses and increases in cortisol level, with the highest level of cortisol expressed by babies with disorganized attachment (depressed or maltreating mothers).

6. I conducted a case study of child care teachers of 3- to 5-year-old children who emphasized individual versus social learning. My research demonstrated that in a social child-rearing environment teachers consistently emphasized creativity, autonomy, and other forms of individual learning. When the children were engaged in prosocial interactions with peers, these teachers rarely observed or affirmed these interactions. In sum, these everyday teacher–child interactions mirrored our society's valuing of individualism. Interestingly, my work with African American Head Start teachers indicated that these teachers more actively promoted child-to-child assistance, social responsibility, and other prosocial interactions in comparison with their Caucasian colleagues in the field (Klass, 1986).

7. This ability to regulate emotions often is not available to babies of depressed mothers, who frequently are not available emotionally to their baby. In contrast to adaptability, these babies often have a restricted range of emotional responses and can be disengaged and/or depressed. Stern (1995) suggested that babies of depressed mothers experience four different "schemes-of-being-with" that make up the baby's representational world. First, in their desire to be with their mother, babies will imitate their mothers' depression and have negative affect, minimal facial expressiveness, and/or minimal motor activity. Second, babies will vocalize, smile, gesture, and be very creative in an effort to reanimate their mother, a strategy that does work sometimes but not all the time. Partial reinforcement, however, is often a strong way to maintain behavior. Third, babies will seek stimulation elsewhere with external events. And fourth, some depressed mothers occasionally overcompensate and engage in a false interaction with their baby, who in turn uses a false self to engage in interaction. Stern noted that babies and their mothers can shuttle back and fourth among these four schemes.

8. Raver (1996) cited research that indicated gender differences in toddlers' emotional regulation strategies and differences in the manner in which adults regulate negative emotions of girls and boys. Research suggested that adults encourage relatedness among girls and independence among boys, and adults regulate girls' negative emotions more so than they do with boys. In turn, toddler girls sought more comfort from their mothers than did boys.

CHAPTER 3

1. Children's communication disorders can stem from biological and/or environmental conditions. Biological conditions can be genetic, such as the chromosomal disorder Down syndrome, the sex-linked chromosomal disorder fragile X syndrome, or the metabolic disorder phenylketonuria (PKU). Congenital conditions include infections such as rubella, fetal exposure to alcohol and/or other drugs, anoxia, and prematurity/low birth weight. Postnatal factors include meningitis, lead poisoning, and chronic ear infections. Environmental conditions include the quality of the environment and the presence of child maltreatment (Prizant et al., 1993).

2. Stern (1985) called babies' ability to understand that experiences are shared *intersubjective relatedness.*

3. The brain of the baby and young child is remarkably plastic. When a child

younger than 10 years old suffers damage to the left cortical hemisphere, which controls language acquisition, neural plasticity allows the right cortical hemisphere to develop a language region; and the child's language continues to develop (Chugani, 1997).

4. Research indicates that "pop-up" books with three-dimensional features invite toddlers to respond to pictures as objects rather than as representations (e.g., children will try to pick up the depicted objects). Instead of helping young children understand the difference between objects and symbolic pictures, these books may actually conceal the difference.

5. Using a mental health perspective, Greenspan (1992) termed the give-and-take interaction between adults and children *opening and closing circles*.

6. Videotaped studies of working-class and upper middle-class mothers in interaction with their 18- to 29-month-old children during mealtimes, dressing, book reading, and toy play show significant social-class differences in these mother–child interactions. Upper–middle-class mothers talked to their children more, asked them more questions, and responded contingently to their children's talk more than did working-class mothers; these patterns were correlated with the upper–middle-class children's vocabulary development. Working-class mothers' speech was more directive and seemed to have a negative effect on their children's language development. These researchers suggested that the interaction context may be a factor in these social-class differences; for example, working-class mothers may have less leisure time leading to less play with their children and more goal-directed conversation (Hoff-Ginsberg, 1991).

7. Hoff-Ginsberg (1991) cited several studies that compared mothers' conversations with children during toy play with their talk during story reading. These studies have found that mothers' speech during story reading is structurally more complex, uses a larger vocabulary, and involves more frequent questioning, all of which stimulate young children's language development.

8. DeLoache (1996) and colleagues' research indicates that young children only gradually understand symbols and their references. Using scale models, the researchers examined how 30- and 36-month-olds could utilize symbols in retrieving hidden toys. The 36-month-olds understood the relation between symbol and referent and how they were related, whereas the 30-month-olds performed very poorly.

CHAPTER 4

1. From Hammarskjöld, D. (1966). *Markings* (p. 129; L. Sjöberg & W.H. Auden, trans.). New York: Alfred A. Knopf; reprinted by permission.

2. Stern (1995) pointed out that emotions are a *temporal* experience, not a static event outside of time. Emotional experiences have a temporal contour, which Stern termed a *temporal feeling shape*. The temporal feeling shape depends on which emotions and which motivations are involved in the experience. Stern illustrated the temporal feeling shape with the universal parent game, "I'm gonna getcha." This game involves increasing suspense, retarding the beat, and then the unexpected, "Gotcha!" Throughout the game the baby experiences waves of excitement, suspense, and pleasure. Listening to music, according to Stern, also is a temporal experience and not a static event.

3. Dahl (1996) explained that the neurobehavioral systems involved in the

regulation of arousal, attention, and emotion overlap with the regulation of sleep. Inadequate sleep influences the emotional state of a baby or young child as well as his or her ability to attend. Babies who experience repeated emotional disturbance or high levels of arousal will have difficulty sleeping. Although most babies and young children are deep sleepers, sleep deprivation of young children at risk has substantive effects on weakening goal-directed behaviors and the ability to regulate emotions.

4. Evidence has shown that vagal tone is central to infants' and young children's emotion regulation ability. Porges, Doussard-Roosevelt, Lourdes Portales, and Greenspan (1996) measured the vagal tone of 24 9-month-old infants during a social/attention task. Those infants with decreasing vagal tone at 9 months had significantly more behavior problems when followed at 3 years of age.

5. Between 6 and 12 months, the period in which the attachment system is forming, elevated levels of cortisol are found. The attachment relationship can dampen or heighten the baby's proneness to being reactive. Utilizing the Ainsworth Strange Situation (Ainsworth, Blehar, Waters, & Wall, 1978), Gunnar (1997) found that babies with insecure attachment have high cortisol levels; and babies with disorganized attachment, abusive caregiving, or depressed mothers have very high cortisol levels.

6. Some malnourished babies suffer from failure to thrive (FTT, also known as *pediatric undernutrition*). FTT babies have growth failure that is caused by malnourishment. Often these babies also have delayed psychomotor development, developmental retardation, and insecure attachments with their mothers. Children younger than 2 years of age who experience multiple risk factors such as poverty and low birth weight can be at risk for FTT (Benoit, 1993; Brazelton, 1992; Kessler & Dawson, 1999).

7. Research shows that aggression and disruptive behavior occur on a regular basis among children as young as 2 years of age. Shaw, Owens, Vondr, Keenan, and Winslow (1996) implemented a longitudinal study of 100 infants 6–11 months old and their mothers. Their study provided information on the pathways leading to the emergence of disruptive behavior of very young children. Those children who experience disorganized attachment (e.g., resulting from maltreatment, the mother's psychological unavailability, or maternal depression), child-rearing disagreements among parents, maternal psychological ill health, and those children who had a difficult temperament as babies were consistently associated with young children's aggression and disruptive behavior problems. Belsky et al.'s (1996) research showed evidence that the externalizing problem behavior of toddlers was related to chronic troubled family interaction.

8. One study found that toddlers who attended low-quality child care differed from those toddlers who attended high-quality child care in their ability to comply and self-regulate. The researchers interviewed and observed 89 families and their toddler-age children at home, in the laboratory, and in child care. Both parents and child care teachers of low-quality programs were less involved and invested in the toddlers' compliance. In turn, the children were less compliant in the child care center and less able to self-regulate in the laboratory. In contrast, children attending high-quality child care programs were more compliant and better able to self-regulate.

9. Crockenberg and Litman (1990) studied 2-year-olds' compliance with their mothers in a laboratory task and during dinnertime at home. Two-year-

olds whose mothers combined control with guidance were most likely to be compliant as well as self-assertive; whereas two-year-olds whose mothers used power-assertive control strategies were defiant in both environments. Findings of this study are congruent with Baumrind's (1972) patterns of authoritative parenting.

10. Farber (1996) recorded the aggressive behavior of 64 4-year-olds in four preschool classrooms. Results indicated that children in social cliques had similar amounts of observed aggressive behavior. These children in social cliques also demonstrated more reciprocal friendships, dominance, and social competence than children not in cliques. Farber suggested that early educators consider focusing their efforts to decrease children's aggression on groups of children instead of on individual children.

11. McGee, Partridge, Williams, and Silva (1990) studied a sample of preschool children over a 12-year period, and their findings indicated troublesome long-term consequences of hyperactivity in preschoolers. The authors found that preschool children who are hyperactive show continued problem behavior during elementary school and adolescence. Hyperactivity seems to be significantly related to poor language skills among preschoolers and lower cognition and reading ability in primary school. A strong association thus appears to exist between inattention and difficulties in cognition and limited language skills.

CHAPTER 5

1. From Gadamer, H.-G. (1993). *Truth and method* (p. 103). New York: Continuum; reprinted by permission.

2. Singer and Singer (1990) have surveyed the range of toys in various cultures and historical periods. The earliest known toys are play rattles from the Middle East that date from 2600 B.C. The Singers found that the most popular playthings across cultures and historical periods were unstructured materials made from natural materials or household items.

3. Young (1997) discussed how tolerable pain and discomfort in infancy and young childhood can be essential ingredients that stimulate creative mastery and that, in fact, creativity can heal.

4. Coleman (1976) identified the multiple functions of games for children. He suggested that in addition to showing that rules must be obeyed by all, games allow a child to see the consequences of one's actions in a predictable and controllable context. Furthermore, games diminish the teacher's role as judge and jury; the outcome is defined by the rules and the play.

5. Researchers have studied whether it is possible to teach children with autism to understand emotion, belief, and pretend play. Hadwin et al. (1996) worked with 30 children with autism. After the children took a pretest on understanding of emotion, belief, and pretend play for 8 consecutive days, researchers engaged in $1/2$-hour teaching activities involving emotion, belief, and pretend play. On Day 10, children were given a posttest. Results of this study indicated that it is possible to teach perspective taking to children with autism. Teaching effects were presented 2 months later. These children, however, could not generalize their learning to other tasks. The children seemed to learn what they were taught without understanding the concept behind it. After teaching, children showed no significant improvement in their ability to engage in spontaneous pretend play.

6. Howes and Rodning (1992) studied 40 3-year-olds enrolled in preschool who were part of a larger, longitudinal sample. At 12 months of age, all of the children had been observed in a standard Ainsworth Strange Situation and were classified according to standard methods. In the sample, 30 children were classified as secure and 10 as insecure. The authors reported that children with insecure attachment found it difficult to engage in social pretend play at all. When they did engage in pretend play, they had difficulty in initiating and maintaining the play and were more likely to have conflicts with their peers.

7. Greenspan and Greenspan (1989) provided a convincing argument of how adults' active engagement as play partners with babies and young children enhances the children's social and emotional selves. The role of the adult as an active participant in young children's play is a relatively new insight among developmental and early education theorists and researchers. Historically, theory promoted adult roles as providers of settings, observers, and periodic participants in play as the need arose, for example, to implement a rule.

8. Flora Thompson, born in 1876, discussed country games of her childhood in the 1880s, games that are parallel to some of the jump-rope games that young girls play outdoors:

> In their ankle-length frocks as they went through the same movements and sang the same rhymes as their mothers and grandmothers had done before them. . . . How long the games had been played and how they originated no one knew, for they had been handed down for a time long before living memory and accepted by each succeeding generation as a natural part of its childhood. Of all of the generations that had played the games, that of the eighties was to be the last. Already those children had one foot in the national school and one on the village green. . . . In ten years' time the games would be neglected and in twenty, forgotten. (1976, p. 456)

CHAPTER 6

1. From Sacks, O.T. (1996). *An anthropologist on Mars: Seven paradoxical tales* (p. xvii). New York: Alfred A. Knopf; reprinted by permission.

2. Researchers observed 24-month-old toddlers of depressed and nondepressed mothers in three play sessions involving two mothers and their children. Researchers also documented mothers' child-rearing practices and mothers' reports of children's behavior at ages 5 and 6 years (Zahn-Waxler, Ianotti, Cummings, & Denham, 1990). Depressed mothers who could anticipate their children's needs; used respectful, reasoned control methods; and provided structure and organization during their child's play had 5- and 6-year-old children who exhibited little aggression. In contrast, depressed mothers who were more inconsistent, negative, and/or unresponsive had 5- and 6-year-old children who exhibited much aggression and other externalizing problems.

3. Toth et al. (1997) administered 10 narrative story stems to 107 preschool children, 72% of whom had experienced multiple subtypes of abuse, and 27% of whom were nonmaltreated children from families receiving Aid for Families with Dependent Children (AFDC; now called Temporary Assistance for Needy Families), similar to the families of maltreated children. Maltreated children's story stems involved negative maternal representation, negative

self-representation, and, with the examiner, were less responsive and more controlling.

4. *The Children of Kauai: A Longitudinal Study from the Prenatal Period to Age 10* (Werner, Bierman, & French, 1971) is about a classic longitudinal study designed to follow the course of prenatal development through adolescence of every pregnancy identified the island of Kauai, Hawaii, between 1954 and 1955. A multidisciplinary team of health care professionals and psychologist followed these children with the aim of discovering predictors of school success and mental health. At age 10, the best predictors were parenting practices of moderate warmth, low physical punishment, responsiveness, and verbal encouragement. Kauai has a diverse multiclass, multiethnic, and multiracial population.

CHAPTER 7

1. Research on child care centers uniformly indicates that accredited centers have a substantively higher quality of child care than do nonaccredited centers. For example, Jorde-Bloom's (1995) comparison of 60 accredited and 320 nonaccredited child care centers in 33 states indicated that accredited centers were substantively higher in quality than nonaccredited centers and had a higher quality of work life for the caregivers.

2. Jackson (1992) classified four ways to assist teacher development: 1) provide principles and techniques to advise teachers how to improve their practice, 2) improve the working conditions of teachers, 3) help teachers handle the psychological stresses of their work, and 4) help teachers gain a broader and more complex understanding of teaching from a variety of perspectives.

3. Butt and colleagues (1992) spoke of how teachers' strong commitments emerge from deeply personal roots.

4. The professional organization ZERO TO THREE: National Center for Infants, Toddlers, and Families has taken the lead in addressing the need for supervision for professionals working with young children and their families. ZERO TO THREE discussed how reflection, collaboration, and consistency are key features of effective supervision. Literature on supervision includes Bertacchi and Stott (1992), Fenichel (1992), and Shahmoon Shanok (1991).

5. With a small grant from a community foundation and 30 home visitors in a large consolidated school district, the author has directed a project of peer mentoring supervision for these home visitors. Each semester the home visitors videotape each other conducting a home visit and then meet together to reflect on the visit. Twice each month the home visitors meet together in teams. Once a month they view each others' videotapes and discuss together the approaches depicted in the video, and once a month they meet with a psychologist to discuss those families experiencing problems they find beyond their professional expertise. In the third year of this project, home visitors are increasingly self-reflective, and professional development is no longer an "add-on." See Poelle (1993) for a discussion of peer mentoring in early education.

6. Cassidy, Buell, Pugh-Hoese, and Russell (1995) have studied the effect of community college coursework on the classroom practices of teachers in child care centers who do not have college degrees. Findings indicate that 15–20 hours of community college coursework influenced significant gains in teachers' beliefs and practices, as measured by Home Observation and

Measurement of the Environment Scale (HOME; Caldwell & Bradley, 1984), as compared with a comparison group of teachers not attending college classes.

7. Networks offer a context for continued professional growth. Networks across geographical areas can be especially helpful for rural early educators. An effective network model in which educators share and learn from one another over time is the Foxfire Teacher Network. In Foxfire, educators come together for summer workshops; and they maintain continued collaboration via electronic and written communications (Lieberman & McLaughlin, 1992).

8. Norton (1996) provided guidelines for in-service education of early education professionals who work with young children and their families.

9. Postmodern early educators have helped us understand that child development knowledge only approximates reality. It reflects a specific sociocultural position while claiming universality and reinforcing the status quo of middle-income Caucasians. If child development knowledge is the only theoretical grounding of early educators, this knowledge becomes what Stott and Bowman spoke of as a "slippery base for practice" (1996). Because children live within specific contexts, other theories such as anthropology and sociology can be helpful frames in teaching. Sally Lubeck (1996) stated that the National Association for the Education of Young Children (NAEYC) Developmentally Appropriate Practices are guidelines that "define a 'universal' child rearing practice to foster this development by distinguishing between appropriate and inappropriate practices, a dualism that makes it difficult to consider other options. Finally, the curriculum serves to foster the development of an isolated being. . . . with the end goal being the autonomous individual. The postmodern challenge, in turn, raises doubts about each of these certainties."

References

Ainsworth, M.D.S., Blehar, M.C., Waters, E., & Wall, S. (1978). *Patterns of attachment*. Mahwah, NJ: Lawrence Erlbaum Associates.

Anderson, T. (1992). *The reflecting team: Dialogues and dialogues about the dialogues.* New York: W.W. Norton.

Barclay, K.D., & Walwer, L. (1992). Linking lyrics and literacy through song picture books. *Young Children, 47*(4), 76–85.

Bates, E., Bretherton, I., & Snyder, L. (1988). *From first words to grammar: Individual differences and dissociable mechanisms.* New York: Cambridge University Press.

Bateson, M.C. (1994). *Peripheral visions: Learning along the way.* New York: Harper-Collins.

Bauer, P.J., & Mandler, J.M. (1990). *Remembering what happened next: Very young children's recall of event sequences.* New York: Cambridge University Press.

Baumrind, D. (1972). Socialization and instrumental competence in young children. In W.W. Hartup (Ed.), *The young child: Reviews of research* (Vol. 2, pp. 202–224). Washington, DC: National Association for the Education of Young Children.

Bausch, W.J. (1984). *Story-telling: Imagination and faith.* Mystic, CT: Twenty-Third Publications.

Behnke, M., & Eyler, F.D. (1994). Issues in prenatal cocaine use research: Problems in identifying users and choosing an appropriate comparison group. *Infant Mental Health Journal, 15*(2), 146–157.

Belsky, J., Woodworth, S., & Crnic, K. (1996). Troubled family interaction during toddlerhood. *Development and Psychopathology, 8*(3), 477–495.

Benoit, D. (1993). Failure to thrive and eating disorders. In C.H. Zeanah, Jr. (Ed.), *Handbook of infant mental health* (pp. 317–333). New York: The Guilford Press.

Berkowitz, C.D., & Senter, S.A. (1987). Characteristics of mother–infant interactions in nonorganic failure to thrive. *Journal of Family Practice, 24,* 377–381.

Bernal, G.R. (1992). How to calm children through massage. *Childhood Education, 74*(1), 9–14.

Bernstein, G.S. (1999). *"Human services? . . . That must be so rewarding.": A practical guide for professional development* (2nd ed.). Baltimore: Paul H. Brookes Publishing Co.

Bertachhi, J., & Stott, F.M. (1992). A seminar for supervisors in infant/family programs: Growing versus paying more for staying the same. In E. Fenichel (Ed.), *Learning through supervision and mentorship to support the development of infants, toddlers, and their families: A source book* (pp. 132–140). Washington, DC: ZERO to THREE: National Center for Infants, Toddlers, and Families.

Bettes, B.A. (1988). Maternal depression and motherese: Temporal and intonational features. *Child Development, 59,* 1089–1096.

Bettleheim, B. (1969). *Children of the dream.* London: Collier Macmillan.

Biber, B. (1984). *Early education and psychological development.* New Haven, CT: Yale University Press.

Boyd, B.J. (1997). Teacher response to superhero play: To ban or not to ban? *Childhood Education, 74*(1), 23–28.

Brazelton, T.B. (1973). *Neonatal Behavioral Assessment Scales.* Philadelphia: J.B. Lippincott.

Brazelton, T.B. (1992). *Touchpoints: The essential reference. Your child's emotional and behavioral development.* Reading, MA: Addison Wesley Longman.

Brazelton, T.B., & Cramer, B.G. (1990). *The earliest relationship: Parents, infants, and the drama of early attachment.* Reading, MA: Addison Wesley Longman.

Brock, D.R., & Dodd, E.L. (1994). A family lending library: Promoting early literacy development. *Young Children, 49*(3), 16–21.

Bronfenbrenner, U. (1970). *Two worlds of childhood: U.S. and U.S.S.R.* New York: Russell Sage Foundation.

Brown, M.W. (1947). *Goodnight moon.* New York: Scholastic.

Bruner, J.S. (1983). Play, thought, and language. *Peabody Journal of Education, 60*(3), 60–69.

Bruner, J.S. (1986). *Actual minds, possible worlds.* Cambridge: Harvard University Press.

Bruner, J.S., & Sherwood, V. (1976). Peekaboo and the learning of rule structures. In J.S. Bruner, A. Jolly, & K. Sylva (Eds.), *Play: Its role in development and evolution* (pp. 277–286). New York: Basic Books.

Bureau of Labor Statistics. (1995). *Employment status of the civilian noninstitutional population by sex, age, presence and age of youngest child, marital status, race and Hispanic origin.* Washington, DC: Author.

Butt, R., Raymond, D., McCure, G., & Yamagishi, L. (1992). Collective autobiography and the teacher's voice. In I.F. Goodson (Ed.), *Studying teachers' lives* (pp. 51–98). London: Routledge.

Caldwell, B., & Bradley, R. (1984). *Home Observation for the Measurement of the Environment (HOME).* Little Rock: University of Arkansas at Little Rock, Center for Research on Teaching and Learning.

Campbell, S.B. (1990). *Behavior problems in preschool children: Clinical and developmental issues.* New York: The Guilford Press.

Carle, E. (1979). *The very hungry caterpillar.* New York: HarperCollins.

Carlsson-Paige, N., & Levin, D.E. (1990). *Who's calling the shots? How to respond effectively to children's fascination with war play and war toys.* Philadelphia: New Society.

Carter, B. (1988). Divorce: His and hers. In M. Walters, B. Carter, P. Papp, & O. Siberstein (Eds.), *The invisible web: Gender patterns in family relationships* (pp. 253–288). New York: The Guilford Press.

Cassidy, D., Buell, M.J., Pugh-Hoese, S., & Russell, S. (1995) The effect of education on child care teachers' beliefs and classroom quality: Year one evaluation of the TECH early childhood associate degree scholarship program. *Early Childhood Research Quarterly, 10,* 171–183.

Chan, I. (1975, April). *New people in new China: As reflected through education and child rearing.* Paper presented at the biennial meeting of the Society for Research in Child Development, Denver, CO.

Chess, S., & Thomas, A. (1987). *Know your child: An authoritative guide for today's parents.* New York: Basic Books.

Children's Defense Fund. (1994). Living in fear: National poll tops children's list of worries. *CDF Reports, 2*, 1–2.

Chugani, H.T. (1997). Neuroimaging of developmental nonlinearity and developmental pathologies. In G.R. Lyon (Ed.), *Developmental neuroimaging* (pp. 187–195). San Diego: Academic Press.

Chugani, H.T. (1998). *Adaptability of the developing human brain. Developmental change: Perspectives from neuroscience and early intervention research.* Chicago: Erikson Institute's Faculty Development Project on the Brain and the University of Chicago's Early Childhood Initiative.

Cicchetti, D., & Lynch, M. (1993). Toward an ecological/transactional model of community violence and child maltreatment: Consequences for children's development. *Psychiatry, 56*, 95–118.

Cicchetti, D., & Rogosch. F.A. (1996). Equifinality and multifinality in developmental psychopathology. *Development and Psychopathology, 8*(3), 597–600.

Cicchetti, D., & Rogosch, F.A. (1997). The role of self organization in the promotion of resilience in maltreated children. *Development and Psychopathology, 9*(4), 797–816.

Clandinin, D.J., & Connelly, F.M. (1994). Personal experience methods. In N.K. Denzin & Y.S. Lincoln (Eds.), *Handbook of qualitative research* (pp. 413–427). London: Sage Publications.

Coleman, J.S. (1976). Learning through games. In J.S. Bruner, A. Jolly, & K. Sylva (Eds.), *Play: Its role in development and evolution* (pp. 460–463). New York: Basic Books.

Constantino, J.N. (1993). Parents, mental illness, and the primary health care of infants and young children. *Young Children, 13*(5), 1–9.

Cox, A.D., Puckering, C., Pound, A., & Mills, M. (1987). The impact of maternal depression on young children. *Journal of Child Psychology and Psychiatry, 28*, 917–928.

Crockenberg, S., & Litman, C. (1990). Autonomy as competence in two-year-olds: Maternal correlates of child compliance, defiance, and self-assertion. *Developmental Psychology, 26*, 961–971.

Cummings, E.M., & Davies, P. (1996). Emotional security as a regulatory process in normal development and the development of psychopathology. *Development and Psychopathology, 8*(1), 123–139.

Curry, N.E., & Arnaud, S.H. (1995). Personality difficulties in preschool children as revealed through play themes and styles. *Young Children, 50*(4), 4–9.

Dahl, R.E. (1996). The regulation of sleep and arousal: Development and psychopathology. *Development and Psychopathology, 8*(1), 3–27.

Damon, W. (1977). *The social world of the child.* San Francisco: Jossey-Bass.

Davenport, Y.B., Zahn-Waxler, C., Adland, M.C., & Mayfield, J. (1984). Early child-rearing practices in families with a manic-depressive parent. *American Journal of Psychiatry, 141*, 230–235.

DeLoache, J. (1996). Shrinking trolls and expanding minds: How very young children learn to understand and use symbols. *ZERO TO THREE Bulletin, 17*(3), 10–16.

Dewey, J. (1922). *Human nature and conduct.* New York: Modern Library

Dilthey, W. (1961). *Patterns and meaning in history: Thoughts on history and society.* New York: HarperCollins. (Edited by H.P. Rickman from Vol. VII of Dilthey's collected works, compiled in 1910).

Dodge, K.A. (1990). Developmental psychopathology in children of depressed mothers. *Developmental Psychology, 26*(1), 3–6.

Drell, M.J., Siegel, C.H., & Gaenbauer, T.J. (1993). Post-traumatic stress disorder. In C.H. Zeanah, Jr. (Ed.), *Handbook on infant mental health* (pp. 291–304). New York: The Guilford Press.

Dunham, P., & Dunham, F. (1992). Lexical development during middle infancy: A mutually driven infant–caregiver process. *Developmental Psychology, 28*(3), 414–420.

Egeland, B., & Sroufe, L.A. (1981). Attachment and early maltreatment. *Child Development, 52*(1), 44–52.

Eiden, R.D., & Leonard, K.E. (1996). Paternal alcohol use and the mother–infant relationship. *Development and Psychopathology, 8*(2), 307–323.

Elshtain, J.B. (1981). *Public man, private woman: Women in social and political thought.* Princeton, NJ: Princeton University Press.

Emde, R.N. (1996). Thinking about intervention and improving socio-emotional development: Clinical perspective and recent trends in policy and knowledge. *ZERO TO THREE Bulletin, 17*(1), 11–16.

Emde, R.N., Biringen, Z., Clyman, R.B., & Oppenheim, D. (1991). The moral self of infancy: Affective core and procedural knowledge. *Developmental Review, 11,* 251–270.

Engle, S. (1997). The guy who went up the steep nicken: The emergence of story telling during the first three years. *ZERO TO THREE Bulletin, 17*(3), 1, 3–9.

Erikson, E. (1950). *Childhood and society.* New York: W.W. Norton.

Fabes, R.A., & Eisenberg, N. (1992). Young children's coping with interpersonal anger. *Child Development, 63*(1), 116–128.

Farber, J.M. (1996). Aggressive behavior in preschoolers' social networks: Do birds of a feather flock together? *Early Childhood Research Quarterly, 11*(3), 333–350.

Fenichel, E. (1992). Learning through supervision and mentorship. In E. Fenichel (Ed.), *Learning through supervision and mentorship to support the development of infants, toddlers, and their families: A source book.* Washington, DC: ZERO TO THREE: National Center for Infants, Toddlers, and Families.

Fernald, A. (1992). Meaningful melodies in mothers' speech to infants. In H.H. Papoušek, U. Jurgens, & M. Papoušek (Eds.), *Nonverbal vocal communication: Comparative and developmental approaches* (pp. 262–282). New York: Cambridge University Press.

Field, T. (1982). Individual differences in the expressivity of neonates and young infants. In R.S. Feldman (Ed.), *Development of nonverbal behavior in children* (pp. 279–298). New York: Springer-Verlag.

Field, T. (1993). Infant massage. *ZERO TO THREE Bulletin, 14*(2), 8–12.

Field, T., Healy, B., Goldstein, S., & Guthertz, M. (1990). Behavior state matching and synchrony in mother–infant interactions of nondepressed versus depressed dyads. *Developmental Psychology, 26,* 7–14.

Fraiberg, S.H. (1980). *Clinical studies in infant mental health.* New York: Basic Books.

Fraiberg, S.H., Adelson, E., & Shapiro, V. (1975). Ghosts from the nursery: A psychoanalytic approach to the problems of impaired mother–infant relationships. *Journal of the American Academy of Child Psychiatry, 14,* 378–421.

French, L.A. (1986). The language of events. In K. Nelson (Ed.), *Event knowledge: Structure and function in development* (pp. 119–136). Hillsdale, NJ: Lawrence Erlbaum Associates.

Gadamer, H.-G. (1993). *Truth and method.* New York: Continuum.

Galinsky, E. (1994). Families and work: The importance of the quality of the work environment. In S.L. Kagan & B. Weissbourd (Eds.), *Putting families first: Amer-*

ica's family support movement and the challenge of change (pp. 112–136). San Francisco: Jossey-Bass.

Garbarino, J. (1989). An ecological perspective on the role of play in child development. In M.N. Block & A.D. Pellegrini (Eds.), *The ecological context of children's play* (pp. 16–34). Greenwich, CT: Ablex Publishing Corp.

Garbarino, J. (1992). *Children and families in the social environment.* Chicago: Aldine.

Garbarino, J. (1993, December 25). Quoted in *St. Louis Post Dispatch,* p. 1.

Garcia, E.E. (1994). Addressing the challenges of diversity. In S.L. Kagan & B. Weissbourd (Eds.), *Putting families first: America's family support movement and the challenge of change* (pp. 243–275). San Francisco: Jossey-Bass.

Gil, E., & Johnson, T.C. (1993). *Sexualized children: Assessment and treatment of sexualized children and children who molest.* Rockville, MD: Launch Press.

Goodman, S.H., & Radke-Yarrow, M., & Teti, D. (1993). Maternal depression as a context for child rearing. *ZERO TO THREE Bulletin, 13*(5), 10–16.

Goodson, I.F. (1992). Studying teachers' lives: Problems and possibilities. In I.F. Goodson (Ed.), *Studying teachers' lives* (pp. 234–249). London: Routledge.

Gordon, T. (1989). *Discipline that works: Promoting self discipline in children.* New York: Penguin USA.

Gottlieb, I., & Hooley, J.M. (1988). Depression and marital distress: Current status and future directions. In S. Duck (Ed.), *Handbook of personal relationships* (pp. 543–570). Chichester, England: John Wiley & Sons.

Greenberg, P. (1987). Child choice—another way to individualize—another form of positive discipline. *Young Children, 43*(1), 48–54.

Greenspan, S.I. (1992). *Infancy and early childhood: The practice of clinical assessment and intervention with emotional and developmental challenges.* Madison, CT: International Universities Press.

Greenspan, S.I., with Benderly, B.L. (1997). *The growth of the mind and the endangered origins of intelligence.* Reading, MA: Addison Wesley Longman.

Greenspan, S.I., & Greenspan, N.T. (1989). *The essential partnership: How parents and children can meet the emotional challenges of infancy and childhood.* New York: Penguin USA.

Gunnar, M.G. (1996a). *Quality of care and the buffering of stress physiology: Its potential role in protecting the developing human brain.* Paper presented at the plenary session of the 11th ZERO TO THREE: National Center for Infants, Toddlers, and Families National Training Institute, Washington, DC.

Gunnar, M.G. (1996b). *Stress and early brain development: The importance of sensitive caregiving.* Paper presented at the plenary session of the 11th ZERO TO THREE: National Center for Infants, Toddlers, and Families National Training Institute, Washington, DC.

Gunnar, M.G. (1997). *Frontiers of science: Stress and coping during infancy.* Paper presented at the plenary session of the 12th ZERO TO THREE: National Center for Infants, Toddlers, and Families National Training Institute, Nashville, TN.

Hadwin, J., Baron-Cohn, S., Howlin, P., & Hill, K. (1996). Can we teach children with autism to understand emotions, belief, or pretence? *Development and Psychopathology, 8*(2), 345–366.

Hammarskjöld, D. (1966). *Markings* (L. Sjöberg & W.H. Auden, trans.). New York: Alfred A. Knopf.

Hart, B., & Risley, T.R. (1999). *The social world of children learning to talk.* Baltimore: Paul H. Brookes Publishing Co.

Heath, S.B. (1983). *Way with words: Language, life and work in communities and classrooms.* New York: Cambridge University Press.

Hitz, R., & Driscoll, A. (1988). Praise or encouragement? New insights into praise: Implications for early childhood teachers. *Young Children, 43*(5), 6–13.

Hochschild, A.R. (1997). *The time bind: When work becomes home and home becomes work.* New York: Henry Holt.

Hoff-Ginsberg, E. (1991). Mother–child conversation in different social classes and communicative settings. *Child Development, 62,* 782–796.

Holdaway, D. (1979). *The foundations of literacy.* Sydney, Australia: Aston Scholastic (distributed in the United States by Heinemann).

Honig, A.S. (1985). Compliance, control, and discipline. *Young Children, 40*(2), 50–58.

Hough, R.A., & Nurss, F.J. (1992). Language and literacy for the limited English proficient child. In L.O. Ollila & M.I. Mayfield (Eds.), *Emerging literacy: Preschool, kindergarten, and primary grades* (pp. 137–165). Needham Heights, MA: Allyn & Bacon.

Howes, C., Matheson, C., & Wu, F. (1992). Friendship and social pretend play: Illustrative study #6. In C. Howes, O. Unger, & C.C. Matheson (Eds.), *The collaborative construction of pretend: Social pretend play functions* (pp. 107–114). Albany: State University of New York Press.

Howes, C., & Rodning, C. (1992). Attachment security and social pretend play negotiation: Illustrative Study #5. In C. Howes, O. Unger, & C.C. Matheson (Eds.), *The collaborative construction of pretend: Social pretend play functions* (pp. 89–98). Albany: State University of New York Press.

Howes, C., Smith, E., & Galinsky, E. (1995). *Florida quality improvement study: Interim report.* New York: Families and Work Institute.

Howes, C., & Unger, O. (1989). Play with peers in child care settings. In M.N. Block & A.D. Pellegrini (Eds.), *The ecological context of children's play* (pp. 16–34). Greenwich, CT: Ablex Publishing Corp.

Howes, C., Unger, O., & Matheson, C.C. (Eds.). (1992). *The collaborative construction of pretend: Social pretend play functions.* Albany: State University of New York Press.

Huttenlocker, R., Haight, J., Bryk, A., Seltzer, M., & Lynos, T. (1991). Early vocabulary growth: Relating to language input and gender. *Developmental Psychology, 27,* 236–248.

Jackson, B.R. (1992). Helping teachers develop. In A. Hargreaves & M.G. Fullan (Eds.), *Understanding teacher development* (pp. 67–74). New York: Teachers College Press.

Jones, N.A., Field, T., Fox, N.A., Lundy, B., & Davalos, M. (1997). EEG activation in 1-month-old infants of depressed mothers. *Development and Psychopathology, 9*(3), 491–507.

Jones, N.B. (1976). Rough-and-tumble play among nursery school children. In J.S. Bruner, A. Jolly, & K. Sylva (Eds.), *Play: Its role in development and evolution* (pp. 352–363). New York: Basic Books.

Jones-Harden, B. (1997). You can't do it alone: Home visitation with psychologically vulnerable families and children. *ZERO TO THREE Bulletin, 17*(4), 10–16.

Jorde-Bloom, P. (1995). The quality of work life in NAEYC accredited and nonaccredited early childhood programs. *Early Education and Development, 7*(4), 301–327.

Kagan, J. (1989). *Unstable ideas: Temperament, cognition, and the self.* Boston: Harvard University Press.

Karr-Morse, R., & Wiley, M.S. (1997). *Ghosts from the nursery.* New York: Atlantic Monthly Press.

Kerr, M.E., & Bowen, M. (1988). *Family evaluation: An approach based on Bowen theory.* New York: W.W. Norton.

Kessen, W. (Ed.). (1975). *Childhood in China.* New Haven, CT: Yale University Press.

Kessler, D.B., & Dawson, P. (1999). *Failure to thrive and pediatric undernutrition: A transdisciplinary approach.* Baltimore: Paul H. Brookes Publishing Co.

Klass, C.S. (1986). *The autonomous child: Day care and the transmission of values.* London: Falmer Press.

Klein, P.S. (1996a). *Early intervention: Cross-cultural experiences with a mediational approach.* New York: Garland.

Klein, P.S. (1996b, December). *Mediated learning: Helping young children understand their world.* Paper presented at the plenary session of the 11th ZERO TO THREE: National Center for Infants, Toddlers, and Families National Training Institute, Washington, DC.

Kontos, S., & Dunn, J. (1993). Caregiver practices and beliefs in child care varying in developmental appropriateness and quality. In S. Reife (Ed.), *Advances in early education and day care* (Vol. 5, pp. 53–74). Greenwich, CT: JAI Press.

Kontos, S., & Wilcox-Herzog, A. (1997). Teachers' interactions with children: Why are they so important? *Young Children, 52*(2), 4–12.

Kounin, J.S. (1970). *Discipline and group management in the classroom.* Huntington, NY: Robert E. Kreiger.

Kulcyzcki, J., & Toohey, M.A. (1997). *Terror in the toy box and on the tube.* Symposium conducted at the Building Good Beginnings for Every Child Conference, St. Louis.

Lally, J.R., Griffin, A., Fenichel, E., Segal, M., Szanton, E., & Weissbord, B. (1995). *Caring for infants and toddlers in groups: Developmentally appropriate practice.* Washington, DC: ZERO TO THREE: National Center for Infants, Toddlers, and Families.

Lansky, V. (1984). *Toilet training.* New York: Bantam Doubleday Dell.

Lee, P. (1989). Is the young child egocentric or sociocentric? *Teacher's College Record, 19*(3), 379–391.

Lester, B.M., & Boukydis, F.Z. (1992). No language but a cry. In H.H. Papoušek, U. Jurgens, & M. Papoušek (Eds.), *Nonverbal vocal communication: Comparative and developmental approaches* (pp. 145–173). New York: Cambridge University Press.

Lester, B.M., & Tronick, E.Z. (1994). The effects of prenatal cocaine exposure and child outcome. *Infant Mental Health Journal, 15*(2), 107–120.

Lieberman, A., & McLaughlin, M.W. (1992). Networks for educational change: Powerful and problematic. *Phi Delta Kappan, 73,* 674–676.

Linder, T.W. (1999). *Read, play, and learn!: Storybook activities for young children. Teacher's guide.* Baltimore: Paul H. Brookes Publishing Co.

Lubeck, S. (1996). Deconstructing "child development knowledge" and "teacher preparation." *Early Childhood Research Quarterly, 11*(2), 147–167.

Lynch, E.W., & Hanson, M.J. (Eds.). (1998). *Developing cross-cultural competence: A guide for working with children and their families* (2nd ed.). Baltimore: Paul H. Brookes Publishing Co.

Mahler, M.S., Pine, F., & Berman, A. (1975). *The psychological birth of the human infant: Symbiosis and individuation.* New York: Basic Books.

Martin, B. (1967). *Brown bear, brown bear, what do you see?* New York: Henry Holt & Co.

Mayer, M. (1983). *I was so mad.* Racine, WI: Western.

Mayes, L.C., Bornstein, M.H., Chawarsk, K., Haynes, O.M., & Granger, R.H. (1996). Impaired regulation of arousal in 3-month-old infants exposed prenatally to cocaine and other drugs. *Development and Psychopathology, 8*(1), 29–42.

McGee, L.M., & Richgels, D.J. (1990). *Literacy's beginnings: Supporting young readers and writers.* Needham Heights, MA: Allyn & Bacon.

McGee, R., Partridge, C.L.P., Williams, B.S., & Silva, P.A. (1990). A twelve-year follow-up of preschool hyperactive children. *Journal of the American Academy of Child and Adolescent Psychiatry, 30*(2), 224–232.

McHale, J.P., & Rasmussen, J.L. (1998). Coparental and family group-level dynamics during infancy: Early family precursors of child and family functioning during preschool. *Development and Psychopathology, 10*(1), 39–60.

Mead, G.H. (1934). *Mind, self, and society from the standpoint of a social behaviorist* (Vol. I). Chicago: University of Chicago Press.

Merriam-Webster's collegiate dictionary. (10th ed.). (1995). Springfield, MA: Merriam-Webster.

Miller, A. (1982). *The drama of the gifted child.* New York: Basic Books.

Milne, A.A. (1924). *The world of Christopher Robin: The complete when we were very young and now we are 6.* New York: Dutton Children's Books.

Morrow, L.M., & O'Conner, E.M. (1995). Literacy partnerships for change with "at-risk" kindergartners. In R.L. Allington & S.A. Walmsley (Eds.), *No quick fix: Rethinking literacy programs in America's elementary schools* (pp. 101–105). New York: Teachers College Press.

Mrazek, M.P.J. (1993). Maltreatment and infant development. In C.H. Zeanah, Jr. (Ed.), *Handbook of infant development* (pp. 159–170). New York: The Guilford Press.

Murphy, L.B. (1997). Creativity in the youngest. *ZERO TO THREE Bulletin, 17*(3), 35–36.

Murray, L. (1992). The impact of postnatal depression on infant development. *Journal of Child Psychology and Psychiatry, 33*(3), 543–561.

Myers, B.J., Olson, H.C., & Kaltenbach, K. (1992). Cocaine-exposed infants: Myths and misunderstandings. *ZERO TO THREE Bulletin, 13*(1), 1–5.

Myers, B.K., & Maurer, K. (1987). Teaching with less talking: Learning centers in the kindergarten. *Young Children, 42*(5), 20–29.

Nelson, K. (1973). Structure and strategy in learning to talk. *Monographs of the Society for Research in Child Development, 38*(Serial No. 149).

Nelson, K. (Ed.). (1989). *Narratives from the crib.* Cambridge, MA: Harvard University Press.

Nelson, K. (1990). Remembering, forgetting, and childhood amnesia. In R. Fivush & J.A. Hudson (Eds.), *Knowing and remembering in young children* (pp. 301–316). New York: Cambridge University Press.

Nelson, K., & Gruendel, J. (1986). Children's scripts. In K. Nelson (Ed.), *Event knowledge: Structure and function in development* (pp. 21–46). Mahwah, NJ: Lawrence Erlbaum Associates.

Nelson, K., Walkenfeld, F.F., & Goldstein, R. (1997). Children's memory for personal experience: Individual and cultural variations in development. *ZERO TO THREE Bulletin, 17*(3), 17–25.

Nias, J. (1989). Teaching and the self. In M.L. Holly & C.S. McLoughlin (Eds.), *Perspectives on teacher professional development* (pp. 155–171). London: Falmer Press.

Noddings, N. (1984). *Caring: A feminine approach to ethics and moral education.* Berkeley: University of California Press.

Noll, S. (1991). *That bothered Kate.* New York: Puffin.

Norman-March, T. (1996). Reflective supervision as a vehicle for individual and organizational development. *ZERO TO THREE Bulletin, 17*(2), 16–20.

Norton, D.G. (1996). Early linguistic interaction and school achievement: An ethnographic, ecological perspective. *ZERO TO THREE Bulletin, 16*(3), 8–14.

Olson, H.C., Burgess, D.M., & Streissguth, A.P. (1992). Fetal alcohol syndrome (FAS) and fetal alcohol effects (FAE): A lifespan view, with implications for early intervention. *ZERO TO THREE Bulletin, 13*(1), 24–29.

Osofsky, J.D. (1993). *Working with infants, toddlers, and caregivers exposed to violence. Tales from two cities: Boston and New Orleans.* Paper presented at the eighth biennial ZERO TO THREE/National Center for Clinical Infant Programs Training Institute, Washington, DC.

Osofsky, J.D. (1996). Islands of safety: Assessing and treating young victims of violence. *ZERO TO THREE Bulletin, 16*(5), 5–8.

Paley, V.G. (1986). On listening to what the children say. *Harvard Educational Review, 56*(2), 122–131.

Paley, V.G. (1990). *The boy who would be a helicopter: The uses of storytelling in the classroom.* Cambridge, MA: Harvard University Press.

Papoušek, M., & Bornstein, M.H. (1992). Didactic interactions: Intuitive parental support of vocal and verbal development in human infants. In H.H. Papoušek, U. Jurgens, & M. Papoušek (Eds.), *Nonverbal vocal communication: Comparative and developmental approaches* (pp. 230–261). New York: Cambridge University Press.

Pawl, J. (1997). Paper presented at the plenary session of the Building Good Beginnings for Every Child Conference, St. Louis.

Pellegrini, A.D., & Jones, I. (1994). Play, toys, and language. In J.G. Goldstein (Ed.). *Toys, play, and child development* (pp. 27–45). New York: Cambridge University Press.

Pellegrini, D.S., & Notarius, C.I. (1988). Marital processes as childhood risk factors: Implications for intervention and prevention. In E.D. Hibbs (Ed.), *Children and families: Studies in prevention and intervention* (pp. 497–509). Madison, CT: International Universities Press.

Piaget, J. (1962). *Play, dreams and imitation in childhood.* New York: W.W. Norton.

Piaget, J. (1967). *The child's conception of the world.* Totowa, NJ: Littlefield, Adams. (Original work published 1929)

Pica, R. (1997). Beyond physical development: Why young children need to move. *Young Children, 52*(6), 4–11.

Pipp-Siegel, S., & Pressman, L. (1996). Developing a sense of self and others. *ZERO TO THREE Bulletin, 17*(1), 17–24.

Poelle, L. (1993). I'll visit your class, you visit mine: Experienced teachers as mentors. In *Growing teachers: Partnerships in staff development* (pp. 120–134). Washington, DC: National Association for the Education of Young Children.

Porges, S.W. (1993). The infant's sixth sense: Awareness and regulation of bodily processes. *ZERO TO THREE Bulletin, 14*(2), 12–16.

Porges, S.W. (1997). Emotion: An evolutionary by-product of the neural regulation of the autonomic nervous system. In C.S. Kirkpatrick & B. Lederhendler (Eds.), The integrative neurobiology of affiliation. *Annals of the New York Academy of Science, 807,* 62–75.

Porges, S.W., Doussard-Roosevelt, J.A., Lourdes Portales, A., & Greenspan, S.I. (1996). Infant regulation of the vagal "brake" predicts child behavior problems: A psychobiological model of social behavior. *Developmental Psychobiology, 29*(8), 697–712.

Prizant, B.M., Wetherby, A.M., & Roberts, J.E. (1993). Communication disorders in infants and toddlers. In C.H. Zeanah, Jr. (Ed.), *Handbook on infant mental health* (pp. 260–279). New York: The Guilford Press.

Pynoos, R.S. (1985). Children traumatized by witnessing of parental violence. In S. Eth & R.S. Pynoos (Eds.), *Posttraumatic stress disorder in children* (Chapter 2). Washington, DC: American Psychiatric Press.

Pynoos, R.S., & Eth, S. (1986). Witness to violence: The child interview. *Journal of the American Academy of Child Psychiatry, 25*, 306–319.

Radke-Yarrow, M., Richters, J., & Wilson, W.E. (1988). Child development in the network of relationships. In R.A. Hinde & J. Stevenson-Hinde (Eds.), *Relationships within families: Mutual influences* (pp. 48–67). Oxford, England: Clarendon Press.

Ramey, C.T., Campbell, F.A., & Blair, C. (1998). *Enhancing the life course for high-risk children: Results from the Abecedarian Project.* New York: The Russell Sage Foundation.

Ramey, C.T. (1998). *Early experience and intervention: Linking brain and behavioral development.* Erikson Institute's Faculty Development Project on the Brain and University of Chicago's Early Childhood Initiative, Chicago.

Raver, C.C. (1996). Relations between social contingency in mother–child interaction and 2-year-olds' social competence. *Developmental Psychology, 32*(5), 850–859.

Reiss, D. (1989). The represented and practicing family: Contrasting visions of family continuity. In A.J. Sameroff & R.N. Emde (Eds.), *Relationship disturbances in early childhood: A developmental approach* (pp. 191–220). New York: Basic Books.

Rice, M.L. (1989). Children's language acquisition. *American Psychologist, 44*(2), 149–156.

Richters, J., & Martinez, P. (1993). The NIMH community violence project: Children as victims and witnesses to violence. *Psychiatry, 56*, 7–21.

Ricœur, P. (1992). *Oneself and another.* Chicago: University of Chicago Press.

Rogers, C.R. (1969). *Freedom to learn.* Columbus, OH: Charles E. Merrill.

Rutter, M. (1990). Commentary: Some focus and process considerations regarding effects of parental depression on children. *Developmental Psychology, 26*(1), 60–67.

Rutter, M., & Quinton, D. (1984). Parental psychiatric disorder: Effects on children. *Psychological Medicine, 14*, 853–880.

Sacks, O.T. (1995). *An anthropologist on Mars: Seven paradoxical tales.* New York: Alfred A. Knopf.

Sameroff, A.J., & Emde, R.N. (Eds.). (1989). *Relationship disturbances in early childhood: A developmental approach.* New York: Basic Books.

Sammons, W.A.H. (1989). *The self-calmed baby: Teach your infant to calm itself—and curb crying, fussing, and sleeplessness.* New York: St. Martin's Press.

Schore, A.N. (1994). *Affect regulation and the origin of the self: The neurobiology of emotional development.* Mahwah, NJ: Lawrence Erlbaum Associates.

Schore, A.N. (1997). Early organization of the nonlinear right brain and development of a predisposition to psychiatric disorders. *Development and Psychopathology, 9*(4), 595–633.

Schore, A.N. (1998). *Early relationship and the developing brain.* Paper presented at the Erikson Institute Faculty Development Institute, Chicago.

Schorr, L. (1997). *Common purpose: Strengthening families and neighborhoods to rebuild America.* New York: Anchor Books.

Schweinhart, L.J., & Weikart, D.P. (1998). The High/Scope preschool curriculum comparison study through age 23. *Early Childhood Research Quarterly, 12*(2), 117–143.

Second step. (n.d.). Seattle: Committee for Children. (Available from the publisher, 22303 Airport Way S., Suite 500, Seattle, WA 98134-2027; 800-634-4449)

Seifer, R., & Dickstein, S. (1993). Parental mental illness and infant development. In C.H. Zeanah, Jr. (Ed.), *Handbook of infant mental health* (pp. 120–142). New York: The Guilford Press.

Selman, R. (1980). *The growth of interpersonal understanding.* New York: Academic Press.

Shahmoon Shanok, R. (1991). The supervisory relationship: Integrator, resource, and guide. *ZERO TO THREE Bulletin, 12*(2), 16–19.

Shaw, D.S., Owens, E.B., Vondr, J.I., Keenan, K., & Winslow, E.B. (1996). Early risk factors and pathways in the development of early disruptive behavior problems. *Developmental Psychpathology, 8*(4), 670–699.

Shore, R. (1997). *Rethinking the brain: New insights into early development* (2nd ed.). New York: Family and Work Institute.

Sidel, R. (1972). *Rethinking the brain: New insights into early development.* New York: Family and Work Institute.

Simon, D., & Burns, E. (1997). *The corner: A year in the life of an inner-city neighborhood.* New York: Broadway Books.

Singer, D.G., & Singer, J. (1990). *The house of make-believe.* Cambridge, MA: Harvard University Press.

Singer, J.L. (1994). Imaginative play and adaptive development. In J.H. Goldstein (Ed.), *Toys, play, and child development* (pp. 6–26). New York: Cambridge University Press.

Slobodkina, E. (1940). *Caps for sale.* New York: W.R. Scott.

Smith, L.M., Klein, P.F., Prunty, J.P., & Dwyer, D.C. (1986). *Educational innovators: Then and now.* London: Falmer Press.

Snyder, M., Snyder, R., & Snyder, R., Jr. (1980). *The young child as person: Toward the development of healthy conscience.* New York: Human Sciences Press.

Sroufe, L.A. (1983). Infant–caregiver attachment and adaptation in the preschool: The roots of competence and maladaptation. In M. Perlmutter (Ed.), *Development of cognition, affect, and social relations* (pp. 41–81). Mahwah, NJ: Lawrence Erlbaum Associates.

Sroufe, L.A. (1996). *Emotional development: The organization of emotional life in the early years.* London: Cambridge University Press.

Stein, A., Bucher, J., Gath, D., Day, A., Bond, A., & Cooper, P.J. (1989). *The relationship between postnatal depression and mother–child interaction.* Unpublished manuscript.

Stern, D. (1985). *The interpersonal world of the infant: A view from psychoanalysis and developmental psychology.* New York: Basic Books.

Stern, D. (1989). The representation of relational patterns: Developmental considerations. In A.J. Sameroff & R. Emde (Eds.), *Relationship disturbances in early childhood: A developmental approach* (pp. 52–69). New York: Basic Books.

Stern, D.N. (1991, April 5–7). *Infant observation and the formation of psychic structure.* Paper presented at the Institute for Psychoanalysis Conference, Chicago.

Stern, D.N. (1995). *The motherhood constellation: A unified view of parent–infant psychotherapy.* New York: Basic Books.

Stott, F. & Bowman, B. (1996). Child development knowledge: A slippery base. *Early Childhood Research Quarterly, 11*(2), 169–184.

Streissguth, A. (1997). *Fetal alcohol syndrome: A guide for families and communities.* Baltimore: Paul H. Brookes Publishing Co.

Sugar, M. (1992). Toddlers' traumatic memories. *Infant Mental Health Journal, 13*(3), 245–251.

Terr, L.C. (1991). Childhood traumas: An outline and overview. *American Journal of Psychiatry, 148*(1), 10–20.

The Annie E. Casey Foundation. (1997) *Kids count: Data on the well-being of children in large cities.* Baltimore: Author.

Thomas, A., & Chess, S. (1977). *Temperament and development.* New York: Brunner/Mazel.

Thompson, F. (1976). Country games in the 1880s. In J.S. Bruner, A. Jolly, & K. Sylva (Eds.), *Play: Its role in development and evolution* (pp. 456–459). New York: Basic Books.

Thompson, R.A., & Calkins, S.D. (1996). The double-edged sword: Emotional regulation for children at risk. *Development and Psychopathology, 8*(1), 163–182.

Thompson, R.A., Flood, M.F., & Lundquist, L. (1995). Emotional regulation: Its relations to attachment and developmental psychopathology. In D. Cicchetti & S.L. Toth (Eds.), *Emotion, cognition, and representation: Rochester symposium on developmental psychopathology* (Vol. 6, pp. 261–298). Rochester, NY: University of Rochester Press.

Tilley, T.W. (1985). *Story theology.* Wilmington, DE: Michael Glazier.

Tomasello, M., & Farrar, M.J. (1986). Joint attention and early language. *Child Development, 57,* 1457–1463.

Toth, S.L., Cicchetti, D., Macfie, J., & Emde, R.N. (1997). Representations of self and other in the narratives of neglected, physically abused, and sexually abused preschoolers. *Development and Psychopathology, 9*(4), 781–796.

Tronick, E.Z., & Gianino, A. (1986). Interactive mismatch and repair: Challenges to the coping infant. *ZERO TO THREE Bulletin, 6*(3), 1–6.

Villarreal, S.F., McKinney, L., & Quackenbush, M. (1992). *Handle with care: Helping children prenatally exposed to drugs and alcohol.* Santa Cruz, CA: ETR Associates.

Vygotsky, L.S. (1962). *Thought and language.* (E. Hanfmann & G. Valar, Trans.). Cambridge, MA: The MIT Press. (Original work published 1934)

Vygotsky, L.S. (1978). *Mind in society: The development of higher psychological process.* (M. Cole, V. John-Steiner, S. Scribner, & E. Souberman, Eds. and Trans.) Cambridge, MA: Harvard University Press.

Wallace, L.B. (1993). Helping young children cope with violence. *Young Children, 48*(4), 4–11.

Wallach, L.B. (1993). Helping children cope with violence. *Young Children, 48*(4), 4–11.

Werner, E., Bierman, J.M., & French, F.E. (1971). *The children of Kauai: A longitudinal study from the prenatal period to age ten.* Honolulu: University of Hawaii Press.

Werner, E.E., & Smith, R.S. (1992). *Overcoming the odds: High risk for children from birth to adulthood.* Ithaca, NY: Cornell University Press.

White, M., & Epston, D. (1990). *Narrative means to therapeutic ends.* New York: W.W. Norton.

Whitebrook, M., Howes, C., Phillips, D., & Pemberton, C. (1989). Who cares? Child care teachers and the quality of care in America. *Young Children, 45*(1), 41–45.

Winnicott, D.W. (1965). *The maturational processes and the facilitating environment.* Madison, CT: International Universities Press.

Wolin, S.J., & Wolin, S. (1993). *The resilient self: How survivors of troubled families rise above adversity.* New York: Villard Books.

Workman, S.H., & Gage, J.A. (1997). Family–school partnerships: A family strengths approach. *Young Children, 54*(5).

Young, B. (1997). Pain and creativity: The complex interplay. *ZERO TO THREE Bulletin, 17*(3), 26–34.

Zahn-Waxler, C., Ianotti, R.J., Cummings, E.M, & Denham, S. (1990). Antecedents of problem behaviors in children of depressed mothers. *Development and Psychopathology, 2,* 271–291.

Zeanah, C.H., Jr. (1993). The assessment and treatment of infants and toddlers exposed to violence. *ZERO TO THREE Bulletin, 14*(3), 29–37.

Zeanah, C.H., Jr., & Burk, G.S. (1984). A young child who witnessed her mother's murder: Therapeutic and legal considerations. *American Journal of Psychotherapy, 38*(1), 132–145.

Zeanah, C.H., Jr., & Scheering, M. (1996). Evaluation of posttraumatic symptomatology in infants and young children exposed to violence. *ZERO TO THREE Bulletin, 16*(5), 9–14.

Zuckerman, B., & Brown, E.R. (1993). Maternal substance abuse and infant development. In C.H. Zeanah, Jr. (Ed.), *Handbook of infant mental health* (pp. 73–86). New York: The Guilford Press.

Supplementary Reading

ADULT–CHILD INTERACTION

Baumrind, D. (1972). Socialization and instrumental competence in young children. In W.W. Hartup (Ed.), *The young child: Reviews of research* (Vol. 2, pp. 202–224). Washington, DC: National Association for the Education of Young Children.

Bernstein, M.H., & Bornstein, H.G. (1995). Caregivers' responsiveness and cognitive development in infants and toddlers: Theory and research. In P.L. Mangione (Ed.), *Infant/toddler caregiving: A guide to cognitive development and learning.* Sacramento: California State Department of Education.

Bowlby, J. (1969). *Attachment and loss: Vol. 1. Attachment.* New York: Basic Books.

Bowlby, J. (1973). *Attachment and loss: Vol. 2. Separation, anxiety, and anger.* New York: Basic Books.

Brazelton, T.B. (1974). *Toddlers and parents: A declaration of independence.* New York: Bantam Doubleday Dell.

Brazelton, T.B. (1983). *Infants and mothers: Differences in development.* New York: Bantam Doubleday Dell.

Brazelton, T.B. (1992). *Touchpoints: The essential reference. Your child's emotional and behavioral development.* Reading, MA: Addison Wesley Longman.

Brazelton, T.B., & Cramer, B.G. (1990). *The earliest relationship: Parents, infants, and the drama of early attachment.* Reading, MA: Addison Wesley Longman.

Bronfenbrenner, U. (1979). *The ecology of human development: Experiments by nature and design.* Cambridge, MA: Harvard University Press.

Cartwright, S. (1998). Caregivers of quality. *Child Care Information Exchange, 18,* 24.

Chess, S., & Thomas, A. (1987). *Know your child: An authoritative guide for today's parents.* New York: Basic Books.

Dunham, P., & Dunham, F. (1992). Lexical development during middle infancy: A mutually driven infant–caregiver process. *Developmental Psychology, 28*(3), 414–420.

Dunst, C.J., Trivette, C.M., & Deal, A. (1988). *Enabling and empowering families: Principles and guidelines for practice.* Cambridge, MA: Brookline Books.

Field, T. (1995). Supporting cognitive development through interactions with young infants. In P.L. Mangione (Ed.), *Infant/toddler caregiving: A guide to cognitive development and learning.* Sacramento: California State Department of Education.

Field, T., Healy, B., Goldstein, S., & Guthertz, M. (1990). Behavior state matching and synchrony in mother–infant interactions of nondepressed versus depressed dyads. *Developmental Psychology, 26,* 7–14.

Hitz, R., & Driscoll, A. (1988). Praise or encouragement? New insights into praise: Implications for early childhood teachers. *Young Children, 43*(5), 6–13.

Hoff-Ginsberg, E. (1991). Mother–child conversation in different social classes and communicative settings. *Child Development, 62,* 782–796.

Klaus, H.M., & Kennell, J.H. (1976). *Maternal–infant bonding.* St. Louis: C.V. Mosby.

Klein, P.S. (1996). *Early intervention: Cross-cultural experiences with a mediational approach.* New York: Garland.

Kontos, S., & Wilcox-Herzog, A. (1997). Teachers' interactions with children: Why are they so important? *Young Children, 52*(2), 4–12.

Lally, J.R. (1995). Discovery in infancy: How and what infants learn. In P.L. Mangione (Ed.), *Infant/toddler caregiving: A guide to cognitive development and learning.* Sacramento: California State Department of Education.

Lally, J.R., Griffin, A., Fenichel, E., Segal, M., Szanton, E., & Weissbourd, B. (1995). *Caring for infants andd toddlers in groups: Developmentlly appropriate practice.* Washington, DC: ZERO TO THREE: National Center for Infants, Toddlers, and Families.

Lieberman, A.F. (1993). *The emotional life of the toddler.* New York: Free Press.

Papoušek, M., & Bornstein, M.H. (1992). Didactic interactions: Intuitive parental support of vocal and verbal development in human infants. In H.H. Papoušek, U. Jurgens, & M. Papoušek (Eds.), *Nonverbal vocal communication: Comparative and developmental approaches* (pp. 230–261). New York: Cambridge University Press.

Radke-Yarrow, M., Richters, J., & Wilson, W.E. (1988). Child development in the network of relationships. In R.A. Hinde & J. Stevenson-Hinde (Eds.), *Relationships within families: Mutual influences* (pp. 48–67). Oxford, England: Clarendon Press.

Raver, C.C. (1996). Relations between social contingency in mother–child interaction and 2-year-olds' social competence. *Developmental Psychology, 32*(5), 850–859.

Reiss, D. (1989). The represented and practicing family: Contrasting visions of family continuity. In A.J. Sameroff & R.N. Emde (Eds.), *Relationship disturbances in early childhood: A developmental approach* (pp. 191–220). New York: Basic Books.

Rogoff, B., Misry, J., Goncu, A., & Mosier, C. (1993). Guided participation in cultural activity by toddlers and caregivers. *Monographs of the Society for Research in Child Development, 58* (8, Serial No. 236).

Sammons, W.A.H. (1989). *The self-calmed baby: Teach your infant to calm itself—and curb crying, fussing, and sleeplessness.* New York: St. Martin's Press.

Sroufe, L.A. (1983). Infant–caregiver attachment and adaptation in the preschool: The roots of competence and maladaptation. In M. Perlmutter (Ed.), *Development of cognition, affect, and social relations* (pp. 41–81). Mahwah, NJ: Lawrence Erlbaum Associates.

Sroufe, L.A. (1989). Relationships, self, and individual adaptation. In A.J. Sameroff & R.N. Emde (Eds.), *Relationship disturbances in early childhood: A developmental approach* (pp. 70–94). New York: Basic Books.

Sroufe, L.A. (1996). *Emotional development: The organization of emotional life in the early years.* London: Cambridge University Press.

Stern, D.N. (1977). *The first relationship: Infant and mother.* Cambridge, MA: Harvard University Press.

Stern, D.N. (1984). Affect attunement. In J. Call, E. Galenson, & R.L. Tyson (Eds.), *Frontiers of infant psychiatry* (Vol. II, pp. 3–14). New York: Basic Books.

Stern, D.N. (1985). *The interpersonal world of the infant: A view from psychoanalysis and developmental psychology.* New York: Basic Books.

Stern, D.N. (1989). The representation of relational patterns: Developmental considerations. In A.J. Sameroff & R.N. Emde (Eds.), *Relationship disturbances in early childhood: A developmental approach* (pp. 52–69). New York: Basic Books.

Stern, D.N. (1991, April 5–7). *Infant observation and the formation of psychic structure.* Paper presented at the Institute for Psychoanalysis Conference, Chicago.

Stern, D.N. (1995). *The motherhood constellation: A unified view of parent–infant psychotherapy.* New York: Basic Books.

Thompson R.A., Flood, M.F., & Lundquist, L. (1995). Emotional regulation: Its relations to attachment and developmental psychopathology. In D. Cicchetti & S.L. Toth (Eds.), *Emotion, cognition, and representation: Rochester symposium on developmental psychopathology* (Vol. 6, pp. 261–298). Rochester, NY: University of Rochester Press.

Tronick, E.Z., Cohn, J., & Shea, E. (1986). The transfer of affect between mothers and infants. In T.B. Brazelton & M.W. Yogman (Eds.), *Affective development in infancy* (pp. 11–25). Greenwich, CT: Ablex Publishing Corp.

Tronick, E.Z., & Gianino, A. (1986). Interactive mismatch and repair: Challenges to the coping infant. *ZERO TO THREE Bulletin, 6*(3), 1–6.

AUTISM SPECTRUM DISORDERS

Charman, T. (1997). The relationship between joint attention and pretend play in autism. *Development and Psychopathology, 9*(1), 1–16.

Greenspan, S.I. (1992). *Infancy and early childhood: The practice of clinical assessment and intervention with emotional and developmental challenges.* Madison, CT: International Universities Press.

Hadwin, J., Baron-Cohn, S., Howlin, P., & Hill, K. (1996). Can we teach children with autism to understand emotions, belief, or pretence? *Development and Psychopathology, 8*(2), 345–366.

Roeyers, H., Oost, P.V., & Bothuyne, S. (1998). Immediate imitation and joint attention in young children with autism. *Development and Psychopathology, 10*(3), 441–450.

BRAIN DEVELOPMENT AND STRUCTURE

Chugani, H.T. (1997). Neuroimaging of developmental nonlinearity and developmental pathologies. In G.R. Lyon (Ed.), *Developmental neuroimaging* (pp. 187–195). San Diego: Academic Press.

Fox, N.A. (Ed.). (1994). The development of emotional regulation: Biological and behavioral considerations. With commentary by J.J. Campos et al. *Monographs of the Society for Research in Child Development, 203*(5, Serial No. 240).

Fox, N.A. (1996). *Early brain organization and infant emotional development.* Paper presented at the plenary session of the 11th ZERO TO THREE: National Center for Infants, Toddlers, and Families National Training Institute, Washington, DC.

Gilkerson, L. (1998). Brain care: Supporting healthy emotional development. *Child Care Exchange, 68,* 66–68.

Gunnar, M.G. (1996a). *Quality of care and the buffering of stress physiology: Its potential role in protecting the developing human brain.* Paper presented at the plenary session of the 11th ZERO TO THREE: National Center for Infants, Toddlers, and Families National Training Institute, Washington, DC.

Gunnar, M.G. (1996b). *Stress and early brain development: The importance of sensitive caregiving.* Paper presented at the plenary session of the 11th ZERO TO THREE: National Center for Infants, Toddlers, and Families National Training Institute, Washington, DC.

Gunnar, M.G., Mangelsdor, S., Larson, M., & Hertsgaard, L. (1989) Attachment, temperament, and adrenocortical activity in infancy: A study of psychoendocrine regulation. *Developmental Psychology, 25*(3), 355–363.

Porges, S.W. (1997). Emotion: An evolutionary by-product of the neural regulation of the autonomic nervous system. In C.S. Kirkpatrick & B. Lederhendler (Eds.), The integrative neurobiology of affiliation. *Annals of the New York Academy of Science, 807,* 62–75.

Porges, S.W., Doussard-Roosevelt, J.A., Lourdes Portales, A., & Greenspan, S.I. (1996). Infant regulation of the vagal "brake" predicts child behavior problems: A psychobiological model of social behavior. *Developmental Psychobiology, 29*(8), 697–712.

Schore, A.N. (1994). *Affect regulation and the origin of the self: The neurobiology of emotional development.* Mahwah, NJ: Lawrence Erlbaum Associates.

Schore, A.N. (1997). Early organization of the nonlinear right brain and development of a predisposition to psychiatric disorders. *Development and Psychopathology, 9*(4), 595–633.

Shore, R. (1997). *Rethinking the brain: New insights into early development.* New York: Family and Work Institute.

Spangler, G., & Grossman, K.E. (1993). Biobehavioral organization in securely and insecurely attached infants. *Child Development, 64,* 1439–1450.

Spangler, G., & Scheubeck, R. (1993). Behavioral organization in newborns and its relation to adrenocortical and cardiac activity. *Child Development, 64,* 622–633.

CULTURAL DIVERSITY

Brunson Phillips, C. (1995). Culture: A process that empowers. In J.R. Lally (Ed.), *Infant/toddler caregiving: A guide to culturally sensitive care.* Sacramento: California State Department of Education.

Chang, H.N., & Pulido, D. (1994). The critical importance of cultural and linguistic continuity for infants and toddlers. *ZERO TO THREE Bulletin, 15*(2), 13–17.

Davis, L.E., & Proctor, E.K. (1989). *Race, gender, and class: Guidelines for practice with individuals, families, and groups.* Upper Saddle River, NJ: Prentice Hall.

Garbarino, J. (1989). An ecological perspective on the role of play in child development. In M.N. Block & A.D. Pellegrini (Eds.), *The ecological context of children's play* (pp. 16–34). Greenwich, CT: Ablex Publishing Corp.

Garcia, E.E. (1994). Addressing the challenges of diversity. In S.L. Kagan & B. Weissbourd (Eds.), *Putting families first: America's family support movement and the challenge of change* (pp. 243–275). San Francisco: Jossey-Bass.

Hoff-Ginsberg, E. (1991). Mother–child conversation in different social classes and communicative settings. *Child Development, 62,* 782–796.

Klein, P.S. (1996). *Early intervention: Cross-cultural experiences with a mediational approach.* New York: Garland.

Locke, D.C. (1992). *Increasing multicultural understanding: A comprehensive model.* Thousand Oaks, CA: Sage Publications.
Lynch, E.W., & Hanson, M.J. (Eds.). (1998). *Developing cross-cultural competence: A guide for working with children and their families* (2nd ed.). Baltimore: Paul H. Brookes Publishing Co.
Mallory, B.L., & New, R.S. (1994). *Diversity and developmentally appropriate practices: Challenges for early childhood education.* New York: Teachers College Press.
Polk, C. (1994). Therapeutic work with African-American families. *ZERO TO THREE Bulletin, 3*(2), 9–11.

EARLY RISK

Belsky, J., Woodworth, S., & Crnic, K. (1996). Troubled family interaction during toddlerhood. *Development and Psychopathology, 8*(3), 477–495.
Benoit, D. (1993). Failure to thrive and eating disorders. In C.H. Zeanah, Jr. (Ed.), *Handbook of infant mental health* (pp. 317–333). New York: The Guilford Press.
Berkowitz, C.D., & Senter, S.A. (1987). Characteristics of mother–infant interactions in nonorganic failure to thrive. *Journal of Family Practice, 24*, 377–381.
Bettes, B.A. (1988). Maternal depression and motherese: Temporal and intonational features. *Child Development, 59*, 1089–1096.
Cicchetti, D., & Lynch, M. (1993). Toward an ecological/transactional model of community violence and child maltreatment: Consequences for children's development. *Psychiatry, 56*, 95–118.
Cicchetti, D., & Rogosch, F.A. (1997). The role of self organization in the promotion of resilience in maltreated children. *Development and Psychopathology, 9*(4), 797–816.
Cohn, J.E., Campbell, S.B., & Matias, R. (1990). Face-to-face interactions of postpartum depressed and nondepressed mother–infant pairs at two months. *Developmental Psychology, 25*, 15–23.
Constantino, J.N. (1993). Parents, mental illness, and the primary health care of infants and young children. *Young Children, 13*(5), 1–9.
Davenport, Y.B., Zahn-Waxler, C., Adland, M.C., & Mayfield, J. (1984). Early child-rearing practices in families with a manic-depressive parent. *American Journal of Psychiatry, 141*, 230–235.
Drotar, D., Eckerle, D., Satola, J., Pallotta, J., & Wyatt, B. (1990). Maternal interactional behavior with nonorganic failure-to-thrive infants: A case-comparison study. *Child Abuse and Neglect, 14*, 41–51.
Egeland, B., & Sroufe, L.A. (1981). Attachment and early maltreatment. *Child Development, 52*(1), 44–52.
Eiden R.D., & Leonard, K.E.. (1996). Paternal alcohol use and the mother–infant relationship. *Development and Psychopathology, 8*(2), 307–323.
Fraiberg, S.H. (1980). *Clinical studies in infant mental health.* New York: Basic Books.
Fraiberg, S.H., Adelson, E., & Shapiro, V. (1975). Ghosts from the nursery: A psychoanalytic approach to the problems of impaired mother–infant relationships. *Journal of the American Academy of Child Psychiatry, 14*, 378–421.
Gadamer, H.G. (1993). *Truth and method.* New York: Continuum.
Garbarino, J. (1990). The human ecology of early risk. In S.J. Meisels & J. P. Shonkoff (Eds.), *Handbook of early childhood intervention* (pp.78–96). New York: Cambridge University Press.
Garbarino, J. (1992). *Children in danger: Coping with the consequences of community violence.* San Francisco: Jossey-Bass.

Gil, E., & Johnson, T.C. (1993). *Sexualized children: Assessment and treatment of sexualized children and children who molest.* Rockville, MD: Launch Press.

Goodman, S.H., Radke-Yarrow, M., & Teti, D. (1993). Maternal depression as a context for child rearing. *ZERO TO THREE Bulletin, 13*(5), 10–16.

Gottlieb, I., & Hooley, J.M. (1988). Depression and marital distress: Current status and future directions. In S. Duck (Ed.), *Handbook of personal relationships* (pp. 543–570). Chichester, England: John Wiley & Sons.

Halpern, R. (1993). *Poverty and infant development.* In C.H. Zeanah, Jr. (Ed.), *Handbook of infant mental health* (pp. 73–86). New York: The Guilford Press.

Helfer, R., & Kempe, C.H. (1976). *Child abuse and neglect: The family and the community.* Cambridge, MA: Ballinger.

Jones, N.A., Field, T., Fox, N.A., Lundy, B., & Davalos, M. (1997). EEG activation in 1-month-old infants of depressed mothers. *Development and Psychopathology, 9*(3), 491–507.

Kempe, C.H., & Helfer, R. (1980). *The battered child.* Chicago: University of Chicago Press.

Klein, N.K., & Campbell, P. (1990). Preparing personnel to serve at-risk and disabled infants, toddlers, and preschoolers. In S. J. Meisels & J.P. Shonkoff (Eds.), *Handbook of early childhood* (pp. 679–699). New York: Cambridge University Press.

Main, M., & Goldwyn, R. (1984). Predicting rejections of her infant from mother's representation of her own experience: Implications for the abused–abusing intergenerational cycle. *Child Abuse and Neglect, 8,* 203–217.

Mayes, L.C., Bornstein, M.H., Chawarsk, K., Haynes, O.M., & Granger, R.H. (1996). Impaired regulation of arousal in 3-month-old infants exposed prenatally to cocaine and other drugs. *Development and Psychopathology, 8*(1), 29–42.

Mrazek, M.P.J. (1993). Maltreatment and infant development. In C.H. Zeanah, Jr. (Ed.), *Handbook of infant development* (pp. 159–170). New York: The Guilford Press.

Murray, L. (1992). The impact of postnatal depression on infant development. *Journal of Child Psychology and Psychiatry, 33*(3), 543–561.

Oates, R.K., Peacock, A., & Forrest, D. (1985). Long-term effects of nonorganic failure to thrive. *Pediatrics, 75,* 36–40.

Olds, D., Henderson, C., Chamberlin, R., & Tatelbaum, R. (1986). Prevention of child abuse and neglect: A randomized trial of nurse home visitation. *Pediatrics, 77,* 65–78.

Olson, H.C., Burgess, D.M., & Streissguth, A.P. (1992). Fetal alcohol syndrome (FAS) and fetal alcohol effects (FAE): A lifespan view, with implications for early intervention. *ZERO TO THREE Bulletin, 13*(1), 24–29.

Osofsky, J.D. (1993). *Working with infants, toddlers, and caregivers exposed to violence: Tales from two cities: Boston and New Orleans.* Paper presented at the eighth ZERO TO THREE/National Center for Clinical Infant Programs Training Institute, Washington, DC.

Papoušek, M. (1992). Early ontogeny of vocal communication in parent–infant interactions. In H. H. Papoušek, U. Jurgens, & M. Papoušek (Eds.), *Nonverbal vocal communication: Comparative and developmental approaches* (pp. 230–261). New York: Cambridge University Press.

Pawl, J. (1994). *Working with infants, parents, and relationship disturbances.* Paper presented at the 9th ZERO TO THREE: National Center for Infants, Toddlers, and Families National Training Institute, Dallas, TX.

Pellegrini, D.S., & Notarius, C.I. (1988). Marital processes as childhood risk factors: Implications for intervention and prevention. In E.D. Hibbs (Ed.), *Children and families: Studies in prevention and intervention* (pp. 497–509). Madison, CT: International Universities Press.

Pynoos, R.S., & Eth, S. (1986). Witness to violence: The child interview. *Journal of the American Academy of Child Psychiatry, 25,* 306–319.

Richters, J., & Martinez, P. (1993). The NIMH community violence project: Children as victims and witnesses to violence. *Psychiatry, 56,* 7–21.

Rutter, M., & Quinton, D. (1984). Parental psychiatric disorder: Effects on children. *Psychological Medicine, 14,* 853–880.

Sameroff, A.J., & Emde, R.N. (Eds.). (1989). *Relationship disturbances in early childhood: A developmental approach.* New York: Basic Books.

Schorr, L.B., with Schorr, D. (1988). *Within our reach: Breaking the cycle of disadvantage.* New York: Bantam Doubleday Dell.

Seifer, R., & Dickstein, S. (1993). Parental mental illness and infant development. In C.H. Zeanah, Jr. (Ed.), *Handbook of infant mental health* (pp. 120–142). New York: The Guilford Press.

Shahmoon Shanok, R. (1997). Giving back future's promise: Working resourcefully with parents of children who have severe disorders of relating and communicating. *ZERO TO THREE Bulletin, 5*(17), 37–48.

Shaw, D.S., Owens, E.B., Vondr, J.I., Keenan, K., & Winslow, E.B. (1996). Early risk factors and pathways in the development of early disruptive behavior problems. *Development and Psychopathology, 8*(4), 670–699.

Simon, D., & Burns, E. (1997). *The corner: A year in the life of an inner-city neighborhood.* New York: Broadway Books.

Singer, L.T., Arendt, R., Farkas, K., Minnes, S., Juang, J., & Yamashita, T. (1997). Relationships of prenatal cocaine exposure and maternal postpartum psychological distress to child developmental outcome. *Development and Psychopathology, 9*(3), 473–490.

Singer, L.T., & Fagan, J.F. (1984). Cognitive development in the failure-to-thrive infant: A three-year longitudinal study. *Journal of Pediatric Psychology, 9,* 363–383.

Sroufe, L.A. (1997). Psychopathology as an outcome of development. *Development and Psychopathology, 9*(2), 251–268.

Sturm, L., & Drotar, D. (1991). Communication strategies for working with parents of infants who fail to thrive. *ZERO TO THREE Bulletin, 12*(5), 25–28.

Sugar, M. (1992). Toddlers' traumatic memories. *Infant Mental Health Journal, 13*(3), 245–251.

Terr, L.C. (1991). Childhood traumas: An outline and overview. *American Journal of Psychiatry, 148*(1), 10–20.

The Annie E. Casey Foundation. (1997). *Kids count: Data on the well-being of children in large cities.* Baltimore: Author.

Thomas, A., Chess, S., & Birch, H.G. (1968). *Temperament and behavior disorders in children.* New York: New York University Press.

Toth, S.L., Cicchetti, D., Macfie, J., & Emde, R.N. (1997). Representations of self and other in the narratives of neglected, physically abused, and sexually abused preschoolers. *Development and Psychopathology, 9*(4), 781–796.

Villarreal, S.F., McKinney, L, & Quackenbush, M. (1992). *Handle with care: Helping children prenatally exposed to drugs and alcohol.* Santa Cruz, CA: ETR Associates.

Wallach, L.B. (1993). Helping children cope with violence. *Young Children, 48*(4), 4–11.

Wieder, S. (1997). Creating connections: Intervention guidelines for increasing interaction with children with multisystem developmental disorder (MSDD). *ZERO TO THREE Bulletin, 5*(17), 19–28.

Wilson, W.J. (1987). *The truly disadvantaged: The inner city, the underclass, and public policy.* Chicago: University of Chicago Press.

Zeanah, C.H., Jr. (1993). The assessment and treatment of infants and toddlers exposed to violence. *ZERO TO THREE Bulletin, 14*(3), 29–37.

Zeanah, C.H., Jr., & Scheering, M. (1996). Evaluation of posttraumatic symptomatology in infants and young children exposed to violence. *ZERO TO THREE Bulletin, 16*(5), 9–14.

Zuckerman, B., & Brown, E.R. (1993). Maternal substance abuse and infant development. In C.H. Zeanah, Jr. (Ed.), *Handbook of infant mental health* (pp. 73–86). New York: The Guilford Press.

GUIDANCE AND DISCIPLINE

Clewett, A. S. (1988). Guidance and discipline: Teaching young children appropriate behavior. *Young Children, 43*(4), 26–36.

Gartrell, D. (1987). Punishment or guidance? *Young Children, 42*(3), 55–60.

Gordon, T. (1970). *PET: Parent effectiveness training: The tested new way to raise responsible children.* New York: New American Library.

Gordon, T. (1989). *Discipline that works: Promoting self-discipline in children.* New York: Penguin USA.

Greenberg, P. (1987). Child choice—another way to individualize—another form of positive discipline. *Young Children, 43*(1), 48–54.

Greenberg. P. (1988). Avoiding "me against you" discipline. *Young Children, 44*(1), 24–29.

Honig, A.S. (1985). Compliance, control, and discipline. *Young Children, 40*(2), 50–58.

Katz, L. (1984). The professional early childhood teacher. *Young Children, 5*(39), 3–23.

Miller, C.S. (1984). Building self-control: Discipline for young children. *Young Children, 39*(7), 15–19.

Nelson, J. (1987). *Positive discipline: A warm, practical, step-by-step sourcebook for parents and teachers.* New York: Ballantine.

Snyder, M., Snyder, R., & Snyder, R., Jr. (1980). *The young child as person: Toward the development of healthy conscience.* New York: Human Sciences Press.

Soderman, A.K. (1985). Dealing with difficult young children: Strategies for teachers and parents. *Young Children, 40*(5), 15–20.

Turecki, S. (1989). *The difficult child.* New York: Bantam Doubleday Dell.

LANGUAGE, COMMUNICATION, AND EMERGENT LITERACY

Arnaud, S. (1973). Introduction: Polish for play's tarnished reputation. In N.E. Curry & S. Arnaud (Eds.), *Play: The child strives toward self realization* (pp. 5–12). Washington DC: National Association for the Education of Young Children.

Barclay, K.D., & Walwer, L. (1992). Linking lyrics and literacy through song picture books. *Young Children, 47*(4), 76–85.

Barclay, L., Benelli, C., & Curtis. A. (1995). Literacy begins at birth: What care-givers can learn from parents of children who read early. *Young Children, 50*(4)24–28.

Bates, E., Bretherton, I., & Snyder, L. (1988). *From first words to grammar: Individual differences and dissociable mechanisms.* New York: Cambridge University Press.

Bates, E., O'Connell, B., & Shore, C. (1987). Language and communication in infancy. In J.D. Osofsky (Ed.), *Handbook of infant development* (2nd ed., pp. 149–203). New York: John Wiley & Sons.

Bruner, J. (1985). *Child's talk: Learning to use the language.* New York: W.W. Norton.

Chang, H.N., & Pulido, D. (1994). The critical importance of cultural and linguistic continuity for infants and toddlers. *ZERO TO THREE Bulletin, 3*(2), 13–17.

DeLoache, J. (1996). Shrinking trolls and expanding minds: How very young children learn to understand and use symbols. *ZERO TO THREE Bulletin, 17*(3), 10–16.

Devine, M. (1991). *Baby talk: The art of communicating with infants and toddlers.* New York: Plenum Press.

Diamond, A. (1996). *Integrating biological and behavioral influences on early development.* Paper presented at the plenary session of the 11th ZERO to THREE: National Center for Infants, Toddlers, and Families National Training Institute, Washington, DC.

Dodge, K.A. (1990). Developmental psychopathology in children of depressed mothers. *Developmental Psychology, 26*(1), 3–6.

Dole, J.D., Duffy, G.G., Roehler, L.R., & Perons, P.D. (1991). Moving from old to the new: Research on reading comprehension instruction. *Review of Educational Research, 61*(2), 239–264.

Engle, S. (1997). The guy who went up the steep nicken: The emergence of story telling during the first three years. *ZERO TO THREE Bulletin, 17*(3), 1, 3–9.

Fernald, A. (1992). Meaningful melodies in mothers' speech to infants. In H.H. Papoušek, U. Jurgens, & M. Papoušek. (Eds.), *Nonverbal vocal communication: Comparative and developmental approaches* (pp. 262–282). New York: Cambridge University Press.

Fields, M.V., & Lee, D. (1989). *Let's begin reading right: A developmental approach to beginning literacy.* Columbus, OH: Charles E. Merrill.

French, L.A. (1986). The language of events. In K. Nelson (Ed.), *Event knowledge: Structure and function in development* (pp. 119–136). Mahwah, NJ: Lawrence Erlbaum Associates.

Galinsky, E., & David, J. (1988). *The preschool years: Family strategies that work—from experts and parents.* New York: Ballantine.

Heath, S.B. (1983). *Way with words: Language, life, and work in communities and classrooms.* New York: Cambridge University Press.

Hoff-Ginsberg, E. (1991). Mother–child conversation in different social classes and communicative settings. *Child Development, 62*, 782–796.

Hough, R.A., & Nurss, F.J. (1992). Language and literacy for the limited English proficient child. In L.O. Ollila & M.I. Mayfield (Eds.), *Emerging literacy: Preschool, kindergarten, and primary grades* (pp. 137–165). Needham Heights, MA: Allyn & Bacon.

Hudson, J.A., & Fivush, R. (1990). Introduction: What young children remember and why. In R. Fivush & J.A. Hudson, (Eds.). *Knowing and remembering in young children.* New York: Cambridge University Press.

Huttenlocker, J., Haight, W., Bryk, A., Seltzer, M., & Lynos, T. (1991). Early vocabulary growth: Relating to language input and gender. *Developmental Psychology, 27,* 236–248.

Kubicek, L.E. (1996). Helping young children become competent communicators: The role of relationships. *ZERO TO THREE Bulletin, 17*(1), 25–30.

Lester, B.M., & Boukydis, F.Z. (1992). No language but a cry. In H.H. Papoušek, U. Jurgens, & M. Papoušek (Eds.), *Nonverbal vocal communication: Comparative and developmental approaches* (pp. 145–173). New York: Cambridge University Press.

Mahoney, B., & Powell, A. (1988). Modifying parent–child interaction: Enhancing the development of handicapped children. *Journal of Special Education, 22*(1), 82–96.

McCartney, K., & Robeson, W.W. (1992). Emergence of communication: Words, grammar, and first conversations. In J.R. Lally, P.L. Mangione, & C.L. Young-Hold (Eds.), *Infant/toddler caregiving: A guide to language development and communication.* Sacramento: California State Department of Education.

McGee, L.M., & Richgels, D.J. (1990). *Literacy's beginnings: Supporting young readers and writers.* Needham Heights, MA: Allyn & Bacon.

Morrow, L.M., & O'Conner, E.M. (1995). Literacy partnerships for change with "at-risk" kindergartners. In R.L. Allington & S.A. Walmsley (Eds.), *No quick fix: Rethinking literacy programs in America's elementary schools.* New York: Teachers College Press.

Nelson, K. (1973). Structure and strategy in learning to talk. *Monographs of the Society for Research in Child Development, 38* (Serial No. 149).

Nelson, K. (1986). Event knowledge and cognitive development. In K. Nelson (Ed.), *Event knowledge: Structure and function in development* (pp. 1–19). Mahwah, NJ: Lawrence Erlbaum Associates.

Nelson, K. (Ed.). (1989). *Narratives from the crib.* Cambridge, MA: Harvard University Press.

Nelson, K., & Gruendel, J. (1986). Children's scripts. In K. Nelson (Ed.), *Event knowledge: Structure and function in development* (pp. 21–46). Mahwah, NJ: Lawrence Erlbaum Associates.

Norton, D.G. (1996). Early linguistic interaction and school achievement: An ethnographic, ecological perspective. *ZERO TO THREE Bulletin, 16*(3), 8–14.

Ollila, L.O., & Mayfield, M.I. (Eds.). (1992). *Emerging literacy: Preschool, kindergarten and primary grades.* Needham Heights, MA: Allyn & Bacon.

Prizant, B.M., Wetherby, A.M., & Roberts, J.E. (1993). Communication disorders in infants and toddlers. In C.H. Zeanah, Jr. (Ed.), *Handbook on infant mental health* (pp. 260–279). The Guilford Press.

Ratner, N., & Bruner, J. (1978). Games, social exchange, and the acquisition of language. *Journal of Child Language, 5,* 391–401.

Rice, M.L. (1989). Children's language acquisition. *American Psychologist, 44*(2), 149–156.

Schickedanz, J.A. (1986). *More than the ABCs: The early stages of reading and writing.* Washington, DC: National Association for the Education of Young Children.

Shatz, M. (1994). *A toddler's life: From personal narrative to professional insight.* New York: Oxford University Press.

Sulzby, E., Teale, W.H., & Kamberelis, G. (1989). Emergent writing in the classroom: Home and school connections. In D.S. Strickland & L.M. Morrow (Eds.), *Emerging literacy: Young children learn to read and write* (pp. 63–79). Newark, DE: International Reading Association.

Thal, D.J. (1992). Emergence of communication: Give and take between adult and child. In J.R. Lally, P.L. Mangione, & C.L. Young-Hold (Eds.), *Infant/toddler caregiving: A guide to language development and communication*. Sacramento: California State Department of Education.

Tomasello, M., & Farrar, M.J. (1986). Joint attention and early language. *Child Development, 57*, 1457–1463.

Vukelich, C., & Golden, J. (1984). Early writing: Development and teaching strategies. *Young Children, 39*(2), 3–8.

Vygotsky, L.S. (1962). *Thought and language* (E. Hanfmann & G. Valar, Trans.). Cambridge, MA: The MIT Press. (Original work published 1934)

Vygotsky, L.S. (1978). *Mind in society: The development of higher psychological process* (M. Cole, V. John-Steiner, S. Scribner, & E. Souberman, Eds. and Trans.). Cambridge, MA: Harvard University Press.

Williams, D. (1996). *Journey to school reform: Moving from reflection to action through story telling*. Washington, DC: NEA Professional Library.

Willamson, G.G, & Anzalone, M. (1977). Sensory integration: A key component of the evaluation and treatment of young children with severe difficulties in relating and communicating. *ZERO TO THREE Bulletin, 17*(5), 29–36.

PLAY, LEARNING, AND DEVELOPMENT

Arnaud, S. (1973). Introduction: Polish for play's tarnished reputation. In N.E. Curry & S. Arnaud (Eds.), *Play: The child strives toward self realization* (pp. 5–12). Washington, DC: National Association for the Education of Young Children.

Biber, B. (1984). *Early education and psychological development*. New Haven, CT: Yale University Press.

Bruner, J.S. (1983). Play, thought, and language. *Peabody Journal of Education, 60*(3), 60–69.

Bruner, J.S., Jolly, A., & Sylva, K. (Eds.). (1976). *Play: Its role in development and evolution*. New York: Basic Books.

Caruso, D.A. (l984). Infants' exploratory play: Implications for child care. *Young Children, 40*(1), 27–30.

Erikson, E. (1950). *Childhood and society*. New York: W.W. Norton.

Fayden, T. (1997). Children's choice: Planting the seeds for creating a thematic sociodramatic center. *Young Children, 52*(3), 15–20.

Fein, G., & Rivkin, M. (Eds.). (1986). *The young child at play: Reviews of research* (Vol. 4). Washington, DC: National Association for the Education of Young Children.

Ford, S.A. (1993). The facilitator's role in children's play. *Young Children, 48*(6), 66–69.

Galinsky, E., & David, J. (1988). *The preschool years: Family strategies that work—from experts and parents*. New York: Ballantine.

Garbarino, J. (1989). An ecological perspective on the role of play in child development. In M.N. Block & A.D. Pellegrini (Eds.), *The ecological context of children's play* (pp. 16–34). Greenwich, CT: Ablex Publishing Corp.

Greenspan, S.I., & Greenspan, N.T. (1989). *The essential partnership: How parents and children can meet the emotional challenges of infancy and childhood*. New York: Penguin USA.

Howes, C., & Unger, O. (1989). Play with peers in child care settings. In M.N. Block & A.D. Pellegrini (Eds.),*The ecological context of children's play* (pp. 16–34). Greenwich, CT: Ablex Publishing Corp.

Howes, C., Unger, O., & Matheson, C.C. (Eds.) (1992). *The collaborative construction of pretend: Social pretend play functions.* Albany: State University of New York Press.

Odoy, H.A.D., & Foster, S.H. (1997). Creating play crates for the outdoor classroom. *Young Children, 52*(6), 12–16.

SEXUALITY EDUCATION

Bernstein, A. (1977). *The flight of the stork.* New York: Delacorte Press.

Brick, P., Davis, N., Fischel, M., Lupo, T., Marshall, J., & MacVicae, A. (1989). *Bodies, birth and babies: Sexuality and education in early childhood programs.* Bergen County, NJ: Center for Family Life Education, Planned Parenthood.

Calderone, M., & Johnson, E. (1988). *The family book about sexuality.* New York: HarperCollins.

Calderone, M., & Rame, J. (1982). *Talking with your child about sex.* New York: Ballantine.

Gordon, S., & Gordon, J. (1982). *Did the sun shine before you were born?* New York: Ed-U Press.

Gordon, S., & Gordon, J. (1983). *Raising a child conservatively in a sexually permissive world.* New York: Simon & Schuster.

TELEVISION

Carlsson-Paige, N., & Levin, D.E. (1990). *Who's calling the shots? How to respond effectively to children's fascination with war play and war toys.* Philadelphia: New Society.

Levin, D.E., & Carlsson-Paige, N. (1994) .Developmentally appropriate television: Putting children first. *Young Children, 49*(5), 38–44.

Index

Page references followed by *t* indicate tables; those followed by *n* indicate endnotes.